Q, the First Writing about Jesus

Q, the First Writing about Jesus

YOSEOP RA

WIPF & STOCK · Eugene, Oregon

Q, THE FIRST WRITING ABOUT JESUS

Copyright © 2016 Yoseop Ra. All rights reserved. Except for brief quotations in critical publications or reviews, no part of this book may be reproduced in any manner without prior written permission from the publisher. Write: Permissions, Wipf and Stock Publishers, 199 W. 8th Ave., Suite 3, Eugene, OR 97401.

Wipf & Stock
An Imprint of Wipf and Stock Publishers
199 W. 8th Ave., Suite 3
Eugene, OR 97401

www.wipfandstock.com

PAPERBACK ISBN 13: 978-1-4982-8386-1
HARDCOVER ISBN 13: 978-1-4982-8388-5

Manufactured in the U.S.A.   04/13/2016

Unless otherwise noted, Scripture quotations contained herein are from the HOLY BIBLE, NEW INTERNATIONAL VERSION® Copyright © 1973, 1978, 1984 by International Bible Society. Used by permission of Zondervan Publishing House. All rights reserved. The "NIV" and "New International Version"'" trademarks are registered in the United States Patent and Trademark Office by International Bible Society. Use of either trademark requires the permission of International Bible Society.

Dedicated to

Mr. Jokwang Jegal and his wife Mrs. Soonok Kim

with thanks in God

Contents

Preface | ix
Abbreviations | xi

Prologue | 1

Part 1: The First Redaction and Later Addition
1 The Ministry of John | 21
2 The Ministry of Jesus | 27
3 Jesus and John | 41
4 Conclusion | 46

Part 2: The Second Redaction and Later Addition
1 The Texts Added to the First Redaction | 51
2 The Followers of Jesus | 56
3 The Manual for Ministry | 60
4 The Lord's Prayer and Its Application | 67
5 Conclusion | 89

Part 3: The Third Redaction and Later Addition
1 The Texts Added to the First Redaction | 95
2 The Texts Added to the Second Redaction | 123
3 The Main Texts of the Third Redaction | 153
4 Conclusion | 174

Part 4: The Fourth Redaction
1 The Texts Added to the First Redaction | 181
2 The Texts Added to the Second Redaction | 205
3 The Texts Interpolated into the Third Redaction | 221
4 Conclusion | 238

Epilogue | 243

Bibliography | 247
Ancient Document Index | 253

Preface

Q is supposed to be the first writing about the historical Jesus. It is, however, not a well-known area even to biblical theological scholars. Furthermore, Q is a hypothetical document reconstructed from the common texts between Matthew and Luke. However, many critical scholars have accepted its existence for more than a hundred years and their number is still increasing in the biblical theological area. Since I was interested in Q during my doctoral research in the joint PhD program at the University of Denver and Iliff School of Theology in 1992, I have studied the process of its redaction. The more Q is studied, the more information about the historical Jesus and his disciples will emerge. In consequence, my study will help build a foundation upon which readers can recognize the stratification of Q.

Q is supposed to be subjected to redaction. Recently, some respected scholars have argued for its triple redaction. However, I would argue that Q has been redacted four times. Its quadruple redaction can be demonstrated through form critical, redaction critical, composition critical, and socio-historical approaches. In this book, I will show how Q went through a process of redaction with different theological emphases reflecting the social environment. Then, it will be seen how each theological theme was developed as the redaction of Q progressed. As for the question that Q underwent quadruple redaction over a short period of time, I would say that it was possible in the beginning of the Jesus movement and the rapidly changing circumstances. The earliest followers of Jesus faced critical situations and responded to them on the basis of his instruction. Thus, I will focus on how four layers of redaction are interwoven in the texts of Q. The diachronic and synchronic approach to Q will result in clear distinctions among them.

Basically, this is a translation from my Korean book published in 2002. However, I made several modifications recently regarding the original order of some texts and added new interpretation to them. Since a number of scholars have studied the redaction of Q, I will not refer to them in every case; rather, when necessary they will be treated in footnotes. In other words, I will concentrate on my own analysis of Q with regard to its redaction and interpretation. My top priority will be on how Q underwent a process of redaction. As a result, it will be shown how a later redactor developed his or her own interpretation based on the previous redactions. I hope my study presents a new interpretation to the academic world of Q.

I have to give thanks to those who helped me. First of all, I owe Dr. Dennis R. MacDonald, who challenged me a lot when I studied theories of the triple redaction of Q at Iliff School of Theology in Denver. He made me study Q more carefully and criticize the contemporary theories. Thus, I could build up my own hypothesis regarding the redaction of Q. Then, I have to show my gratitude to thank Dr. Kychun So who is in charge of "Q Room" in Seoul Korea. He generously allowed me to use the academic resources during my translation and edition of this book. In addition, I would like to thank Miss Unmi Lee, who helped me improve my writing in English. Especially, I am grateful to Dr. Daniel SungYul Kim DDS and Mrs. Hooja Chon Kim for their financial support in order that this book be published. They were enthusiastic for the publication of this book in English. Finally, I would like to thank Mr. Jim Tedrick, managing editor at Wipf and Stock Publishers, for allowing my manuscript to be published. This book is dedicated to Mr. Jokwang Jegal and his wife Mrs. Soonok Kim who have taken part in my suffering on account of obedience to God with finance and prayer.

Yoseop Ra
October 27, 2015

Abbreviations

BETL	*Bibliotheca ephemeridum theologicarum Lovaniensium*
BTB	*Biblical Theological Bulletin*
CBQ	*Catholic Biblical Quarterly*
ETL	*Ephemerides Theologicae Lovanienses*
EvT	*Evangelische Theologie*
HTR	*Harvard Theological Review*
ICC	International Critical Commentary
Int	*Interpretation*
JBL	*Journal of Biblical Literature*
JSNT	*Journal for the Study of the New Testament*
JSNTSS	*Journal for the Study of the New Testament Supplement Series*
LXX	Septuagint
NovTSup	Supplements to Novum Testamentum
NTS	*New Testament Studies*
SBLSP	*Society of Biblical Literature Seminar Papers*
SNTSMS	Society for New Testament Studies Monograph series
WMANT	Wissenschaftliche Monographien zum Alten und Neuen Testament
WUNT	Wissenschaftliche Untersuchungen zum Neuen Testament

Prologue

In the prologue, I will explain the preliminary information to understand Q better. First of all, the Christian Scripture itself bears witness to the existence of Q. Second, scholarly studies will be surveyed, so that we might see how the redaction of Q has been studied. The recent studies have focused on the triple redaction of Q. However, since they carry some weaknesses, an alternative will be suggested in order to understand the redaction of Q better. Third, methodology will be discussed in order to identify the layers of redaction. Form critical approach will be dealt with first; then, redaction critical, composition critical, and socio-historical approaches will be explained. They will make it possible to detect the quadruple redaction of Q. In this respect, the prologue will help build a foundation upon which readers can understand what I am going to argue in this book.

1. THE EXISTENCE OF Q

Critical biblical scholars have believed that there was a document about Jesus before the gospels. This belief is detected from Luke 1:1–3:

> Many have undertaken to draw up an account of the things that have been fulfilled among us, just as they were handed down to us by those who from the first were eyewitnesses and servants of the word. Therefore, since I myself have carefully investigated everything from the beginning, it seemed good also to me to write an orderly account for you, most excellent Theophilus.

The above text clearly announces that there were many who wrote about Jesus before Luke was written. In other words, Luke used previous sources and traditions for the biographical description of Jesus. With regard to the sources, according to the two-document theory, Luke used Mark and

Q.[1] Although Q is a hypothetical document yet to be determined, the majority of critical scholars have admitted its existence in the form of a document.[2] As people get to know the process of how the Synoptic Gospels were formed, they come to accept the existence of Q.

Q is basically reconstructed from the texts commonly found in Matthew and Luke but not in Mark. An abundance of texts are included in this category. It is, however, noteworthy that critical scholars have recently argued for Mark's use of Q.[3] Then, the two-document hypothesis must be modified as follows: Mark selectively used Q, and then Matthew and Luke used both Q and Mark. Thus, it is not easy to reconstruct Q without profound knowledge of the Synoptic Gospels. For the study of Q's redaction, I will take the position that the texts of Q were used by Matthew and Luke and are to be reconstructed from them on the basis of common words, themes, and literary forms.

Q conveys various instructions through the sayings and actions of John and Jesus. They are, however, not necessarily to be considered the genuine sayings and actions of John and Jesus. Critical scholars have believed that the majority of them were created by the later redactor(s).[4] In this respect, it could be said that Q "has also been thought to be testimony to the circumstances and theological outlook of a particular author or community."[5] This means that while some texts of Q carry the genuine sayings and actions of John and Jesus, the rest of them were created by the later redactor(s) in order to deliver his or her instruction to the audience. At this moment, it is necessary to reconsider that "a single group was responsible

---

1. "Q" was originated from the German word "Quelle," which means "source." Jacobson argues that Paul Wernler was the first scholar who raised the question about the existence of Q (*First Gospel*, 21).

2. Kloppenborg, *Q*, 65; and Brown, *Introduction*, 116–22.

3. To them several texts belong. For example, the role of John the Baptist (Mark 1:2–5, 9), the baptism of Jesus (1:10–11), the temptation (1:12–13), the list of the twelve disciples (3:16–19), the Beelzebul controversy (3:22–29), the parable of the lamp (4:21–22), the parable of the leaven (4:30–32), the sermon for missionary journey (6:7–11), and the demand for a sign (8:11–12). More texts can be found in Mark according to the reader's theological perspective. Cf. Lambrecht, "John the Baptist," 357–84. See also Fleddermann, *Mark and Q*, and Labahn and Schmidt, *Jesus, Mark and Q*. Against this opinion, see Neirynck, "First Synoptic Pericopae," 41–74. Jacobson also lists the common texts used by both Q and Mark ("Literary Unity," 378–84).

4. There is an argument for "fourfold development of the tradition in Q." In other words, the four stages of development can be categorized as follows: (1) Die Redenkompositionen, (2) Strukturierte Kompositionen, (3) Spruch-Paare, (4) Spruch-Gruppen (Schürmann, "Komposition," 325–42).

5. Allison, *Jesus Tradition*, 2.

for its various stages."⁶ Thus, this makes readers think about the distinction between the teaching of the historical Jesus and the theological interpretation of redactor(s).

It is not easy to reconstruct the original texts of Q. However, thanks to scholars' efforts, critical editions came to the world. For the study of Q's redaction, I will use *The Critical Edition of Q*, edited by Robinson, Hoffmann, and Kloppenborg. However, this does not mean that I agree with them in every text of Q. To my judgment, this book still needs to pay more attention to the original order and text of Q because it also reflects their theological presuppositions. If there is a problem that needs to be discussed theologically and textually, it will be dealt with during my interpretation of it.

2. STUDIES OF Q'S REDACTION

Q is supposed to be a well-structured document from a literary perspective. However, some critical scholars have detected a possibility that Q underwent a process of redaction.⁷ Although single and double redactions have often been alleged, recently a triple redaction has gained the support of scholars.⁸ However, their studies are not exempt from critiques because they do not explain everything regarding the redaction of Q. In this chapter, I will survey the hypothesis for the triple redaction of Q and point out some problems, so that I could provide a theoretical basis for an alternative.

John S. Kloppenborg

John S. Kloppenborg is the first scholar who argued for the triple redaction of Q. He adopts the literary genres of sapiential sayings and prophetic judgment sayings as the criteria for the analysis of redaction.⁹ His study is a

---

6. Arnal, *Jesus*, 162.

7. Jacobson, "Apocalyptic," 413. On the contrary, there are some who argue for the unity of Q. Cf. Tuckett, "Stratification," 213–21.

8. As for those who argue for the single redaction of Q, refer to Lührmann, *Redaktion*. And as for the double redaction, refer to Schulz, *Q*, and Polag, *Christologie*. For the brief summary of their argument for the double redaction, see Allison, *Jesus Tradition*, 2–3.

9. Kloppenborg was able to take literary genre as the criterion for the analysis of Q's redaction on account of previous studies such as James M. Robinson and Helmut Koester. Robinson argues that Q was composed of the sapiential sayings ("LOGOI SOPHON," 84–130). This kind of argument was already proclaimed by the German scholars such as Vielhauer, *Geschichte*, 316–19. On the other hand, Koester argues that the early Christianity shows a variety of local and literary characteristics and that

foundational work for the triple redaction of Q. However, his argument has both merit and weakness.

Kloppenborg argues that Q consists of three redactions. According to him, the first redaction is composed of sapiential sayings, and the second redaction consists of prophetic judgment sayings. And then, he assigned the temptation story to the third redaction.[10] In this respect, Q completed the biographical description of Jesus. In other words, from a literary perspective, Kloppenborg adopts audience, motif, and literary form as the criteria for distinguishing the redactions. For example, the second redactor considered "this generation" as the audience who had opposed the Q community and had not accepted the instruction of Jesus. Then, Kloppenborg puts forth the "judgment on this generation" as the motif for the redaction. For this, the pronouncement was used most frequently. On the contrary, he argues that the first redactor regarded the members of the Q community as the audience, the proclamation of the kingdom of God for the poor as the motif, and the sapiential saying as the genre. In this way, Kloppenborg distinguishes three layers of redaction. To the first redaction belong: (1) Q 6:20b–23b, 27–29; (2) 9:57–62; 10:2–11; (3) 11:2–4, 9–13; (4) 12:2–7; (5) 12:22b–34; (6) 13:24; 14:26–27; 17:33; 14:34–35. Five groups of prophetic judgment sayings are found in the second redaction: (1) 3:7–9, 16–17; (2) 7:1–10, 18–23, 24–28; 16:16; 7:31–35; (3) 11:14–26, 29–32, 33–36, 39–52; (4) 12:39–40, 42–46, 49, 51–53, (54–56), 57–59; (5) 17:23–24, 26–30, 34–35, 37. In addition, 6:23c; 10:12–15, 21–24; 12:8–10; 13:25–30, 34–35; 14:16–24 were used to connect the prophetic judgment sayings to the first redaction at the stage of the second redaction. It seems that the disciples of Jesus faced the rejection and persecution of their fellow Jews and responded to them. In addition, Kloppenborg insists that 4:1–13 belongs to the final redaction heading for the biographical description of Jesus. His analysis turns out to be a sophisticated hypothesis regarding the triple redaction of Q.

Kloppenborg has been influential to American scholars with regard to the study of Q's redaction. However, his hypothesis is not exempt from critique. As Richard A. Horsley points out, the traditions of sapiential sayings and prophetic judgment sayings were interwoven at the time of the writing of Q in the first half of the first century CE.[11] His critique can be supported

---

Q includes the apocalyptic and eschatological sayings ("GNOMAI DIAPHOROI," 114–57). On the basis of these kinds of opinions, Kloppenborg was able to insist on the triple redaction of Q.

10. Kloppenborg, *Formation*, 102–245. Cf. Kloppenborg, "Formation of Q," 443–62. Mack is heavily dependent upon Kloppenborg (*Lost Gospel*, 4).

11. Horsley, "Questions," 186–203; Horsley, "Logoï Prophētōn?," 195–200; and Horsley, "Q and Jesus," 175–209. Horsley points out that the book of Daniel contains

by Burton L. Mack, who points out that Q 6:22–23b should not belong to the sapiential sayings because it reflects the rebuke and persecution of the outsiders.[12] Then, the criteria to distinguish the sapiential saying from the prophetic judgment saying is too vulnerable.[13] In other words, it is difficult to make a clear cut between the sapiential saying and the prophetic judgment saying.[14] Although the hypothesis of Kloppenborg is subject to more critique, it will not be discussed further.[15]

Migaku Sato

Migaku Sato is another scholar who argued for the triple redaction of Q. He takes into consideration how the book was manufactured in the first century CE. Although his argument also has its own weakness, it is convincing with regard to the fact that the literary analysis is combined with the process of manufacturing a book.

---

both the sapiential sayings and the judgment sayings (Cf. Attridge, "Reflections," 224–27). Horsley suggests an alternative that each pericope of Q is to be interpreted in relationship with its social situation. Jacobson also points out that it is difficult to distinguish the sapiential tradition alone (*First Gospel*, 51, 257). See also Allison, *Jesus Tradition*, 4–6.

12. Mack, "Kingdom," 610n4. Cf. Tuckett, Q, 142.

13. In some cases, Kloppenborg assigns the prophetic judgment saying to the sapiential one according to his intention. For instance, he assigns Q 14:34–35 to the sapiential saying. However, it could belong to the prophetic sayings because it proclaims the judgment against those who lost the nature of disciples. This means that it is not easy to make a clear cut between the sapiential saying and the prophetic judgment saying (cf. Boring, "Sayings," 137–82; and Jacobson, *First Gospel*, 257).

14. There are opinions that Q consists of prophetic sayings. Cf. Sato, "Wisdom Statement," 139–58; Boring, "Sayings," 132–87; Horsley, "Logoi Prophetōn?," 195–200; and Williams, "Parable," 85–114. On the other hand, Williams argues that there is no "firm basis for delineating redactional strata in Q" ("Parable and Chreia," 105).

15. Kloppenborg induces two redactions with omission of some texts which are supposed to belong to Q. For instance, Q 3:2–4, 21–22; 13:18–21; 17:33 do not appear in his study. Although Kloppenborg does not explain why they were not included, it is probably because he would not accept the possibility that Mark also knew Q. To my judgment, the texts listed above should be included in Q. In particular, 13:18–21 reveals both aspects: the sapiential saying in terms of parable and the prophetic judgment saying in that the kingdom of God is indispensably related with the eschatological judgment. In this respect, Kloppenborg cannot help but modify the criteria of distinction for the redaction of Q to explain the texts listed above. With regard to this, later Kloppenborg admitted that some texts' distinguishing characteristics are ambiguous (*Formation*, 69). In order to meet the critique against ambiguous distinction, Kloppenborg admits the mixed form of both sapiential and prophetic judgment sayings in his later article ("Symbolic," 291–92).

Sato insists that Q was developed like a parchment notebook bound with strips of leather—that is, a "looseleaf book."[16] According to him, Q was a prophetic document in general, developed section by section. He divides the content of Q into three sections.[17] Above all, Q 3:7—7:28 constitutes the first section. It primarily deals with John and Jesus and belongs to the first redaction [Redaction A] with exception of 4:1–13 and 7:27. Then, Sato assigns most of 9:57—10:24 to the second section which describes the mission of disciples. However, 10:(12), 13–15, 22 are regarded as later addition. Thus, the rest of them belong to the second redaction [Redaction B]. Finally, Sato attributes 11:14–32, 39–52; 12:2–34; 13:23–35; (17:23–27) to the third section which focuses on "this generation." Thus, they belong to the third redaction [Redaction C]. According to Sato, some texts were invented to connect the new section to its preceding ones at the time of the writing of the third redaction. For example, 7:31–35 was created to connect the second section to the first, and 10:12–15 was added to the second section. Then, he lists some texts such as 4:2b–13; 6:39–40, 43–45; 7:27; 10:22; (17:23–27) as the texts added at the unknown time. According to Sato, however, it is logically too unstable to conclude that they constitute another redaction.

Sato contributed the process of supplementary composition to the study of Q's redaction. It is possible that Q was expanded section by section. However, his hypothesis is not free from critique, either. Above all, it is doubtful whether each section was written by a writer or redactor except the texts used to connect the later section to its preceding one. It seems that a more complicated process of redaction is found in each section than Sato alleges. In other words, while a later redactor copied the texts of the preceding redaction, he or she could insert some texts into them. Thus, if a certain number of texts are determined as the interpolated ones in more places than Sato suggested above, his hypothesis could be in jeopardy. For instance, a process of multiple additions is found among the beatitudes in Q 6:20b–23. Above all, 6:20b–21 and 6:22–23 seem to have originated in different redactions because they show differences in literary form and theological focus.[18] It seems that 6:22–23 was added to 6:20b–21 later because the latter carries a simpler form of beatitude than the former.[19] In addition,

---

16. Sato, Q, 64–65; and Sato, "Shape," 178–79.

17. Sato, Q, 33–47, 62–76, 320–22, 391–93; and Sato, "Shape," 166–77. For the summary of his argument, see Jacobson, *First Gospel*, 53–60, esp. 57. However, there are some who oppose to it. Cf. Lührmann, "Sayings Collection Q," 65; and Robinson, "Logienquelle," 367–89.

18. Schürmann, *Gottes Reich*, 160; reprinted in English in Schürmann, "Observations," 80.

19. Jacobson, "Literary Unity," 373–74; and Jacobson, *First Gospel*, 99.

each of them seems to be a combination of two different redactions. While the first beatitude is written with the present tense verb in 6:20b, the second and third beatitudes are with the future tense verb in 6:21. It seems that 6:21 was added to 6:20b because they reflected different reasons for writing at different stages; in other words, although Jesus proclaimed the presence of the kingdom of God in 6:20b, it did not come as soon as his disciples expected. Thus, a later redactor postponed the moment of fulfillment of the kingdom to the future in 6:21. In addition, it is also plausible that 6:23c was added to 6:22–23b.[20] While 6:22–23b refers to the blessing of those who were insulted and hated by their opponents on account of the Son of Man, 6:23c mentions the persecution of prophets by their forefathers. If my observation is right, it can be said that four different redactions are interwoven in 6:20b–23. It should not be neglected that this kind of redaction is also found in other sections which are considered a literary unity. Then, Sato's hypothesis turns out to require more careful work on the redaction of each section.

Arland D. Jacobson

Arland D. Jacobson also provides an alternative hypothesis with regard to the triple redaction of Q. Having paid attention to its literary unity, he divides Q into four sections and then analyzes them from a compositional perspective.[21] This made him distinguish the three layers of redaction embedded in each section.

Jacobson distinguishes the compositional stage from the tradition and intermediate redaction. According to him, the compositional stage reflects the understanding of Israel based on the failure of disciples in their mission to the Israelites. Thus, the redactor wrote the compositional stage from the background of the Deuteronomistic tradition that deals with "the violent fate of prophets" in connection with the wisdom tradition that condemns "Israel for her impenitence and resistance to God's messengers."[22] Then, Jacobson argues that two other redactions are found; one of them was supposed to be written earlier than the compositional stage and the other was later than that. In this way, he insists on the three redactions of Q at least. Jacobson lists the texts of each layer of redaction. The first section which is about "John and Jesus" includes Q 3:1–6, 7–9, 16–17; 6:20b–49; 7:1–10, 18–35; 16:16. Among them, 3:1–6, 7–8a, 9, 16a, 17; 6:20b–23b, 27–38,

---

20. Jacobson, *First Gospel*, 62, 100, 223.

21. Jacobson, "Literary Unity," 383–39; and Jacobson, *First Gospel*, 77–250.

22. Jacobson, "Literary Unit," 374, 378, 387. Jacobson lists the characteristics of the Deuteronomistic tradition in 384–35 (*First Gospel*, 72–76).

40–41, 43–49; 7:24–27 have been passed down to the redactor through tradition, and then they were added to the texts of the compositional stage, such as 3:8c; 6:23c, 39, 42; 7:1–10; 16:16; 7:31–35, which reflects the Deuteronomistic tradition. Then, later, they were added to the texts of intermediate redaction such as 3:16c; 7:18–23, 28, and 4:1–13. The second section includes 9:57–60a; 10:2–12, 13–15, 16, 21–22, which is about "the Mission and Welcoming." Among them, 9:59–60a; 10:3–11, 16 belong to the tradition and then were added to the texts of the compositional stage such as 9:57b–58; 10:2, 12–15. Later, the text of the intermediate redaction, 10:21–22, was added to the texts of the compositional stage. The third section is about "Against This Generation." The tradition handed down the texts of 11:14–20, 23, 24–26, 33–36, and then they were added to the texts of the compositional stage, such as 10:23–24, 29–32; 11:39–40, 42, 44, 46, 47–51, which reflect the Deuteronomistic tradition. And then the texts of the intermediate redaction, such as 11:2–4; 11:9–13, were interpolated into the texts of the compositional stage. The fourth section includes the rest of the texts, which can be named "For the Community." The texts of 12:31–34, 35–39, 51, 53, 58–59; 13:24–27 had been transmitted as the tradition. And then, the texts of 12:49–53, 54–56; 13:18–19, 20–21; 13:24–35; 14:16–24, 26–27; 17:33; 14:34–35 were added to the compositional stage. And finally, the texts of 12:40, 42–46 were interpolated into the preceding texts at the stage of intermediate redaction. It is noteworthy that Jacobson approaches the content of Q from a literary perspective.

Jacobson contributes the compositional approach to the study of Q's triple redaction. Especially, he should be credited with a unique achievement in his application of the Deuteronomistic tradition to the texts of the compositional stage.[23] However, his argument cannot avoid critique. First of all, it is illogical to think that the Deuteronomistic tradition was applied to the compositional stage—that is, the main layer of Q's redaction. Rather, it should be applied to the last stage of the composition when the persecution reached its peak being represented by martyrdom. For instance, there is a possibility that 6:23c, which reflects the Deuteronomistic tradition, was added to 6:20b–22b at the fourth stage of redaction. This implies that the Deuteronomistic tradition was applied to Q at the last stage of redaction. Second, the division of Q into four parts is an exceptional job in that Jacobson looked at Q from a literary perspective. It is, however, to be noted that his division is somewhat arbitrary. For instance, Q 12:2–3 should not belong to the fourth section, rather to the third section, because it is to be connected with 11:33–34 regarding the disclosure of the hidden thing. Then, in

---

23. Cf. Kloppenborg, Q, 92–93.

the middle of them, 11:39–42 shows that the hidden aspect of the Pharisees would be revealed. To my judgment, following Sato, it is better to divide the content of Q into three sections. I would rather categorize them as follows: Jesus and John (3:2—7:35), Jesus and his disciples (9:57—12:34; 16:13; 17:3–4), and Jesus the Son of Man and the kingdom of God (12:39—22:30).

Dale C. Allison Jr.

Dale C. Allison Jr. also argues for the triple redaction of Q from a literary perspective. He depends upon the tradition that the content of Q has been generally divided into five sections. It is, however, to be noted that his argument pays too much attention to the terminological, thematic, and literary similarities among the five sections rather than the stratification of each section.

Allison explains how it went through a process of composition from a literary perspective.[24] First of all, he starts with the tradition that Q used to be divided into five sections. Then, he pays attention to how each section consists of units. According to him, the first section Q 3:7—7:35 consists of five units (1–5). Then, 9:57—11:13 is assigned to the second section which is composed of five units (6–10), 11:14-52 is attributed to the third section consisting of six units (11–16), 12:2-32 is allocated to the fourth section, composed of two units (17–18), and 12:33—22:30 is arranged to the fifth section, consisting of fifteen units (19–33). Then, Allison takes into consideration how common terms, themes, and literary patterns appear among the five sections. As a result, he argues that the first and third sections have many similarities in their terminological, thematic, and literary perspective.[25] Then, based on the common theme of encouraging itinerant missionaries and the common structure between 11:9-11 and 12:4-7, 22-31, he asserts that the second and fourth sections were written by the same editorial hand.[26] However, Allison points out that the common words, themes, and literary patterns are rare in the fifth section.[27] Therefore, he concludes that the second and fourth sections were redacted first probably by and for the itinerant preachers, then the fifth section was attached to the previous two sections at the second redaction, and finally the first was attached in front of them and the third section was interpolated between

---

24. Allison, *Jesus Tradition*, 8n39. Q has been divided into five sections since T. W. Manson (*Sayings*, 5).

25. Allison, *Jesus Tradition*, 17-21.

26. Ibid., 24–25.

27. Ibid., 29–30.

the second and fourth sections at the stage of the third redaction by settled communities. In this respect, Allison argues for the triple redaction of Q.

Allison should be credited with a significant achievement in that Q shows many common literary patterns in various places. He contributed the literary approach to the study of the triple redaction of Q. However, his theory is not free from critiques. First of all, he is too obsessed with literary aspects such as term, theme, and patterns. Although they are helpful in distinguishing the redaction among sections, they are not sufficient to decide it, because the later redactor could have written in a similar manner as the previous redactor with regard to terms, theological themes, and literary patterns. For instance, although the first section conveys the proclamation of John in Q 3:7–9 and 3:16–17, they reveal a difference in terms of temporal aspect. This informs readers of the possibility that they originated in different redactions. Thus, it is necessary to look carefully at the thematic, theological, and literary difference in the designated section in order to separate the layers of redaction in it.[28] It is hard to conclude that Q was redacted section by section. Second, Allison is too obsessed with the traditional division of Q into five sections. He is right when he says that critical scholars must pay attention to the flow of content. However, the criteria to decide how to divide the content of Q is to be more considerate of its overall structure. The threefold division of Q mentioned by Sato is more suitable to explain how the story advances naturally from a literary perspective than the fivefold one.[29] Thus, I would like to prefer Sato's work to Allison's regarding the literary unit of Q. Nevertheless, no one can underestimate Allison's attempt to reconstruct the compositional history of Q.

Summary

Scholars have attempted to explain how Q went through a process of redaction as time passed. Kloppenborg was the first scholar who argued for the triple redaction of Q. Then, Sato followed him; later, Jacobson and Allison joined them. Although their studies have their own merit, no one provides us with a satisfactory hypothesis. Thus, an alternative hypothesis is necessary

---

28. Cf. Arnal, *Jesus*, 6.

29. For example, Allison regards Q 11:14–52 as an interpolated section in between 9:57—11:13 and 12:2–32. This could be right. However, he neglects the possibility that 11:11–13 is an explanation about the "father" used in vocative form of the Lord's Prayer, 11:14–26 is an explanation about the second petition, 11:16, 29—12:3 are about the fifth petition, 12:4–12 is about the first petition, and 12:22–34 is about the third petition. To my judgment, the Lord's Prayer plays the key role in the middle of Q. In this respect, Allison's division of Q into five sections is to be modified.

to see how the redaction of Q progressed. As a result, this will show how the earliest author or redactor left the writing about Jesus.

3. METHODOLOGY

Q was not written at once. Rather, it seems to have been subjected to redaction. This is detected in various ways. The literary forms are different from each other, logical inconsistency is found among the adjacent texts, the flow of content changes suddenly, and the different circumstances are reflected in many texts. These elements make readers think about the possibility that Q went through a process of redaction. It is, then, necessary to see how it can be distinguished. This is the reason that the methodology is to be examined in order to identify the process of Q's redaction. For the separation of different redactions, form critical, redaction critical, composition critical, and socio-historical approaches will be discussed.

Form Critical Approach

Form critical approach is a useful tool for the distinction of redaction. It pays attention to the literary form used for the composition of a certain sentence or paragraph. Then, it identifies the literary differences among the designated sentences or paragraphs. As a result, it provides a theoretic basis to recognize the different stages of redaction.

Form critical approach can be applied to the various forms of the literary unit. For instance, differences are found among the beatitudes in Q 6:20b–23. First of all, two different forms are found; while the Greek word ὅτι [because] is used in 6:20b–21, ὅταν [when] is adopted in 6:22–23. This could provide us with a clue about the different strata of redaction. In addition, as mentioned before, a present tense verb is used in 6:20b, whereas a future tense verb is adopted in 6:21. The literary and temporal differences provide glimpses of a literary stratification between 6:20b and 6:21. It is most likely that 6:21 was added to 6:20b by a later redactor because the kingdom of God promised to the poor by Jesus had not come as soon as his disciples expected. Moreover, while the third person plural pronoun is used in the main clause of 6:20b–21, the second person plural is adopted in 6:22–23. Whereas the third person plural refers to the undesignated persons in the former, the second person plural is used for the designated persons in the latter. This kind of difference could also provide a theoretic basis upon which readers can recognize the possibility that 6:20b–21 and 6:22–23 originated in different redactions at different times. Form critical approach can be also applied to a pericope. The pericope could be composed of various literary forms such as metaphor, simile, beatitude, woe, healing miracle story, pronouncement story, etc.[30] It is necessary to distinguish the different forms among them. Although the distinction of literary form itself does not ensure the different strata of redaction, form critical approach is useful enough to identify them. In conclusion, the distinctive qualities of form must be discerned because they could contribute to the redactional activity.[31]

Redaction Critical Approach

Redaction critical approach is also a useful tool to detect the process of Q's redaction. According to Jacobson, it aims

> to explore how the theological convictions of the author of the document shaped the editing of the material; correspondingly, from the way an editor (or redactor) shaped the material one might discern the theological assumptions at work in the redaction.[32]

In order to detect the theological conviction of the author or redactor, it is necessary to pay attention to the different literary form, term, grammatical change, change of tone, theological theme, intended reader, compositional purpose, etc.; then, they will provide the logical foundation upon which readers can notice how and why the redactor composed the sentence or pericope.[33] According to Mack, theme, literary style, rhetorical strategy, form of address to a particular audience, similarity of literary genre, and organization of material are important in order to recognize the process of Q's redaction.[34] As a result, readers will be able to acknowledge the different meanings among the texts intended by the redactor.

Q reveals various traces of redaction in many places. For instance, the preaching of John appears in Q 3:7–9 and 3:16–17. First, 3:7–9 left a trace of redaction in that 3:8bc breaks the literary flow from 3:7–8a to 3:9. While 3:7–8a and 3:9 treat the instruction about repentance and its fruits, 3:8bc deals with the descendants of Abraham. When 3:8bc is erased, the logic

---

30. Cf. Kloppenborg, *Formation*, 9; Jacobson, *First Gospel*, 44; and Zeller, "Redaktionsprozesse," 396–99.
31. Jacobson, "Literary Unity," 373.
32. Jacobson, *First Gospel*, 34.
33. Kloppenborg, *Formation*, 99; and Jacobson, *First Gospel*, 45.
34. Mack, *Lost Gospel*, 108.

flows naturally from 3:7–8a to 3:9.[35] This makes readers conclude that 3:8bc was interpolated later in between 3:7–8a and 3:9. Thus, it can be said that 3:7–9 consists of two redactions. Second, although 3:16–17 follows 3:7–8a, 9 by the theme of eschatological judgment, they show many different aspects, especially with regard to the moment of judgment. While 3:7–8a, 9 conveys the ongoing judgment with present tense verbs, 3:16–17 displays the futuristic one with future tense verbs. It seems that the moment of eschatological judgment was postponed as the redaction of Q progressed. In addition, while the former designates God as the eschatological agent with the divine passive voice verbs, the latter describes Jesus as the eschatological agent who comes after John with active voice verbs. This implies that the divine and eschatological role was imposed to Jesus later from a theological perspective. Thus, it can be concluded that 3:7–8a, 9 and 3:16–17 originated from different redactions; in addition, it seems that 3:16–17 was added to 3:7–8a later because the eschatological judgment did not occur as soon as John proclaimed. Third, it seems that 3:8bc was added to 3:7–8a, 9, 16–17 later because 3:8bc treats the theme of the descendants of Abraham, which is irrelevant to the theme of eschatological judgment. Then, it can be concluded that 3:7–9, 16–17 is a combination of three different redactions. In this way, redaction critical approach can be used for the separation of layers of redaction.

The redaction critical approach to Q is possible on account of scribal characteristics. It seems that a later scribe did not modify the texts of earlier scribes according to the Jewish tradition. This tendency is found in various places of the Bible.[36] It seems that the redactors of Q were accustomed to their traditional way of redaction which did not modify the preceding tradition.[37] In other words, following their predecessors, the later redactor(s) of Q did not change the previous texts, thus preserving the sources written by their predecessors. As a result, we can isolate a redaction from others.

---

35. Jacobson, *First Gospel*, 82.

36. A good example is found in Gen 6:19–20; 7:2–3, 9, 15. The use of different numbers appears regarding clean and unclean animals. On the one hand, 7:2–3 describes seven pairs of clean animals and one pair of unclean animals to be on board; on the other hand, only one pair are allowed to be on board for both clean and unclean animals in 6:19–20; 7:9, 15. The difference has made the scholars believe that two different documents were interwoven in 6:19–20; 7:2–3, 9, 15 by a compiler.

37. Mack, *Lost Gospel*, 107.

Composition Critical Approach

The composition critical approach is also a useful tool to identify the layer of Q's redaction. While form and redaction critical approaches can be designated as the diachronic method, composition critical approach will be attributed to the synchronic one. As a result, this makes it possible to treat Q as a whole.

The composition critical approach focuses on the composition of Q as a whole. As a result, the literary structure will be revealed and how the content of Q advances will be shown from a literary perspective. On the other hand, composition critical approach makes it possible to connect the texts separated by form and redaction critical approaches.[38] In this respect, it can be understood as the synchronic approach. Jacobson defines the term composition criticism as "composition in the sense of the arrangement of traditional material into a larger whole"; and then he explains further as follows:

> Technically, composition criticism includes not only observations of how materials have been brought together and arranged but also the discovery of the compositional tendencies typical of other literature of the day. This is because material was usually assembled according to patterns which can be detected by comparison with other literature. However, this study is largely limited to two aspects of the composition of Q: the sequence of the material and the thematic relationships among the various pericopaes.[39]

The composition critical approach makes it possible to connect the texts distinguished by the form and redaction critical approaches, so that they might show a certain tendency with regard to the theology and the literary peculiarity.

The composition critical approach makes it possible to see how Q is composed regarding its content. As shown before, Sato divides the content of Q into three sections, Jacobson into four sections, and Allison into five. However, I would like to divide it into three, following Sato, because his

---

38. Jacobson, *First Gospel*, 45. This is similar to what Robbins suggests as logical form and quantitative form (*Jesus*, 9). Kloppenborg also wrote a brief explanation about this (*Formation*, 94).

39. Jacobson, *First Gospel*, 43. Jacobson introduces the concept about the literary unity relying upon Thrall and Hibbard who say, "The concept that a literary work shall have in it some organizing principle in relation to which all its parts are related so that, viewed in the light of this principle, the work is an organic whole" (Thrall and Hibbard, *Handbook*, 500; quoted in Jacobson, "Literary Unity," 372).

literary analysis explains how the content of Q flows naturally. The first section focuses on the ministry of John and Jesus in Q 3:2—7:35. Then, the second section describes the ministry of Jesus in his relationship with the disciples in 9:57—12:34. He commissioned them as the worker for the proclamation of the kingdom of God and taught them the manual for ministry and prayer. Finally, the third section deals with the coming Son of Man and the kingdom of God with the pattern of *inclusio* in 12:35—22:30. The composition critical approach makes readers see the different emphasis in each section.

The composition critical approach shows how a theological theme was developed in a certain redaction. For instance, as shown before, the redaction critical approach has shown that 3:8bc was interpolated in between 3:7–8a and 3:9 by a later redactor. The text of 3:8bc introduces the theme of Abraham's descendants for the first time. Then, this text can be connected with the temptation story by the theme of Abraham's descendants because Jesus represented the twelve tribes of the Israelites who had been tempted in the wilderness (4:1–13). Next, the names of the twelve apostles are listed as those who replaced the twelve patriarchs of the Israelites (6:12–16). Finally, the theme of Abraham's descendants is also found at the end of Q in that Jesus promised his disciples the twelve thrones to reign over the twelve tribes (22:30).[40] In this way, the texts listed above share the theme of Abraham's descendants and develop it step by step. Thus, all the texts mentioned above seem to originate from the same editorial hand. In this respect, the composition critical approach makes it possible to separate a certain layer of redaction. It can be used in order to show how tradition was developed as the redaction progressed.

Socio-Historical Approach

The socio-historical approach is also a useful tool to identify the layer of redaction. This can be applied to some texts which reflect the social or historical setting at the time of redaction. In this respect, the socio-historical approach can be also considered as synchronic method.

The socio-historical approach can be applied to a text which reflects the social situation. A certain text can be connected with others that show the same situation. For instance, Q 6:23c is a good case that shows a social

---

40. Unfortunately, Jacobson argues that there is no clue for the twelve tribes of Israel beyond Q 22:30 (*First Gospel*, 249). I would rather argue that 22:30 is the climax about the allusion to the twelve tribes of Israel based on the texts such as 3:8bc; 4:1–13; and 6:12–16.

experience of persecution. As mentioned before, while 6:20–23 reveals at least three different layers of redaction, the majority of scholars detect another redaction in 6:23c. In other words, this seems to be added by the fourth redactor to 6:20–23b because the persecution of the prophets is a totally new theme. This theme is found in 11:47–51 which describes the martyrdom of Abel and Zechariah in the temple. Moreover, the martyrdom of those sent by the Wisdom to Jerusalem is clearly announced in 13:34–35. In this way, the fourth redactor developed the description about the persecution and martyrdom of the prophets as the redaction of Q progressed. As a result, it can be said that as the story advances, the social experience of persecution is well described and developed.

In addition, the socio-historical approach can be applied to a certain text reflecting the historical situation. Although not many texts reflect their historical situation, some texts tell people about it. Then, its date of composition can be determined. For instance, socio-historical approach can be applied to the temptation story (4:1–13). According to Theissen, it reflects the crisis caused by the Roman emperor Gaius Caligula, who attempted to erect his statue in the Jerusalem temple in 40–41 CE.[41] The descriptions that the temple was used as the place of temptation and that the devil had the authority to give the earthly kingdom remind readers of the Roman emperor's attempt to erect his statue. On the contrary, the quotation from Deuteronomy reflects the Jews' resistance against the Roman emperor by relying upon the law. In this respect, the temptation story is supposed to be written during or after the crisis occurred in 40–41 CE. Then, the texts that belong to the redaction from which the temptation story originated can be understood to be written around 41 CE. In this respect, the socio-historical approach is a useful tool to identify the date of a certain layer of redaction.

Summary

As time passed, Q was expanded by the redactors. Various critical approaches make it possible to distinguish the redactions of Q. Form critical, redaction critical, composition critical, and socio-historical approaches are useful to identify them. It is, however, not necessary to apply each approach to each text independently; rather, they would be used in combination. Form critical and redaction critical approaches can be used diachronically to distinguish one text from the other. Then composition critical and socio-historical approaches can be used synchronically to connect the isolated texts by the form and the redaction critical approaches, so that they might

---

41. Theissen, *Gospels*, 206–21.

build up the layers of redaction. It will be a tedious work like a puzzle that requires use of trial and error.

Part 1

The First Redaction and Later Addition

As mentioned in the prologue, Q can be divided into three sections according to the role of Jesus. The first section is composed of Q 3:2—7:35 focusing on the ministry of John and Jesus. However, it can be divided into three parts: the ministry of John (3:2–17), the ministry of Jesus (3:21—7:10), and Jesus and John (7:18–35). Although the first redaction of Q is mostly found in this section, it also includes the texts added by later redactors. In other words, they inserted their texts into the first redaction on purpose. As a result, my study will show how the first section was composed by redactors. Form critical, redaction critical, and composition critical approaches will be used to separate four layers of redaction in the first section. Then, the first redaction will be isolated. It will be seen that the radical instruction was delivered regarding the repentance for the preparation of impending wrath and the reciprocal relationship among human beings. As a result, it can be said that the texts of the first redaction stand for the words and activities of the historical John and Jesus. However, we will be surprised by its smaller amount of texts than we generally expected.

1

The Ministry of John

The first section of Q begins with the debut and proclamation of John in Q 3:2–17—that is, the first part. It primarily describes the ministry of John who proclaimed the preparation for the way of God and the fruit worthy of repentance. The first part provides the sources for the first redaction; of course, it will also show some texts inserted by later redactors. When the texts of the first redaction are isolated, its theology will be revealed. The first redactor described John as a servant of God for the impending wrath of God.

A. THE DEBUT OF JOHN (Q 3:2–4)

The title of Q has been missing. When Mark, Matthew, and Luke used Q as their source, they did not need to preserve it. Thus, no clue is left to trace the title of Q. As a result, the debut of John appears first in Q 3:2–4 (Luke 3:2–4; Matt 3:1–3, 5–6).[1] Although his origin has been unknown, Q describes that John appeared in the wilderness of the Jordan. The fact that John was introduced earlier than Jesus implies that John was more important than Jesus when this text was written. Probably, he was the primary leader. Nevertheless, his origin was probably not important to his followers when the redactor collected the words of John for the first time.

---

1. Most scholars agree that Q 3:2–4 is the beginning text (Catchpole, "Beginning," 205–21; Lambrecht, "John the Baptist," 357–84; and Marcus, *Way*, 12). On the contrary, there are some who would not agree with it (Fleddermann, "Beginning," 153–59; and Neirynck, "Minor Agreement," 49–72). I would argue that the debut of John is in Q because Mark knew it.

Q describes John working in the wilderness of the Jordan. Although its exact location has not been known, wilderness used to be the place of God's trial and salvation according to the Jewish tradition. For instance, Moses had led the Israelites to the wilderness and wandered for forty years enduring God's trial before they crossed the River Jordan. In addition, Elijah had spent forty days in the wilderness before he reached Mount Horeb and heard the voice of God. Later, Elijah also crossed the River Jordan before his ascension. Of course, it is to be admitted that Elijah was described under the light of Moses in the wilderness. In a similar manner, it seems that the Jewish tradition serves a mirror for the description of John in Q. In this way, he was defined as a servant of God who brought the divine salvation. Then, it can be said that the redactor of this text tried to describe the coming of a new era for the salvation of God through John from a typological perspective.

According to Q, John proclaimed the repentance of sins and asked people to be baptized. Baptism is inseparable from repentance of sins which was an important element for the righteousness before God. Then, it can be said that baptism was performed as a religious ritual among the crowds who approached John. They seemed to regard baptism as a means of cleansing their sins after repentance.[2] It is, however, not clear whether baptism was performed once in a life or occasionally. In addition, its origin has not been known, either.[3] John was probably the first person who performed baptism as a religious ritual.

Q introduces the role of John. For this, Q cites a verse from Isa 40:3; in other words, John is described in the fashion of Isaiah the prophet.[4] Having quoted Isaiah directly, Q describes John as a servant of God who prepared the way for the Lord in the wilderness.[5] The Lord is none other than YHWH in this text. It is interesting to observe that Isaiah the prophet played the role

---

2. Some scholars disagree with the opinion that baptism was a ritual (Cf. Schulz, Q, 372; and Jacobson, *First Gospel*, 81).

3. The baptism mentioned in Q was probably different from the cleansing ritual practiced every evening at the Qumran community (CD 10:11–13; Rule of Community 5:13–14; 6; 16–17). Although many scholars have worked on the relationship between John and the Qumran community, they have not reached a conclusion regarding it yet.

4. Robinson, Hoffmann, and Kloppenborg think that the quotation was not in Q (*Critical Edition*, 6–7). Rather, they seem to believe that it came from Mark 1:3. This kind of opinion probably resulted from their belief that Mark did not know Q. To my judgment, Mark adopted Mal 3:1 from Q 7:27 and Isa 40:3 from Q 3:4 and then put them together in Mark 1:2–3. Then, this argument rather supports the hypothesis that Mark also knew Q.

5. Jacobson, *First Gospel*, 80. The Qumran community also cited Isa 40:3. See 1QS VIII, 14–16.

of mirror for John; in this respect, he was a prophetic servant of God like Isaiah the prophet. John was most likely understood to be "a voice of one calling in the wilderness." In addition, it is important to take a look at the context of Isa 40:3. It has been believed to be part of Second Isaiah, written after Cyrus of Persia defeated Darius III of Babylonia (Isa 45:1–3). As a result, the Jews in Babylon were able to have the hope of being freed from bondage and returning to their hometown. This was considered to be the second Exodus which symbolized the salvation of God. Based on the Jewish tradition, Q could describe that John was the prophetic servant of God who would lead people to the salvation of God. Then, the quotation from Isa 40:3 is the result of the redactor's theological interpretation about the role of John and informs readers of the possibility that there was a scribe who was able to interpret it under the light of the Bible. On the one hand, John was a respected prophet who raised his voice in the wilderness for the salvation of people; on the other hand, repentance of sins was how to prepare the way for the Lord and make straight paths for YHWH.

B. THE FIRST PROCLAMATION OF JOHN (Q 3:7–9)

The first proclamation of John is written in Q 3:7–9 (Luke 3:7–9; Matt 3:7–10). This text follows Q 3:2–4 by the connecting word "baptism" and the implication that his proclamation refers to the voice calling in the wilderness. However, as shown in the prologue, 3:7–9 leaves a clue about the different hands for redaction. From a redaction critical perspective, it can be said that the flow of content from 3:7–8a to 3:9 is interrupted by 3:8bc.[6] This implies that 3:8bc was interpolated in between 3:7–8a and 3:9 by a later redactor.[7] Thus, when 3:7–8a is connected with 3:9, the content naturally flows with regard to the theme of "fruit worthy of repentance." Then, it can be concluded that 3:7–8a, 9 originated from the redaction to which 3:2–4 belongs; on the other hand, 3:8bc belongs to a later redaction.

The proclamation of John is introduced by the phrase "He said." No particular introductory formula is used for his proclamation. This means that the redactor of this text simply wanted to deliver the proclamation of John. Although Q introduces the crowds as his audience, their identity is not known because they are simply depicted as those who came to John to be baptized. Probably, they were the marginal people in the region of the

---

6. Kloppenborg, *Formation*, 103–4; and Jacobson, *First Gospel*, 82. On the contrary, Tuckett argues for the unity of Q 3:7–9 (Q, 110–14).

7. Davies and Allison, *Gospel according to St. Matthew*, 317; and Uro, "John the Baptist," 244.

Jordan, were disregarded by the ordinary people, and would not participate in the ritual service held at the synagogue or the temple. On the other hand, they could be those who had waited for the new era of God because they were disappointed with the contemporary religious system. This implies that the baptism was allowed to anyone who repented his or her sins. However, it is indefinite whether they constituted a community or not. Nevertheless, it was possible that after a while, a group of followers gathered together around John. It seems that they started collecting his words and activities.

The proclamation of John begins with the rebuke against those coming to him. Having called them "You, brood of vipers," John revealed his spiritual power strong enough to rebuke them. In this way, the redactor depicted John as an authoritative agent of God. In addition, John emphasized the fruit of worthy of repentance in order to avoid the impending wrath—that is, the eschatological judgment of God. In this way, the precondition to avoid the impending wrath is indirectly suggested. However, the redactor does not definitely explain how the impending wrath will be and what the fruit worthy of repentance is, yet. It is, however, clear that John's proclamation of impending wrath and repentance is the way to prepare the way for God the Lord (Q 3:4). In this respect, John is described as the eschatological agent.[8]

The proclamation of John conveys the metaphor of an ax (Q 3:9). It is said that an ax is lying [κεῖται] at the root of the trees and that every tree not bearing good fruit is being chopped down [ἐκκόπτεται] and being thrown [βάλλεται] into the fire. It is important to observe that the present tense of verbs is used in three places. It seems that the ax stands for John's preaching to bear fruit worthy of repentance and that the trees refer to the crowds who heard his message about repentance. In this way, the present aspect of eschatological judgment is emphasized here. It is, however, noteworthy that the trees are not distinguished from their origin. It means that everyone was born of equal status before God. However, what is important is that the redactor focuses on the effort to bear the fruit worthy of repentance. From the context, it can be said that bearing the fruit worthy of repentance means doing what is right. In this respect, everyone is responsible for it. Then, fire is described as the tool of eschatological judgment as it has been used in the Jewish tradition. Without doubt, the eschatological judgment is being performed by God. At last, the conclusion can be drawn that the eschatological judgment of God is being passed on to those who would not bear the fruit worthy of repentance in response to the proclamation of John.[9]

---

8. Jacobson, *First Gospel*, 82.
9. Cf. Fledderman, "Beginning," 158.

C. THE SECOND PROCLAMATION OF JOHN (Q 3:16–17)

The second proclamation of John is introduced in Q 3:16–17 (Luke 3:16–17; Matt 3:11–12). This text follows Q 3:7-8a, 9 by common themes: the role of John, baptism, and eschatological judgment.[10] However, differences are found with regard to the agent of baptism, tool for the eschatological judgment, and tense of verb. First, while John is described as the servant of God in 3:7-8a, 9, he is understood to be the forerunner of Jesus in 3:16–17. Second, the baptism of John with water is understood to be inferior to that of Jesus with the spirit and fire. In this way, the role of John suddenly changed, and he was subordinate to Jesus. Third, ax and fire were introduced as the tools for the eschatological judgment in 3:7-8a, 9; on the other hand, pitchfork and fire are mentioned as its tools in 3:16–17. Fourth, the tense of verbs used for the judgment is different; while the present tense verbs are used in 3:7-8a, 9, the future tense verbs are adopted in 3:16–17. Using the future tense verbs, 3:16–17 informs readers of the postponed judgment from present to future. This indicates that 3:7-8a, 9 and 3:16–17 were written from different perspectives, reflecting different occasions for writing about the eschatological judgment. It is unreasonable to think that an author described two different eschatological judgments as if they would happen simultaneously. Therefore, it can be concluded that 3:7-8a, 9 and 3:16–17 originated in different redactions from each other. It is, however, generally believed that 3:16–17 was added to 3:7-8a, 9 by a later redactor because a later redactor described the delay of eschatological judgment which did not happen as soon as John proclaimed.[11]

D. SUMMARY

The above study shows us that three different layers of redaction are detected in Q 3:2-4, 7-9, 16–17. First of all, the first redaction seems to be composed of 3:2-4, 7-8a, 9, because they were written prior to any other texts. Then, 3:16–17 was probably attached to 3:2-4, 7-8a, 9; in addition, 3:8bc was possibly interpolated into its current place. It is, however, difficult to decide yet which one was added earlier to 3:2-4, 7-8a, 9. It will be decided later. At any rate, it can be said that 3:2-4, 7-9, 16–17 went through a process of redaction a couple of times. It is, however, plausible that the first redaction begins with the debut and proclamation of John written in 3:2-4, 7-8a, 9. He was a prophet who came to prepare the way for the Lord God and asked people

---

10. Cf. Kloppenborg, *Formation*, 105.
11. Jacobson, *First Gospel*, 84–85. Cf. Vassiliadis, "Function," 408.

for repentance of sins and the fruit worthy of it. The baptism was a symbolic ritual for those who repented and bore the fruit worthy of repentance in order to be exempted from the impending wrath.

2

The Ministry of Jesus

The ministry of Jesus is depicted in Q 3:21—7:10, which is the second part of the first section. The words and actions of Jesus are exclusively found here. It is, however, noteworthy that the text of his ministry consists of several layers of redaction. In order to distinguish them, it is necessary to take a look at the differences regarding the linguistic characteristics, literary patterns, theological themes, grammatical changes, etc. Then, Jesus will be known as a sage rather than a prophet in the first redaction of Q. Moreover, we will be surprised by his instruction, which is very radical when compared with that of his Jewish contemporaries.

A. PREPARATION FOR MINISTRY (Q 3:21—6:16)

Preparation for the ministry of Jesus is described in Q 3:21—6:16. This includes his baptism (3:21–22), temptation (4:1–13), and selection of the twelve apostles (6:12–16). It will be, however, seen that they also consist of two layers of redaction.

The baptism of Jesus is depicted in Q 3:21-22 (Luke 3:21-22; Matt 3:16-17).[1] This text follows Q 3:16-17 by linking words such as "baptism" and "spirit." Q describes the baptism of Jesus with the Spirit in order to define him as the one whom John foretold in the previous text. As a result, these two texts share a theological theme regarding the promised one to

---

1. There are some who do not agree with the opinion that Q 3:21-22 belongs to Q (Jacobson, *First Gospel*, 85–86; and Kloppenborg, *Q Parallels*, 16). They probably think that Q 3:21-22 came from Mark 1:10-11. It is, however, noted that they did not acknowledge Mark's use of it.

come. Then the natural flow from 3:16–17 to 3:21–22 indicates that they originated from the same redaction. It seems that 3:21–22 as well as 3:16–17 were added to Q¹ 3:2–4, 7–8a, 9 by a later redactor. Then, 3:21–22 will be dealt with later along with 3:16–17 regarding the stage of their redaction.

The temptation of Jesus is introduced in Q 4:1–13 (Luke 4:1–13; Matt 4:1–11). This follows Q 3:21–22 by the linking word "spirit" and the common theme of "God's Son." It is natural to describe that the Spirit descended from heaven led Jesus to the devil to be tempted. It is, however, noteworthy that there are significant differences between the two stories. First, the title of Jesus is slightly different; while the heavenly voice called him "my [God's] Son" (3:22), the devil used "a Son of God" (4:3, 9). Second, the temptation story shows characteristics of a better developed pericope than the baptism story. While the baptism story introduces the unilateral announcement from heaven, the temptation story describes three sets of dialogue between Jesus and the devil. This strengthens the aspect of narrative and implies that the baptism and the temptation stories originated in different redactions from each other. In consequence, it can be said that 4:1–13 was written later than 3:21–22 and attached to it. In addition, the temptation of Jesus recalls the Israelites being tempted by God in the wilderness during the exodus. This allusion is supported by the quotation from Deut 6:13, 16; 8:3 in Q 4:4, 8, 12. The temptation story seems to depict Jesus as the representative of the Israelites who were tested by God in the wilderness. This is strengthened by the fact that the Israelites were often called the "son of God" (Exod 4:22; Isa 65:1; Hos 11:1, etc.). In this respect, Jesus represents the Israelites from a typological perspective, and the temptation story conveys the theme of descendant of Abraham written in 3:8bc. This is supported further by the linking word "stone" in 3:8c and 4:3. Therefore, it can be said that 4:1–13 belong to the redaction in which 3:8bc was included.[2]

The twelve apostles are listed in Q 6:12–16 (Luke 6:12–16; Matt 5:1a; 10:2–4).[3] The text follows Q 4:1–13 by the connecting word "mountain."

---

2. There are many who regard the story of Jesus' temptation as belonging to the last redaction of Q (Kloppenborg, *Formation*, 247–48; Jacobson, *First Gospel*, 90; and Theissen, *Gospels in Context*, 206–9). On the other hand, there are some who would disagree with that argument (Humphrey, "Temptation," 43–50).

3. Many scholars think that the list of the twelve apostles was absent in Q. For example, Kloppenborg does not introduce the list at all. Jacobson also does not think that the list was in Q (*First Gospel*, 251). Robinson, Hoffmann, and Kloppenborg also do not consider the list a part of Q in their book *The Critical Edition of Q*. On the contrary, there are some who argue for the historicity of Jesus that he called the twelve on the basis of 1 Cor 15:5. Although he agrees with it, Attridge does not definitely say that the list was in Q ("Reflections," 233). Its existence in Q will be treated more in detail later when the texts of the fourth redaction will be explained. Without Q 6:12–16, it is

It is natural that Jesus summoned his disciples on the mountain where he finally defeated the devil. After Jesus had been described as the representative of the Israelites in the temptation story, it is reasonable to describe that he selected the twelve apostles as those who replaced the twelve tribes of the Israelites. This makes the comparison between Jesus and Moses possible in that the latter called the twelve tribes, the descendants of Abraham, on Mount Sinai and Nebo. In this way, Q introduces the twelve apostles as the descendants of Abraham mentioned in 3:8bc for the first time. Then, 6:12–16 seems to belong to the redaction which includes 3:8bc and 4:1–13 with regard to the theme of "descendants of Abraham." If the temptation story belonged to the last stage of redaction as Kloppenborg insists, 3:8bc and 6:12–16 also seem to belong to it.

Q introduces three episodes for the description of Jesus' preparation for ministry: baptism, temptation, and the selection of the twelve apostles. It is, however, noteworthy that they were plausibly written later than the first redaction. It can be said that Q has shown three layers of redaction so far. The first redaction consists of Q 3:2-4, 7-8a, 9. Then, later redaction includes 3:16-17, 21-22. In addition, the latest one has 3:8bc; 4:1-13; 6:12-16. Although the analysis is not thorough enough, it is possible to say that the texts listed above show three different redactions.

B. THE INSTRUCTION OF JESUS

A bundle of Jesus' instructions is found in Q 6:20-49. This text follows 3:21—6:16 by the theme of Jesus' ministry. However, the instruction is also composed of several redactions. When we isolate the texts of the first redaction, they will show what the instructions of the historical Jesus were.

The Disciples (Q 6:20a)

The reference to the disciples is found in Q 6:20a (Luke 6:20a; Matt 5:1b). This text follows Q 6:12-16 by the theme of "disciples." Although it is natural to describe the disciples at the beginning part, it seems to be created at the last stage of redaction.

The term "disciple" appears for the first time in Q 6:20a. The disciples undeniably refer to the twelve apostles selected by Jesus on the mountain (6:12-16). In this respect, the content flows naturally from 6:12-16 to 6:20a. In other words, 6:20a seems to belong to the redaction in which 6:12-16

---

impossible to mention the twelve thrones and tribes in 22:30.

was included. However, a difference is found between "apostles" and "disciples." It seems that the twelve apostles were those chosen from the disciples. In this respect, 6:20a seems to originate in the latest redaction along with 3:8bc; 4:1–13; 6:12–16.

The Beatitudes (Q 6:20b–23)

Four beatitudes are listed in Q 6:20b–23 (Luke 6:20b–23; Matt 5:3–4, 6). As treated briefly in the prologue, they seem to consist of four redactions. Therefore, it is necessary to see which belongs to the first redaction and identify the characteristic of each redaction.

The first beatitude is described in Q 6:20b. It is said, "Blessed are you who are poor, for yours is the kingdom of God."[4] The poor are promised to possess the kingdom of God—that is, the eschatological place. No other precondition is required of them. Then, the kingdom of God is connected with the present tense verb ἐστίν in order to describe its present aspect. This recalls the first proclamation of John because the present tense verb is used three times in order to depict the present aspect of eschatological judgment (Q[1] 3:7–8a, 9). In other words, both the first proclamation of John and the first beatitude of Jesus share a common element with regard to the temporal aspect—that is, a present aspect of eschatological matter. Another common element is plausible in that the kingdom of God and the impending wrath are related to God's judgment. It seems that John and Jesus shared a perspective on the realized eschatology. Moreover, the content flows from 3:7–8a, 9 to 6:20b naturally in that "the poor" could refer to the crowds who came to John in the wilderness of the Jordan. The elements mentioned above tell people about the possibility that 6:20b followed 3:2–4, 7–8a, 9 in the first redaction. Then, the first redactor emphasized the present aspect of eschatological matter with regard to the impending wrath and the kingdom of God.

The first beatitude characterizes the kingdom of God. The kingdom of God relates to the economic affluence that gives contentment to them.[5] Generally then, the kingdom of God stands for the situation or circumstance that gives contentment to those who look for a better life. In this respect, Jesus was supposed to proclaim the kingdom to the marginal people

---

4. While Matthew used the third person plural pronoun (Matt 5:3), Luke adopted the second person plural (Luke 6:20b). It seems that the Lucan version represents the original wording of Q (Robinson et al., *Critical Edition*, 46). This kind of difference is also found in the second and third beatitudes in Q 6:21.

5. Ra, *Origin*, 100.

from a socio-religious perspective. It is interesting that economic poverty was suggested as the precondition in order to belong to the kingdom of God. This implies that the audience of Jesus was probably the poor people who could not help but depend upon God at that time. The poor wished that their economic poverty could end soon. They seemed to be not much different from the crowds who came to John in the wilderness to hear his preaching and to be baptized. At any rate, it was Jesus who mentioned the kingdom of God for the first time.[6]

Two more beatitudes are listed in Q 6:21. As mentioned in the prologue, they are different from the first beatitude in many aspects (6:20b). First of all, they adopted future tense verbs rather than present tense. As a result, the moment of being blessed is postponed to the future. Second, the subject appears in a different form in that the substantive function of the present participle is used here. The content of blessing is specific in that the hungry will be satisfied and those who mourn will laugh. This implies that the second and third beatitudes originated in a redaction other than the first one, to which the first beatitude belongs. To my judgment, the second and third beatitudes were added to the first beatitude by a later redactor because the kingdom of God did not come as soon as Jesus promised. Then, it can be said that while the first beatitude belonged to the first redaction, the second and third beatitudes originated in the later redaction. It is, however, not yet clear whether they were created or redacted when 3:16–17 was done.

The fourth beatitude is described in Q 6:22–23. However, differences are found in various ways. First, while the previous three beatitudes use the conjunctive particle ὅτι [because] (6:20b–21), the fourth beatitude uses ὅταν [when] (6:22–23). Second, the precondition to be blessed changed from the "general human afflictions"—such as poverty, hunger, or mourning—to a specified situation—such as insult, hatred, and maltreatment on account of the Son of Man. One's relationship with Jesus the Son of Man comes to the fore as the precondition to be blessed. Third, the characteristic of reward changed from an earthly one (6:20b–21) to a heavenly one (6:22–23). These differences imply that 6:22–23 originated in a redaction different from that to which 6:20b–21 belongs. In other words, the fourth beatitude was added to the first three by a later redactor. The fourth beatitude seems to originate from the redaction to which 3:16–17, 21–22 belong because of the following reasons. First, the heavenly aspect of blessing is to be pointed out; while 3:21–22 deals with the heavenly voice announced to Jesus, 6:22–23b mentions the reward in heaven. Second, the role of Jesus is getting more

---

6. The term "kingdom of God" does not appear in the Bible or in the intertestamental writings penned prior to the first century CE (Collins, "Kingdom of God," 81).

focused; while he is the one coming after John in 3:16–17, the relationship with him is introduced as the criterion to be blessed or not in 6:22–23b. These common characteristics evince the possibility that 6:22–23b belongs to the redaction from which 3:16–17, 21–22 originated. Then, it can be concluded that 3:16–17, 21–22; 6:22–23b originated from the third redaction, while 3:2–4, 7–8a, 9; 6:20b belong to the first one, 6:21 to the second one, and 3:8bc; 4:1–13; 6:12–16, 20a to the fourth one.

As discussed in the prologue, many scholars have assigned Q 6:23c to the later addition to 6:22–23b. The persecution of the prophets is mentioned for the first time in connection with their forefathers having done the same. Then, this saying implies that the disciples of Jesus were also persecuted by their fellow people. This reveals a couple of different aspects from 6:22–23b. First of all, the intensity of opposition enhanced from insult and maltreatment to persecution. Such a change reflects the worsened environment of the disciples. Second, they understood themselves as similar to the prophets persecuted by the forefathers. This implies that the redactor of 6:23c understood the persecution of the disciples of Jesus from the Deuteronomistic tradition.[7] In consequence, 6:23c is to be considered a later addition to 6:20b–23b.[8] Then, it is necessary to see to which redaction 6:23c belongs. For this, the mentioning of "forefathers" tells people about the plausible connection with 3:8bc, because "forefathers" appears in both texts and they are inevitably related with the theme of "descendants of Abraham." Then, the above explanation leads us to the conclusion that 6:23c belongs to the fourth redaction along with 3:8bc. In conclusion, the fourth redaction consists of 3:8bc; 4:1–13; 6:12–16, 20a, 23c at the beginning part of Q.

To sum up, the above study has shown that the beatitudes consist of four redactions. It seems that Q 6:20b originated from the first redaction; and then two beatitudes were added in 6:21 that belongs to the second redaction. Later, 6:22–23b was attached to 6:20b–21 at the stage of the third redaction. Finally, the fourth redactor put 6:20a in front of and 6:23c at the back of 6:20b–23b. It can be concluded that so far, the text 6:20–23 has shown the possibility of four redactions.[9] In this way, the beatitudes were expanded by supplementary redaction as time passed. Thus, 6:20–23

---

7. Cf. Steck, *Israel*, 20–26, 257–60; and Jacobson, *First Gospel*, 72, 100–101. Neh 9:26 is the best candidate that reflects the Deuteronomist historical perspective. See also Seeley, "Jesus' Death," 223.

8. Cf. Jacobson, *First Gospel*, 62, 100–101; and Mack, "Kingdom," 610n4.

9. Cf. Jacobson, *First Gospel*, 100; Kloppenborg, *Formation*, 173; Kloppenborg, "Blessing," 36–37, 45; and Horsley, "Questions," 194. However, they fail to say that the four texts belong to different redaction from each other.

provides the theoretic basis for the distinction of four redactions in the following texts.

The Ethical Instruction (Q 6:27–38)

A series of commandment about ethical behavior is introduced in Q 6:27–38 (Luke 6:27–38; Matt 5:39–40, 42, 44–48; 7:1–2, 12). This text follows Q 6:20–23 by the implication that it is also an instruction of Jesus. This text reveals the instruction regarding the reciprocal relationship among people. Then, it can be divided into three paragraphs 6:27–30; 6:31–36; and 6:37–38, and a less radical instruction regarding the intensity of reciprocity is reflected in the texts according to this order.

The most radical commandment about human relationship is written in Q 6:27. For this, the introductory formula λέγω ὑμῖν [I tell you] is used at the beginning. This leads readers to the instruction about ethical behavior of people. Then, the main thesis follows immediately saying, "Love your enemies." This is a unique type of instruction by Jesus, which is not found among the Jewish documents. The instruction about loving one's enemy was most radical and extraordinary, no matter who the enemy was. It is, however, noteworthy that this instruction was addressed to everyone.[10] The imperative form of instruction reminds readers of 3:8a, in which John commanded the crowds to bear the fruit worthy of repentance with the imperative verb. In addition, the second person plural pronoun recalls that used in 6:20b. Although this does not ensure that they originated from the same redaction, it sheds light on their similarity. In this respect, 6:27 seems to be written by the same editorial hand as that of 3:8a and 6:20b at the stage of the first redaction.

The instruction about prayer for others is written in Q 6:28. It is said that people have to pray for those who maltreated them.[11] The theme of prayer appears for the first time here. For this, the imperative form is used following its preceding commandment in Q¹ 6:27. It is, however, to be noted that the term "mistreat" reminds readers of Q³ 6:22–23b, which puts forth the maltreatment of disciples by their fellows in the society. It can be said

---

10. The instruction about the love of enemies is contrasted with the saying, "Love your neighbor," written in Lev 19:18 (Allison, *Intertextual Jesus*, 30).

11. Matthew mentions those who persecuted the disciples (Matt 5:44b), while Luke deals with those who mistreated them (Luke 6:28). I prefer the Lucan version as the original wording of Q because the term "mistreat" fits better with the surrounding context of Q 6:28. It is difficult to say that the disciples of Jesus were persecuted at the very beginning of his ministry.

that 6:28 was added to 6:27 by the redactor who also wrote 6:22–23b. In this respect, 6:28 seems to originate from the third redaction.

Three applications of loving one's enemy are written in Q 6:29–30. First, the instruction about non-retaliation is dealt with as the first application in 6:29a. It is said that one has to offer the other as well when someone slaps him or her on the cheek. It is clear that one can slap others who are subordinate. In other words, the superior could slap the inferior. No matter whether the Lucan or Matthean version represents the original wording of Q (Luke 6:29a; Matt 5:39b), according to the Jewish tradition, being slapped on the right cheek with the back of one's right hand is more shameful than being slapped on the left cheek with its front.[12] Thus, one should endure the less shameful slapping after he or she suffered the more shameful. It seems that the slapped were those who were not allowed to protest. In this way, those who followed Jesus were required to live a non-retaliatory lifestyle. The instruction about non-retaliation reaches its culmination in this verse. In other words, it is a way of loving one's enemy.

The second application of loving one's enemy is introduced in Q 6:29b. It is said that when someone wants a shirt, one has to give his or her coat as well. It seems to be a matter between the creditor and the debtor. It has been well known that the law taught the Jews to return the coat to the poor by sunset, so that he or she might sleep in it (Exod 22:26–27; Deut 24:12–13). It is, however, to be reminded that an ordinary but poor person cannot observe the instruction to give his or her coat voluntarily in case of legal obligation. Even if a person is deprived of his or her shirt, he or she has to take off the coat ahead. Although it is not easy to give the coat that was already taken off, it is said that one has to do that. This instruction emphasizes voluntary donation rather than forced deprival. In this way, the followers of Jesus were required to live a sacrificial life. This is the second application of how to love one's enemy. In this respect, the teaching about voluntary sacrifice reaches its acme in this saying.

The third application is described in Q 6:30. It is said that one should give to everyone who asks, and if something is taken, not to demand it back. This reminds readers of Exod 22:25 which prohibits one from charging any interest. This is how to love and help those who are in need from an economical perspective. The instructions listed above have a common element that one should do with love more than what he or she was asked. It seems that these radical instructions are the application of how to love one's enemy. They can be the way how to bear the fruit worthy of repentance and

---

12. Cf. Mishnah Baba Qamma 8:6. Wink paid attention to the slapping with the back of one's hand as a means of punishing inferiors ("Neither Passivity," 5–27, esp. 8).

avoid the impending wrath (Q¹ 3:7–8a. 9).[13] In addition, those who were slapped on their cheek and deprived of their coats seem to be the marginal and poor people. Then, it can be said that they were those to whom Jesus promised the kingdom of God (6:20b). Then, it can be said that the text of 6:27, 29–30 also originated from the first redaction.

The less radical commandment regarding the human relationship is written in Q 6:31–36. The so-called Golden Rule is addressed as another principle for ethical behavior with the positive imperative: "Do to others as you would have them do" (6:31). This commandment also carries the reciprocal relationship among people as the text of 6:27, 29–30 does. It is, however, noteworthy that this commandment is less radical than the preceding one. Then, the redactor introduced a pair of instruction in 6:32–34 in order to support the commandment in 6:31. It is said that if a person loves only those who love him or her, he or she does not receive the reward. Even the tax collectors love those who love them (6:32).[14] In the same manner, the matter of lending money is treated (6:34).[15] This seems to be a repetition of the preceding instruction (6:30); in this way, the redactor revealed a Jewish characteristic in shaping dual examples which reflects the number of witnesses (Deut 19:15). There are two things on the agenda with regard to reciprocity and reward. First, the matter of loving one and lending money are mentioned with regard to the reciprocal relationship. It is, however, noteworthy that the Golden Rule is easier to be observed than the commandment to love one's enemy. In other words, the Golden Rule and its related instructions lower the religio-ethical burden of loving others including enemies. However, one should do more than loving only those who love him or her. Second, the redactor mentioned the reward. Those who observe the commandment may become sons of God the Father (Q 6:35). The redactor opened the way to the tax collectors and the sinners to be the children of God although they could be regarded as "the brood of vipers" (3:7). The filial relationship is emphasized for the first time here. It

---

13. Cf. Sato, Q, 33–34; and Jacobson, *First Gospel*, 81.

14. It is not easy to decide which version represents the original wording of Q because Luke adopted "sinners" while Matthew mentioned "tax collector." To my judgment, the term "tax collectors" is preferred to "sinners" because the latter is too ambiguous and vague to be used in this context. The tax collectors can be categorized as one of those who had to repent their sins (Q¹ 3:8a). In this vein, Robinson seems to adopt the Matthean version (*Critical Edition*, 68).

15. Once again, it is not easy to decide the original wording of Q between the Matthean and the Lucan versions. It seems that Lucan version is preferred to the Matthean because the similar matter was already treated in the previous texts in Q 6:30. It is, however, difficult to consider "the Gentiles" to be part of Q; rather, the term "sinners" fit in the context better.

is, however, to be reminded that the ordinary Jews considered themselves "sons of God" according to their tradition (Exod 4:22; Hos 11:1; Isa 63:16, etc.). Then, it seems that although the redactor raised a question about who were the true sons of God with this instruction, he or she did not segregate the followers of Jesus from the Jewish society yet. It seems that they were identified as those who belong to the kingdom of God (Q^1 6:20b). In this respect, 6:31–35 seems to be a part of the first redaction as 6:20b does.

In consequence, the redactor made a conclusion to the less radical instruction regarding the reciprocal relationship in Q 6:36. It is said that one should be merciful as God is merciful. This is the way to be like God the Father who is generous to both the good and evil.[16] The inclusive characteristic of God is the mirror for those who listened to the sage instruction of Jesus. In this respect, the filial relationship with God is connected with the imitation of him. It seems that the imitation of God was the top priority of the first redactor.

The least radical instruction regarding human relationship is described in Q 6:37–38. It is said in the form of negative imperative: "Do not judge, and you will not be judged" (6:37). In a similar manner, it is said that one will be measured with the measurement that he or she used to measure out. (6:38). The redactor listed a pair of sayings regarding the reciprocal relationship among people.[17] It is, however, noteworthy that one of them is written in the negative imperative form.[18] The negative imperative form delivers a strong prohibition. Nevertheless, it is to be remembered that not doing something is much easier than doing something that has been asked for. It is sufficient enough for people that they stop judging or criticizing others. In this sense, the commandment written in 6:37–38 is the least radical instruction among the three groups regarding the human relationship. Then, from the fact that the text of 6:37–38 deals with the instruction about reciprocal relationship, it can be said that this also originated in the first redaction along with 6:27, 29–36. In addition, the fact they adopted verbs of the present tense indicates the importance of practicing the ethical decree in their life. This recalls the usage of present tense verbs in Q^1 3:7–8a, 9; 6:20b. This strengthens the possibility that 6:37–38 originated from the first redaction.

In conclusion, the content of Q 6:27, 29–38 is as radical as that of 3:7 and 6:20b. In other words, Jesus taught the crowds how to live with a non-retaliatory and sacrificial attitude (6:27, 29–38) as he promised the kingdom

---

16. This reminds readers of Lev 19:2 regarding the imitation of God (Allison, *Intertextual Jesus*, 29–30).

17. Kee, *Jesus*, 92.

18. It is, however, noteworthy that this saying is reminiscent of Lev 19:15 in the fact that there is a striking contrast (Allison, *Intertextual Jesus*, 33).

of God to the poor (6:20b) and John proclaimed the impending wrath to the crowds calling them "You brood of vipers" (3:7). There is a possibility that the text 6:27, 29–38 was introduced as the way to bear the fruit worthy of repentance and avoid the impending wrath (3:7–8a, 9). It seems that the redactor tried to describe the instruction of Jesus in connection with that of John. In this respect, the text of 6:27, 29–38 seems to belong to the first redaction with 3:7–8a, 9 and 6:20b.[19]

To sum up, Q 6:27–38 consists of two redactions. In other words, 6:27, 29–38 was written as the way of bearing the fruit worthy of repentance at the first stage of redaction. Then, 6:28 was interpolated in between 6:27 and 6:29–38 by the third redactor in order to instruct the disciples of Jesus to pray for those who mistreated them. The same way of redaction is found in 3:7–9 in that the fourth redactor inserted his or her source 3:8bc in between 3:7–8a and 3:9 which were the texts of the first redaction. It is clear that the interpolation was a common way of supplement.

The Instruction about the Conflict (Q 6:39–49)

A group of instruction regarding the conflict is found in Q 6:39–49 (Luke 6:39–49; Matt 7:3–5, 16, 18, 21, 24–27; 10:24–25; 12:33–35; 15:14). This text follows Q^1 6:27, 29–38 by the fact that it also deals with relationships among people. However, from the fact that the text 6:39–49 shows a different context from Q^1 6:27, 29–38,[20] it can be said that this text originated in a redaction other than the first one. Q 6:39–49 can be divided into four paragraphs—namely, 6:39–40, 41–42, 44–45, 46–49—according to the different expressions of competition and conflict.

A proverbial saying appears regarding the blind in Q 6:39. It is said, "Can a blind man lead a blind man? Will they not both fall into a pit?" The term "blind" appears for the first time here. The blind stands for those who do not know what they should know. In this respect, the term "blind" reflects that the occasion for writing was a context of competition and conflict with the opponents. This recalls the occasion of insult and hatred written in Q^3 6:22–23b. In this respect, it seems that 6:39 originated from the third redaction with 6:22–23b.

The relationship between a teacher and disciple is mentioned in Q 6:40. It is said, "It is enough for the student [disciple] to be like his teacher" (cf. Matt 10:25). This text also reflects competition with opponents. This is

---

19. Q 6:27–38 "rewrites Leviticus 19" and "puts the Q unit firmly within a tradition" (Allison, *Intertextual Jesus*, 37).

20. Jacobson, *First Gospel*, 106.

different from what was taught regarding the reciprocal relationship among people written in Q¹ 6:27, 29–38. From the fact that the theme of conflict appeared in Q³ 6:22–23b, it can be said that 6:39–40 also belongs to the third redaction. In other words, the third redactor identified the opponent as the blind teacher and student who hated and insulted the disciples of Jesus.

A metaphor about eye is described in Q 6:41–42. This deals with the matter of more intensified conflict between two groups in that reproach is described in this text. Jesus criticized those who did not recognize the beam in their eyes but saw the speck in their brother's eyes. They are identified as hypocrites; therefore, they are demanded to take the beam first out of their eyes. This reflects that Jesus and his disciples had a different view from their fellows. In this respect, 6:41–42 also belongs to the third redaction along with 6:22–23b and 6:39–40 because of the tension between Jesus and his fellows in their normal life.[21]

The parable of the good and bad trees is described in Q 6:43–45. This parable reminds readers of the proclamation of John with regard to the common element "tree" (Q¹ 3:7–8a, 9). There is, however, a difference between them with regard to the origin. John did not deal with the origin of the tree; rather he mentioned the fruit worthy of repentance. On the other hand, this parable mentions two different trees from their origin. In other words, while John's proclamation focuses on different kinds of fruit from the same tree (3:8a, 9), this parable is concerned with different fruits from different trees (6:43–44).[22] Then, the difference between the two trees is applied to the two different kinds of human beings in 6:45. It seems that 6:43–45 also reflects a situation of conflict between the followers of Jesus and their opponents. The theme of difference from one's origin reminds readers of 3:16–17 in that the wheat and chaff are different from their origin. From the fact that 6:43–45 also carries the theme of distinction between two groups of people, it goes along with its previous texts such as 6:22–23b; 6:39–40; and 6:41–42. In addition, the term πονηρός [evil] is commonly used in both 6:22–23b and 6:45. The common elements listed above make it possible to think that 6:43–45 also belongs to the third redaction along with 3:16–17; 6:22–23b;

---

21. Some scholars point out that the connection between Q 6:39 and 6:41–42 is obvious. Cf. Jacobson, *First Gospel*, 104, 106–7. Jacobson thinks that 6:39 and 6:41–42 belong to the redactional work added to the tradition.

22. On the other hand, some scholars insist that Q 6:43–44 is used as an example of how to bear fruit worthy of repentance (cf. Sato, *Q*, 33–34; and Jacobson, *First Gospel*, 104–5). Their insistence could be understandable when the third redaction was complete.

6:39–40; and 6:41–42. The further the redaction of Q progressed, the clearer the distinction between good and evil was made.

The instruction about observance of the Lord's words appears in Q 6:46–49. The identification of Jesus as the "Lord" differs from the text that defined God as the Lord in the first redaction (Q^1 3:4). This implies that the title began to be applied to Jesus by a later redactor. On the other hand, his identity as the Lord recalls "the one coming after me" (Q^3 3:16) and "the Son of Man" (6:22) in that the identification of Jesus was made. It seems that as time passed, more and more focus was being placed on Jesus' identity. In addition, the parable of the two builders drew a contrast between the wise and unwise. The sharp contrast calls our attention to that between the wheat and chaff in 3:17, the beam and speck in 6:42, the healthy and decayed in 6:43, and the good and evil in 6:45. In addition, the theme of obedience to Jesus comes to the fore for the first time in 6:46–49. The parable of the two builders is introduced as an example of those who observed what Jesus had said and those who did not. The concentration on Jesus the Lord reminds readers of 6:22–23b regarding one's relationship with Jesus the Son of Man. Moreover, the instruments that destroyed the house on sand—such as strong wind and flood—signify the attack of the opponents on the followers of Jesus—such as insult and hatred—listed in 6:22–23b. From the observation above, it can be said that 6:46–49 originated from the third redaction in which 3:16–17; 6:22–23b, 41–45 are included.

In conclusion, it seems that Q 6:39–49 is composed of texts that belong to the third redaction. This was attached to Q^1 6:27, 29–38 by the third redactor in order to strengthen the instruction of Jesus focusing on competition and conflict with opponents. In this respect, the instruction of Jesus also went through a process of redaction as time passed.

C. THE ACTIVITY OF JESUS (Q 7:1–10)

The story about the Gentile centurion is introduced in Q 7:1–10 (Luke 7:1–10; Matt 8:5–10, 13). This text follows Q^3 6:46–49 by linking words such as "Lord" and "word," and the theme of obedience to his words.[23] It seems, however, that this story was created by the third redactor.

This story describes the lordship of Jesus over the centurion. This is seen in that the centurion obeyed the words of the Lord Jesus. Then, the centurion is the example of those represented by the wise builder (Q^3 6:46–49).[24] In addition, the identification of Jesus as the Lord calls our attention to what

---

23. Lührmann, *Redaktion*, 58; and Jacobson, *First Gospel*, 109.
24. Cf. Jacobson, *First Gospel*, 109–10; and Kloppenborg, *Formation*, 117.

is written in 3:16–17; 6:22–23b and 6:46. The obedience of the centurion to the Lord Jesus is contrasted with those who insulted and hated his followers in 6:22–23b.[25] Moreover, it is necessary to take into consideration that the term "worthy" [ἱκανός] appears in 3:16 and 7:6.[26] This implies that 7:1–10 originated in the third redaction along with 3:16–17; 6:22–23b, 46–49.

D. SUMMARY

The ministry of Jesus is described in Q 3:21—7:10. It is, however, to be noted that it consists of four redactions. For instance, the first redactor wrote the instruction of Jesus in 6:20b, 27, 29–38. Then, the second redactor attached two beatitudes in 6:21. Later, the third redactor added the texts concentrated on the relationship with Jesus in 3:21–22; 6:22–23b, 28, 39–49; 7:1–10. Finally, the fourth redactor interpolated his sources describing Jesus into the background events of the forefathers in 4:1–13; 6:12–16, 20a, 23c. It is clear that each redactor had his or her own purpose in supplementing the sources to the previous redactions.

---

25. Horsley, "Questions," 187.
26. Catchpole, "Centurion's Faith," 536.

3

Jesus and John

After the separate description about John and Jesus, Q defines their relationship in the third part of the first section (Q 7:18–35). This part can be divided into three paragraphs: the evaluation of Jesus on John (7:18–28), the role of John (7:29–30), and the response of this generation to Jesus and John (7:31–35). John is evaluated from both positive and negative perspectives. In this respect, this part plays the role of conclusion to the previous two parts. It seems that this text is also composed of three redactions. When we examine this part, it will be shown that John was depicted as the servant of God for righteousness in the first redaction. However, as the redaction of Q progressed, Jesus was described as the one superior to John.

A. THE EVALUATION ON JOHN (Q 7:18–28)

A series of Jesus' words about John appears in Q 7:18–28 (Luke 7:18–28; Matt 11:2–11). John is depicted as a prophetic figure. However, this text seems to consist of two redactions. It is noteworthy that John was depicted as the one inferior to Jesus.

The doubt of John about Jesus is written in Q 7:18–23. John sent his disciples to Jesus and asked him whether he was the one promised to come. This recalls the proclamation of John about the one coming after him (Q³ 3:16–17). In addition, 7:18–23 mention the miracles that Jesus performed. Although this text does not describe miracles in detail, the mentioning of "the blind" calls our attention to 6:39 in which a reference to it appears. Moreover, the relationship between John and his disciples reminds readers of 6:40 in which the terms "teacher" and "disciple" appear. Furthermore, when Jesus mentions miracles in 7:22, it probably calls our attention to the healing event for the Gentile centurion (Q^3 7:1–10). In this respect, John is contrasted with the centurion regarding the faith in and the obedience to Jesus. Finally, one's relationship with Jesus is suggested as the criterion to be blessed or not in 7:23. This reminds readers of the beatitude written in 6:22–23b because it also emphasizes the importance of one's relationship with Jesus the Son of Man as the criterion to be blessed or not. In consequence, John is described as the one who heard about Jesus but actually did not believe in him. In this sense, he represented those who received the instruction of Jesus but did not obey (6:46–47). This indicates that 7:18–23 also originated from the third redaction, to which the texts mentioned above belong.

The evaluation of Jesus on John is found in Q 7:24–27. This follows Q^3 7:18–23 by the theme of relationship between John and Jesus. Jesus talked about John after his disciples left Jesus. This implies that Jesus was in the superior position so as to make an evaluation on John. Whereas John was supposed to be depicted as the primary leader in the first redaction, he is a little bit downgraded in this text in that he had been evaluated by Jesus.[1] As time passed, it seems that John was losing his influence on the followers in comparison to Jesus. In addition, the quotation that describes John as the one coming before Jesus reminds readers of his proclamation about the coming one after him (3:16–17).[2] This reinforces the possibility that 7:24–27 originated in the third redaction along with 3:16–17 and 7:18–23.[3]

The status of John is disregarded in Q 7:28. John is described as the one who was the greatest among those born of women but was less than the least in the kingdom of God. This saying implies that he was excluded from the kingdom of God. John is probably depicted as the one inferior to the disciples of Jesus who represented the descendants of Abraham—that is, the entrants of the kingdom of God (Q^4 3:8bc; 6:12–16).[4] This is the worst description about the status and role of John so far and collides with the positive description about his status as the one better than the prophets

---

1. Pointing out the fact that Q describes the superiority of Jesus to John in 7:18–35, Robinson argues for the Christian characteristic in this text ("Sayings," 362). It is, however, to be noted that the title "Christ" does not appear in Q. In this sense, it has been doubted whether Q is a Christian document. I do not agree with that; rather Q is a Jewish document.

2. Tuckett, *Q*, 125.

3. Jacobson, *First Gospel*, 114.

4. Mack insists that the redaction of Q shows a distorted eulogy for John (*Lost Gospel*, 157–58). See also Tuckett, *Q*, 137.

and as the messenger sent by God ahead of Jesus (Q³ 7:24–27). Here we must ask whether it was possible that a redactor was able to have a different understanding of John. The different perspective on the status of John makes us think about the possibility that 7:28 was probably added to Q³ 7:24–27 by a later redactor.[5] In other words, as the redaction of Q progressed, the status of John was getting worse. Then, it can be said that 7:28 belongs to the fourth redaction along with 3:8bc and 6:12–16.

B. THE ROLE OF JOHN (Q 7:29–30)

The positive role of John is described in Q 7:29–30 (Luke 7:29–30; Matt 21:31–32). This text follows Q 7:18–28 by the fact that John was chosen as a medium for the servant of God. It is, however, noteworthy that this text shows somewhat different aspects of John from the previous texts in that he was depicted from a positive perspective. This tells people about the possibility that 7:29–30 originated in a redaction other than the third and fourth.

It is interesting to observe that the term "tax collectors" is mentioned as the audience of John. They are depicted as those who responded positively to the proclamation of John; in other words, they believed in the righteousness of God proclaimed by John.[6] It is, however, noteworthy that the tax collectors were already mentioned when Jesus instructed how to love others (Q¹ 6:32); in other words, the audience of Jesus' instruction had to be better than the tax collectors who loved those who had loved them. Then, it is very plausible that the text of 7:29–30 originated from the first redaction in which 6:32 is also included. It has been well known that the tax collectors were despised by the ordinary people due to their traitorous loyalty to the Roman Empire by collecting taxes excessively. Then, they could be one of those designated as "the brood of vipers" and asked to repent and bear the fruit worthy of repentance (Q¹ 3:7). It seems that the tax collectors responded to the proclamation of John; thus, they probably repented their sins and were baptized by John. This is why the first redactor depicted the tax collectors as those who believed in the righteousness of God proclaimed by John at the ending part of the first section. In this respect, the text of

---

5. Jacobson, "Literary Unity," 381n45; and Jacobson, *First Gospel*, 116. It was suggested that Q 7:28b is to be regarded as a correction to 7:27 (Wink, *John the Baptist*, 24–25).

6. While the Lucan version mentions "God's way was right" (Luke 7:29), the Matthean version reads "the way of righteousness" (Matt 21:32). It seems that Q contained the term "righteous" or "righteousness." On the other hand, Robinson does not include this term in Q (*Critical Edition*, 138).

7:29–30 seems to recapitulate the role of John described in the texts of the first redaction.

John is introduced in relationship to God. It is said that he came to the world for the righteousness of God.[7] Here John is depicted as the servant of God leading people to it. Righteousness is an important element for the Jews to be the people of God. This reminds readers of the proclamation of John about preparation for the way of the Lord God who would come to his people (Q¹ 3:4). Then, the way and path of God were no other than John's work to lead people to the righteousness of God. In other words, John did not separate himself from the Jewish religious environment. In this respect, the text of 7:29–30 seems to originate in the redaction which also includes 3:4.

There were some who did not accept the proclamation of John (Q 7:30). Although their identity has not been known, they were in contrast to the tax collectors in their attitude toward John. Probably, they were people of privileged class. They were not deficient of religious need. They could be those who came to John but did not repent their sins and were not baptized by him. In this respect, 7:29–30 seems to originate from the first redaction along with 3:2–4, 7–8a, 9; 6:32. Then, it can be said that 7:29–30 is the conclusion to the texts which mention the relationship between John and Jesus in the first redaction (3:2–4, 7–8a, 9; 6:20b, 27, 29–38).

C. THE OPPOSITION TO JOHN AND JESUS (Q 7:31–35)

The relationship between John and Jesus is described in Q 7:31–35 (Luke 7:31–35; Matt 11:16–19). However, this seems to be composed of two redactions. Jesus seems to be depicted as the one superior to John at the time of the writing this text.

The controversy of this generation over John and Jesus is written in Q 7:31–34. This text follows Q¹ 7:29–30 by the linking word "tax collectors." There is, however, a significant difference between the two texts from a perspective of literary form. The parable of the children in the marketplace is described in 7:31–32. This recalls the parable of the two builders (Q³ 6:48–49) in that they share the literary genre "parable" and commonly draw a sharp contrast between the two groups. In this respect, the parable of the marketplace seems to belong to the third redaction in which the parable of the two builders is also included. John and Jesus are in parallel against this generation in 7:33–34. They seemed to constitute the common front. However, Jesus is described as the one superior to John by applying the title

---

7. Jacobson, *First Gospel*, 256.

"Son of Man" to Jesus.[8] There turns out to be unequal relationship between the forerunner John and the coming one, Jesus (Q³ 3:16–17; 7:18–27). The title "Son of Man" makes us think of that used in Q³ 6:22–23b where he is depicted as the central figure. The text 7:31–34 reflects the controversial situation with the outsiders and reminds readers of their opposition mentioned in Q³ 6:39–45. It seems that 7:31–34 belongs to the third redaction along with 3:16–17; 6:22–23b; 6:39–49 and 7:18–27.

An enigmatic saying appears in Q 7:35. This saying follows Q³ 7:31–34 by the theme of "children."[9] There is, however, a significant difference in that wisdom is introduced for the first time. The enigmatic saying about wisdom has been believed to be an independent saying. "Wisdom" probably refers to Jesus, and the children were none other than his followers—namely the disciples of Jesus.[10] In this respect, Q 7:35 is closely associated with the twelve apostles (Q⁴ 6:12–16). The filial relationship between wisdom and her children recalls the phrase "descendants [children, τέκνα] of Abraham" written in 3:8bc.[11] The term was not used without purpose. Therefore, it can be said that 7:35 belongs to the fourth redaction along with 3:8bc and 6:12–16.

---

8. Jacobson, *First Gospel*, 123.

9. Schulz, *Q*, 386; and Cotter, "Parable," 294.

10. Some scholars believe that John and Jesus represent wisdom as the bearers of her message. Cf. Jacobson, *First Gospel*, 124–125.

11. Allison, *Jesus Tradition*, 9.

4

Conclusion

The first section of Q concentrates on the ministry of John and Jesus (Q 3:2—7:35). However, it shows inconsistencies among the texts in terms of theological logic. This leads readers to the possibility that the first section consists of four layers of redaction.

Critical analysis shows the literary structure and the redaction of the first section. From a literary perspective, the first section consists of three parts regarding John and Jesus: the ministry of John in Q 3:2–17; the ministry of Jesus in 3:21—7:10; and the relationship between John and Jesus in 7:18–35. In addition, the critical analysis makes us see this section consisting of four redactions. The first redaction includes 3:2–4, 7–8a, 9; 6:20b, 27, 29–38; 7:29–30; the second, 6:21; the third, 3:16–17, 21–22; 6:22–23b, 28, 39–49; 7:1–10, 18–27, 31–34; and the fourth, 3:8bc; 4:1–13; 6:12–16; 6:20a, 23c; 7:28, 35.

The texts of the first redaction show its own literary and theological characteristics. John probably initiated the new religious movement and then Jesus joined it. While John proclaimed repentance in order to prepare the way for God's eschatological judgment, Jesus provided the people with instruction on how to bear the fruit worthy of repentance in order to circumvent the impending wrath and enter the kingdom of God. They can be listed as follows:

1. The Ministry of John

    Q^1 3:2–4 (Luke 3:2–4 / Matt 3:1–3, 5–6)

    Q^1 3:7–8a, 9 (Luke 3:7–8a, 9 / Matt 3:7–9a, 10)

2. The Ministry of Jesus

    Q^1 6:20b (Luke 6:20b / Matt 5:2b, 3)

    Q^1 6:27 (Luke 6:27 / Matt 5:44a)

    Q^1 6:29–38 (Luke 6:29–38 / Matt 5:39–40, 42, 45–48; 7:1–2, 12)

3. Jesus and John

    Q^1 7:29–30 (Luke 7:29–30 / Matt 21:31–32)

It seems that the first redactor simply collected the source in order to preserve what John and Jesus had said and done. The texts of the first redaction seem to stand for the words and actions of the historical John and Jesus. While John was described as a prophet for repentance and eschatological judgment, Jesus was identified as a sage who demonstrated how to bear the fruit worthy of repentance. If this argument is acceptable, then fewer words and activities of the historical John and Jesus are known than people generally think and expect. In fact, there is not much tangible historical information left about John and Jesus.

The texts of the second through fourth redactions do not show a consistency with regard to the literary shape and theological characteristic yet in the first section. It is then necessary to see whether there are more texts that can belong to the second through fourth redactions. When we examine the rest of Q, it will be shown that they have their own literary shape and theological characteristics. This requires us to study the rest of Q.

PART 2

The Second Redaction and Later Addition

The second section describes Jesus giving instructions for ministry and prayer to his followers in Q 9:57—12:34 and 17:3-4. This section can be divided into three parts from a literary point of view: the summoning of followers (9:57–60a), the manual for their ministry (10:2–24), the Lord's Prayer and its application (11:2—12:34; 17:3-4). It is noteworthy that the second section focuses on the teaching of Jesus for his followers. When we apply form critical, redaction critical, and composition critical approaches to this section, they will show that this section consists of three layers of redaction. Although the second redaction of Q is mostly found in it, it also includes texts added by later redactors. Henceforth, 6:21 will be included as having been interpolated into the main texts of the first redaction by the second redactor. Then, the texts of the second redaction will reveal its theology about total dependence upon God. In addition, they will also show the social environment at the time of the second redaction; that the followers of Jesus went out to the local neighbors for the proclamation of the kingdom of God.

1

The Texts Added to the First Redaction

As discussed before, the second redactor inserted a pair of beatitudes into the main texts of the first redaction. They were added to the first beatitude of the first redaction in Q² 6:21. By doing so, the second redactor tried to show his or her theological interpretation that the moment of fulfilling the blessing was postponed.

A. THE SECOND BEATITUDE (Q 6:21A)

The second redactor added a beatitude to the first one in Q² 6:21a (Luke 6:21a; Matt 5:6). This text follows Q¹ 6:20b with the phrase μακάριοι οἱ . . . ὅτι [blessed are who . . . because]. It seems that the second redactor created the second beatitude in order to adjust the theology revealed through the first beatitude of the first redaction.

The second redactor created the second beatitude (Q² 6:21a). The term πεινῶντες [the hungry] appears as the beneficiary of blessing. The second redactor seemed to choose it intentionally because "the hungry" is an aspect of "the poor" that is the beneficiary of blessing in the first beatitude (Q¹ 6:20b). From a theological point of view, the second redactor was able to create the second beatitude on the basis of some texts of the first redaction, such as Q¹ 6:27, 29–30, in which those who were deprived of clothes are depicted. They could not help but be hungry because they lost what they had. This reflects the social environment at the time of the writing of the second redaction; that the hungry were around Jesus. On the other hand, the second beatitude became the theoretic basis for those who had been deprived of clothes forcefully, since Q¹ 6:27, 29–30 comes later than Q² 6:21 at the stage of the second redaction. In this way, the second redactor supplements the meaning of the poor by adding the hungry. The hungry lack food; thus, they do not eat as much as they need daily. In this respect, the second redactor introduced the hungry right after the poor mentioned in the first beatitude. The hungry were not necessarily the disciples of Jesus at the stage of the second redaction. It seems to be addressed to the crowds who approached Jesus, as it is described in the first redaction (Q¹ 3:7). Some of them were probably hungry; in this respect, they were the marginal people at that time. They probably represent the audience to whom the second redactor tried to deliver the instruction of Jesus. They seem to be the anonymous followers of Jesus, not necessarily the twelve disciples of Jesus. In other words, those who were around Jesus were the disadvantaged people at the time of the second redaction from a socio-economical perspective.

The second redactor introduced the second blessing with the future tense verb χορτασθήσεσθε [you will be satisfied with food] (Q² 6:21a). As mentioned before, it is to be noted that the future passive verb was used in the second beatitude in comparison to the present active verb used in the first beatitude (Q¹ 6:20b). In consequence, the hungry will be satisfied with food in the future. Then, there are three things on the agent: the moment, agent, and content of blessing. First, the future verb indicates that the blessing will be fulfilled in the indefinite future. While the first redactor promised the presence of the kingdom of God with the present verb, the second redactor postponed the moment of being blessed to the future. This reflects the belief of the second redactor that the blessing would not be given in the present anymore. In this respect, the moment of being blessed is postponed from present in the first redaction to future in the second redaction. Therefore, it can be said that while the first redactor conveyed the present aspect of the eschatological judgment and the kingdom of God (Q¹ 3:9; 6:20b), the second redactor reveals the futuristic aspect of the eschatological reward (Q² 6:21). The reason that the second redactor postponed the moment of fulfilling the blessing to the indefinite future was because the expectation of the kingdom of God was fading away at the time of the second redaction.

Second, the passive verb indicates that God is the agent who will give the reward. It seems to be a divine passive form used by the Jews in order to avoid mentioning the name of God. Whereas the first beatitude mentions the term "God" with "the kingdom," the second one implicitly describes him as the agent of giving the reward. It is noteworthy that the passive form was once used in the first redaction regarding the eschatological judgment (Q¹ 3:9). Although it appears in the literary form of metaphor, there is no doubt that God is the one who chops down the tree and throws it into the fire. In this respect, the second redactor was able to depict God as the giver of blessing in the second beatitude (Q² 6:21a).

Third, the content of blessing is to be taken into consideration. It is noteworthy that the blessing of the second beatitude is parallel to possessing the kingdom of God when the second redaction was completed. In other words, being satisfied with food is one of the rewards that will be given at the kingdom of God in the future. This indicates that no transcendental aspect was attributed yet to the kingdom of God at the time of the second redaction. It is, however, noteworthy that the term χορτασθήσεσθε is used for the second beatitude. According to Alexander A. Di Lella, the term χορτάζω "is cognate with the noun χορτοῦ, 'green crops,' in Gen 1:11-12 (LXX). It is noteworthy that the phrase βοτανὴν χορτοῦ occurs precisely in the account of the fourth work of creation."[1] If his interpretation is correct, the term χορτασθήσεσθε could be connected with the fruits abundant enough for the daily food of Adam and Eve in the garden of Eden (Gen 2:9, 16). In other words, the second redactor had the garden of Eden in his or her mind as the background for the description of the kingdom of God and its abundant amount of fruit could be the mirror for the blessing of being satisfied with food. Although this kind of typological interpretation is not thorough enough yet, its connection with the primordial times is not to be denied at the stage of the second redaction.

B. THE THIRD BEATITUDE (Q 6:21B)

The second redactor added one more beatitude in Q² 6:21b (Luke 6:21b; Matt 5:6). This text follows Q² 6:21a by the same literary form of beatitude. With this addition, the second redactor strengthened his or her theological interpretation on the blessing.

The second redactor created the third beatitude, as he did the second one (Q² 6:21b). It seems that the third beatitude was also made on the basis of Q¹ 6:20b, 27, 29-30 in which those who were poor, slapped on the cheek and deprived of clothes, are mentioned. They could not help but mourn on account of their damaged self-esteem. This reflects the social environment at the time of the writing of the second redaction, that those who mourned were around Jesus. On the other hand, the third beatitude became the theoretic basis for the description of those who had been slapped on the cheek and deprived of clothes, since Q¹ 6:27, 29-30 comes later than Q² 6:21b when the second redaction was complete. In this way, the second redactor

---

1. Di Lella, "Structure," 240.

supplemented the meaning of the poor in connection with the mourner. They mourned because their hearts were hurt; thus, they are promised to be consoled in the future.

The second redactor introduced blessings with the future tense verb in the third beatitude (Q^2 6:21b). Although the conjunctive particle ὅτι is used for the third beatitude following the second one, the second redactor took the future passive verb once again. It is noteworthy that the terms πενθοῦντες [those who mourn] and παρακληθήσεσθε [will be consoled] are used for the third beatitudes.[2] Those who mourn will be consoled in the future. Then, there are three things on the agent again: the moment, agent, and content of blessing. In other words, consolation will be given by God in the future. In consequence, "the mourner" is parallel to "the hungry"; in the same manner, "will be consoled" is parallel to "will be satisfied with food" that is the eschatological reward in the second beatitude. As the term "will be satisfied with food" characterizes an aspect of the kingdom of God, so does "will be consoled" in the second redaction. The blessing of consolation also alludes to the benefit enjoyed at the kingdom of God. Although no description about the consolation for Adam and Eve in the garden of Eden is found in the Bible or the intertestamental writings penned prior to 40 CE, the second redactor could have had it in his or her mind at the time of the writing of the third beatitude as well as the second beatitude.[3] It seems that the third beatitude also reflects that the reason for writing was the theological intention of interpreting the kingdom of God in light of the garden of Eden. If this interpretation is acceptable, it is clear that the second redactor reinterpreted the theology of the first redactor regarding the characteristics of the kingdom of God. The characteristics of the kingdom of God were defined according to the situation of the time of the redactor.

---

2. Tuckett, "Beatitudes," 198–99; cf. Robinsion et al., *Critical Edition*, 48.

3. It seems that the terms πενθοῦντες and παρακληθήσεσθε were adopted by the second redactor in order to refer to the elements of the beginning of the world. In other words, the term πενθοῦντες can be also related with the garden of Eden when we take a look at the intertestamental documents in the first century CE. According to *Apocalypse of Moses* which is supposed to be written around 70 CE, before Adam and Eve were expelled from the garden, they lamented and wept severely; in addition, he intended to beseech God's forgiveness (*Apoc. Mos.* 27:2–3). In response, God offered some form of consolation to them: if they would guard themselves from evil, he would give them the fruit of the tree of life (28:4). Then, Adam and Eve mourned (πενθῆσαι) for seven days on account of their sin after their expulsion from the garden of Eden (29:7). It is, however, to be noted that *Apo. Mos.* was written later than the second redaction of Q.

C. SUMMARY

The second redactor added two more beatitudes to the first redaction in Q^2 6:21. In this way, when the second redaction was completed, there were three of them in total. According to the Jewish tradition, the number three symbolizes the complete situation. The second redactor probably wished to express the complete situation of blessing. On the other hand, it is to be noted that the moment of fulfilling the blessing was postponed from present time to future by using the future tense verb. In addition, God is defined as the agent who will give the blessing by using the passive voice verbs. This implies that the second redactor reflected that the occasion for writing was the faded expectations about the presence of the kingdom of God adding the allusion to the garden of Eden.

2

The Followers of Jesus

The second section begins with the story about the follower of Jesus (Q 9:57–60a).[1] Of course, this part also underwent a process of redaction. Thus, it is necessary to distinguish the text that belongs to the second redaction of Q. Then, the theology of the second redactor will be discerned. This part can be divided into two paragraphs: the voluntary follower (9:57–58) and the invited follower (9:59–60a).

A. THE VOLUNTARY FOLLOWER (Q 9:57–58)

The story about the voluntary follower appears in Q 9:57–58 (Luke 9:57–58; Matt 8:19–20). This text follows Q^3 7:31–35 by the title "Son of Man." It is, however, noteworthy that while this title appears in the context of opposition in 7:31–35, it does not in 9:57–58. The fact that Jesus is less theologically interpreted in 9:57–58 than in 7:31–35 implies that this text was written earlier than Q^3 7:31–34. It seems that 9:57–58 followed 6:21 in the second redaction because they reflect the similar economic situation in that the hungry and the mourner can be related with the follower who should live without a place to lay his head.

The story about a voluntary follower of Jesus is written in Q^2 9:57–58. It is noteworthy that the description about his follower appears for the first

---

1. While there are some scholars who regard Luke 9:61–62 as part of Q, there are also some who do not. I do not regard it as part of Q because it was written against the backdrop of 1 Kgs 19:19–21. Cf. Fleddermann, "Demands," 548–52. The Gospel of Luke reflects the influence of the Elijah-Elisha story in many places. To my judgment, Luke 9:61–62 is one of them.

time. If my previous analysis of the first redaction is acceptable, there was no mention of disciples or followers in it. From a literary point of view, it is awkward to deal with the follower after the selection of the twelve disciples in Q^4 6:12–16. However, when we consider 6:12–16 as part of the fourth redaction, it is understandable to describe the summoning of the follower at the beginning of the main texts of the earlier redaction. The follower of Jesus who does not have a place to lay his head represents the hungry and the mourner described in the second and third beatitudes (Q^2 6:21). Then it is natural to describe the summoning of the follower at the very beginning of the second redaction.

A set of dialogue between Jesus and the voluntary follower is written in Q^2 9:57–58. According to the second redactor, a person came to Jesus and said that he would follow him. Jesus responded to the person, saying, "Foxes have holes and birds of the air have nests, but the Son of Man has no place to lay his head." The first two metaphors form an antithesis with the last one. Those who would like to follow Jesus had to endure the wandering life with confidence that God would provide daily food, as reflected in the second beatitude (Q^2 6:21).[2] Although daily food is not guaranteed, he or she should follow Jesus being voluntarily a hungry person. This implies that the person would like to be one of those who were hungry and mourning with the promise of blessing in the future. In consequence, the second redactor asked the audience to go wherever Jesus would go. This reflects the social situation of the first group of people who gathered around Jesus at the time of the writing of the second redaction.

The story about the voluntary follower conveys several theological instructions. First, it is noteworthy that a set of animals appears such as foxes and birds. The parallel between foxes and birds reminds readers of a set of beatitudes used at the beginning of the second redaction (Q^2 6:21). The second redactor seems to be fond of using parallelism. Foxes and birds are contrasted with the tree used in the first redaction (Q^1 3:9). The second redactor broadened the range of comparison for the description of Jesus' instruction. Second, foxes and birds are in contrast with the Son of Man for the first time in the second redaction regarding lifestyle. The second redactor used the "specific residents of land and sky" in order to deliver the matter of shelter.[3] The reason that the second redactor began using the image of animal was because Jesus changed his lifestyle from a settled residence to a wandering journey for his ministry. This means that the second redactor taught the followers to go wherever Jesus would move around. In reality, the second

---

2. Cf. Casey, "Son of Man," 15.
3. Jacobson, *First Gospel*, 135.

redactor wanted the audience to go anywhere Jesus would visit because they had to follow him. It is, however, noteworthy that the title "disciple" is not yet applied to the voluntary follower. Third, it is necessary to look at the title "Son of Man" used for the identification of Jesus. The Son of Man seems to be used as a substitute for the first person here. We acknowledge that the "son of man" was often used for the third person in the Bible (Ps 8:4; 58:1; 80:17; Prov 8:31; Jer 49:33; 50:40; 51:43, etc.). In addition, it was used by God to refer to Ezekiel the prophet as a substitute for the second person (Ezek 2:1; 3:1; 4:1; Prov 8:4, etc.). Moreover, it was occasionally used as a substitute for the first person (Job 16:21, etc.). In the background of the Bible, the second redactor used the title "Son of Man" [ὁ υἱὸς τοῦ ἀνθρώπου] for Jesus for the first time. However, no messianic meaning was imposed to the title "Son of Man" yet. The Son of Man is an earthly human figure. Fourth, it has not been known whether the voluntary follower was with Jesus or not. However, the second redactor seems to indicate that the person followed him. This probably reflects the contemporary custom regarding how to recruit followers. In this respect, the second redactor showed that the followers of Jesus gathered together according to their own will.[4] In other words, as time passed, there were some who followed Jesus.

B. THE INVITED FOLLOWER (Q 9:59–60A)

Another story about the follower of Jesus is described in Q 9:59–60a (Luke 9:59–60a; Matt 8:21–22). This text follows Q^2 9:57–58 by the linking word "follow." However, they display differences that provide a theological basis for the redactional origin.[5] First, the direction of initiative is different in the process of being a follower. While the man took the initiative by saying that he would follow Jesus in Q^2 9:57–58, Jesus took the initiative by asking to be followed in 9:59–60a. The difference recapitulates their different origins from the perspective of redaction. Second, the precondition to follow Jesus is different in each. While Jesus suggested to him a wandering life in 9:57–58, the man asked Jesus to allow him to hold a funeral for his dead father in 9:59–60a. The theme of death recalls the temptation story in which Jesus was seduced to throw himself from the pinnacle of the temple (Q^4 4:1–13). In addition, the authority to summon a person reminds readers of

---

4. It seems that the calling of the disciples at the shore of the Lake Galilee was created by Mark (Mark 1:16–20). With this description, Mark would like to emphasize the authority and initiative of Jesus.

5. Jacobson, *First Gospel*, 136.

the commissioning of the twelve apostles in Q^4 6:13–16. In this respect, it is possible that 9:59–60a originated in the fourth redaction with 4:1–13 and 6:13–16.

C. SUMMARY

It seems that Q 9:57–60a conveys two kinds of followers: the voluntary and the invited. It is, however, noteworthy that there is a theological gap between the two. In consequence, the text seems to consist of two layers of redaction. The text of 9:57–58 originated in the second redaction, while 9:59–60a came from the fourth redaction. In this respect, Q reveals the development of theology regarding the way of summoning the followers of Jesus.

3

The Manual for Ministry

The manual for ministry is described in the second part of the second section of Q (10:2–24). First of all, this part can be divided into four paragraphs from a literary perspective: the commissioning of eschatological workers (10:2–3), the manual for ministry (10:4–12), the woe against the Galilean towns (10:13–15), and the origin of mission (10:16–24). It is, however, noteworthy that 10:2–24 also underwent a process of redaction. Thus, it is necessary to distinguish the second redaction from others. Then, it will show how its theology was formed and developed as the redaction of Q progressed.

A. THE COMMISSIONING OF ESCHATOLOGICAL WORKERS (Q 10:2–3)

The commissioning of eschatological workers is described in Q 10:2–3 (Luke 10:2–3; Matt 9:37–38; 10:16a). It seems that this text was interpolated into the main texts of the second redaction. It is, however, noteworthy that this text consists of two different redactions.

Q 10:2 follows 9:57–60a by the theme of "follower." However, it is not so strong to connect them from a thematic perspective. Rather, 10:2 shares the theme of "sending the servant" with Q^3 7:27. Then, it carries a common image of harvest with 3:16–17. While the image of wheat stocked in the granary is used in 3:16–17, that of workers for the eschatological harvest appears in 10:2. The theme of "end time" appears in both texts. In addition, the text of 10:2 shares the title "Lord" applied to Jesus with 6:46–49 and 7:1–10.

These common elements inform readers of the possibility that 10:2 belongs to the third redaction along with 3:16–17; 6:46–49; 7:1–10; and 7:24–27.

Q 10:3 most likely follows Q^3 10:2 by the linking word "send." However, there are some differences between them. Especially, the Lord of harvest seems to be different in that while Jesus said, "Ask the Lord of the harvest, therefore, to send out workers into his harvest field," in 10:2, he said, "Go! I am sending you out like lambs among wolves," in 10:3. Whereas God is depicted as the Lord of harvest in 10:2, Jesus is described as the sender of workers in 10:3.[1] The difference shows a tension between 10:2 and 10:3. Thus, it could be said that they belong to different redactions and that 10:3 was added to 10:2 later. As the redaction of Q progressed, the status of Jesus was getting more important. In addition, the image of sheep among wolves reminds readers of the theme of death implied in Q^4 4:9–12 and 9:59–60a. The eschatological workers had to run the risk of death when following Jesus. Moreover, the sending of the disciples recalls the "apostle" [ἀποστόλος] whose meaning is the one who was sent [ἀποστέλλω] (Q^4 6:12–16). Then, it can be concluded that 10:3 belongs to the fourth redaction with 4:1–13; 6:12–16 and 9:59–60a.

B. THE MANUAL FOR MINISTRY (Q 10:4–12)

The manual for ministry is written in Q 10:4–12 (Luke 10:4–12; Matt 10:7–15). This text follows Q 10:2–3 by the theme of "workers for Jesus." On the other hand, 10:4–12 seems to follow 9:57–58 in the second redaction by the common element about the wandering life. The followers of Jesus have to observe the instruction during their ministry written in 10:4–12.

The followers of Jesus were asked to be contented with honest poverty in Q 10:4. They should not carry a purse, pouch, or sandals during the missionary journey. This means that the followers of Jesus should be voluntarily poor and hungry (Q^1 6:20b; Q^2 6:21); thus, they cannot help but depend upon God. This means that the followers of Jesus began to leave their hometown for ministry. This describes their characteristic as itinerants for the first time. Then, this shows the social situation of the followers of Jesus at the time of writing 10:4. They voluntarily gathered together around Jesus and then went out for the missionary journey being completely dependent upon God. In this respect, 10:4 reflects the characteristic of voluntary poverty at the time of writing the second redaction.

It is said that the followers of Jesus should find a house to stay during their ministry in Q 10:5. The term "house" is a place to lay one's head. In this

---

1. Jacobson, *First Gospel*, 147.

respect, the house is parallel to the hole of foxes and the nest of birds; on the contrary, it reminds readers of the saying that the Son of Man had no place to lay his head (Q^2 9:57–58). The house plays the role of outpost for the followers of Jesus during their mission to the people of neighboring towns. This instructs the followers of Jesus to be dependent upon God with regard to the place to lay their heads during their missionary journey.[2] God will provide them with a place to dwell while they are engaged in his mission. In this respect, being welcomed to the house refers to the providence and protection of God. Then, it can be said that 10:5 was a part of the second redaction with 9:57–58.

A reciprocal relationship is described in Q 10:6. The followers of Jesus were taught that they had to say, "Peace to this house," when they looked for a house to stay. In this respect, they were the workers for peace. If there is a person who welcomes them, then the peace will rest on him or her. If not, the peace will return to them. In this respect, the reciprocal aspect appears in the relationship between the followers of Jesus and the household. This recalls the instruction about the reciprocal relationship among people in Q^1 6:27, 29–38. It is, however, noteworthy that a less radical instruction is found in this text than in the first redaction regarding the intensity of sacrifice. The fact that Jesus taught people to do good for others regardless of their attitude in the first redaction reflects the social relationship between the ruling class and the being-ruled class who acknowledged each other in a closed society. On the other hand, the fact that Jesus taught his followers the principle of reciprocal relationship that does not lose anything in case of being refused in 10:6 indicates the social situation in the open society. The followers of Jesus had to meet those whom they did not know. The less radical instruction of this text implies that it was written later than the first redaction, probably in the second redaction.

The principle of reception is written in Q 10:7–8. First, the followers of Jesus were allowed to eat and drink whatever the household provided during their stay at the house because they were worthy of reward. Second, they were encouraged to stay at the house during the ministry at the village or town; therefore, they were prohibited from moving from a house to the other. Although many biblical scholars argue that the wandering followers of Jesus are to be understood against the backdrop of the Cynics,

---

2. Batten argues that although some of the followers of Jesus "probably left their families, many of them would have remained attached to their households while still advocating the primacy of discipleship over domestic affairs" ("More Queries," 47). Her argument is based on the fact that the lower Galilee was not big enough to travel for a long time.

their relationship is not explained with complete satisfaction.³ On the other hand, they can be compared to the ancient Jewish prophets such as Elijah who was poor and hungry enough to rely on a widow of Zarephath and wandered in the wilderness for forty days being supplied with food by the angel (1 Kgs 17:7–16; 19:7–8). To my judgment, it is not necessary to find the background of iteneracy outside the Jewish tradition. At any rate, Q 10:7–8 describes how God supplies food to his hungry workers as promised in Q² 6:21. In this respect, 10:7–8 seems to belong to the second redaction with 6:21.

The mission of the followers of Jesus is listed in Q 10:9. They were commanded to heal the sick and proclaim the coming of the kingdom of God. First, the healing ministry was usual to the servants of God in the Jewish tradition. In this respect, the followers of Jesus were also asked to heal the sick. Although healing ministry is mentioned for the first time, the sort of sickness is not mentioned yet. Second, the followers of Jesus were entrusted with the proclamation of the coming of the kingdom of God. While the kingdom of God was promised to the poor by Jesus in the first redaction (Q¹ 6:20b), its proclamation was assigned to the followers of Jesus in 10:9. Everyone can hear the proclamation about the kingdom of God and respond to it. This indicates the changed strategy for the expansion of the people of God. In addition, it is noteworthy that a difference is found between the two redactions; while the first redactor mentioned the presence of the kingdom of God with the present tense verb ἐστίν (Q¹ 6:20b), the perfect tense verb ἤγγικεν is used in 10:9. This indicates that the kingdom of God had already begun to come but had not yet been fulfilled among the people. Its arrival seems to be postponed from the present to the immediate future. This means that the presence of the kingdom of God was not assured at the time of the writing of this text. This is in accordance with the description of the second and third beatitudes referring to the futuristic fulfillment of the reward (Q² 6:21). Therefore, it seems that 10:9 belongs to the second redaction along with 6:21.

The instruction about the case of being refused is described in Q 10:10–11. This is parallel to 10:8–9 in terms of literary form; on the other hand, this is in contrast to it in regard to the theme of acceptance and

---

3. The Cynics would not accept the virtue of contemporary society by warning the establishment of their unrighteousness; rather they took the wandering lifestyle with non-possession of materials and delivered sapiential words (Mack, *Lost Gospel*, 114–21; Seeley, "Blessings," 131–35; Theissen, *Studien*, 90–91; and Downing, "Quite," 196–225). However, this opinion does not go without critique (Jacobson, *First Gospel*, 144). Although the Greek culture was influential in Palestine, it is not sure whether the philosophical movement, such as the Cynics, was strong enough among the Jewish religious people (Horsley, "Questions," 197).

refusal.[4] If the followers of Jesus are not welcomed by the people, they have to get out of the town and shake off the dust from their feet. It is, however, noteworthy that they were required to shake off the dust. It is natural that the native would not easily accept the foreign. In this respect, it can be said that Jesus and his followers were not easily welcomed by their fellows. However, no animosity was given to the followers of Jesus yet, from a socio-religious perspective. No severe opposition or persecution is mentioned although this kind of instruction could have caused challenges from those who heard their proclamation and healing ministry. While John rebuked the crowds saying, "The brood of vipers," in the first redaction (Q^1 3:7), the followers of Jesus faced refusal from their neighbors as reflected in 10:10–11. In this respect, 10:10–11 seems to originate in the later redaction than the first of one—namely, the second redaction.

The warning against those who refuse the proclamation of the kingdom of God appears in Q 10:12. It is said, "It will be more bearable on that day for Sodom than for that town." First of all, Q uses the phrase "I tell you" [λέγω ὑμῖν] here. This is usually regarded as the introductory formula used by the prophets in the Bible (Isa 1:11, 18; 3:16; Jer 1:11; 2:5; 44:11; Ezek 3:16; 7:1; etc.). While this phrase was once used to introduce the sapiential saying in the first redaction (Q^1 6:27), it is used for the prophetic saying here because 10:12 carries eschatological judgment. It seems that the prophetic aspect was attributed to Jesus here. Second, a judgment saying is found here. It is said that the town which would not accept the proclamation about the kingdom of God will be punished more severely than Sodom was. The comparative form tells people about the severity of eschatological judgment at the end of the world. The eschatological warning calls our attention to the second and their beatitudes in that the eschatological reward is described with the future tense verb. This supports the possibility that 10:12 belongs to the second redaction with 6:21. Third, Sodom is mentioned for the first time from a typological perspective. Sodom is a place which represents the punishment of God with burning sulfur (Gen 19:24). With a typological description, the second redactor emphasized the severe judgment at the end of time upon those who would not accept the instruction of Jesus. In this respect, Q 10:12 seems to play the role of conclusion to 10:4–11 in the second redaction.

---

4. Jacobson, *First Gospel*, 142.

C. LATER ADDITION

A pair of woes are written against the Galilean cities in Q 10:13-15 (Luke 10:13-15; Matt 11:21-23). This text follows Q² 10:12 with the phrase "will be more bearable." The literary form "woe" is used for the first time. It is necessary to take the object of condemnation into consideration; while the towns were its object in Q² 10:12, the specific cities are mentioned in 10:13-15. They were condemned because they had opposed the followers of Jesus. In addition, the names of the cities mentioned in both texts have different characteristics. While unknown towns were compared with Sodom in Q² 10:12, Chorazin and Bethsaida were compared with Tyre and Sidon. It seems that 10:13-15 was originally independent from 10:12 but was connected to it by a later redactor.[5] The text of 10:13-15 shares common elements with the texts that belong to the third redaction in many points. First, the mentioning of miracles recalls the healing miracle performed by Jesus for the servant of the centurion at Capernaum in Q³ 7:1-10 and the miracle mentioned in 7:22. Second, the interest in the Gentile cities such as Tyre and Sidon in 10:13-15 calls our attention to the Gentile centurion at Capernaum in 7:1-10. Third, the comparative form used in 10:14 is reminiscent of that in 3:16-17 because it is connected with the theme of eschatological judgment. In this respect, 10:13-15 seems to belong to the third redaction with 3:16-17; 7:1-10, 22.

The mediatory role of Jesus is described in Q 10:16 (Luke 10:16; Matt 10:40). This text was placed after Q² 10:4-12 by the linking word "receive."[6] Q 10:16 seems to be attached to Q³ 10:13-15 as a conclusion in order to show that those who do not accept the servant sent by God will be punished at the end of the world. At any rate, in 10:16 Jesus is defined as the mediator between God and his followers. God has ultimately sent the disciples through Jesus. Whoever receives the followers of Jesus are those who receive God. It seems that 10:16 was written on the basis of many previous sayings. For instance, it has a common theme of "sending" with 3:16-17 and 7:18-27. In addition, Jesus is described as the mediator between God and the followers of Jesus as it is written in 10:2.[7] Moreover, the central role of Jesus between God and his followers remind readers of the role of the Son

---

5. Some scholars argue that Q 10:12 was made when 10:13-15 was added to 10:4-11 (Lührmann, *Redaction*, 62; Jacobson, *First Gospel*, 145). There is, however, an opinion that 10:13-15 was added much later (Catchpole, "Mission Charge," 155).

6. Jacobson argues that the Lucan version is to be preferred to the Matthean in Q 10:16 (*First Gosepl*, 143). On the other hand, Robinson prefers the Matthean version (*Critical Edition*, 188).

7. Cf. Catchpole, "Mission Charge," 155.

of Man in 6:22-23b. All the descriptions above evince the possibility that 10:16 originated from the third redaction along with the texts listed above.

Jesus is described as the mediator between his followers and God in Q 10:21-22 (Luke 10:21-22; Matt 11:25-27). This follows Q^3 10:16 by the theme that Jesus is the mediator between them. Jesus is the only channel between God and the followers through whom they can know about God. Then, the heavenly aspect of God reminds readers of the heavenly voice at the baptism which identified Jesus as his Son (Q^3 3:21-22). In addition, it is noteworthy that the phrase ἔμπροσθέν σου [before you] is found in 7:27 and 10:21. Moreover, the mentioning of children calls our attention to those who were sitting at the marketplace and saying of something mysterious to the crowds (7:31-34). Furthermore, the mediatory role of Jesus recalls the image of Jesus who asked God to send the workers for the harvest (10:2). In this respect, 10:21-22 belongs to the third redaction along with 3:21-22; 7:24-27, 31-34; 10:2; and 10:16.

The blessing for the followers of Jesus is described in Q 10:23-24 (Luke 10:23-24; Matt 13:16-17). The fact that the beatitude is mentioned in the form of the second person plural recalls the fourth beatitude written in the same manner (Q^3 6:22-23b). Then, the themes of seeing and hearing appear to be in connection in the beatitude, pointing to the fact that the same connection is found in 7:18-23.[8] In addition, the reference to the king and the prophet leads us to the description that John mentioned in the wilderness (7:24-27).[9] In this respect, 10:23-24 seems to also originate from the third redaction with 6:22-23b; 7:18-23; and 7:24-27.

D. SUMMARY

The text of Q 10:2-16, 21-24 consists of three different redactions. First of all, the second redactor composed 10:4-12 as the manual for ministry for the followers of Jesus. Later, the third redactor put 10:2 in front of Q^2 10:4-12 and attached 10:13-16, 21-24 to its end. Finally, the fourth redactor interpolated 10:3 in between Q^3 10:2 and Q^2 10:4-12. As the redaction of Q progressed, the manual for ministry was being added to by later texts in order to emphasize the eschatological role of Jesus.

---

8. The beatitude is formed without the conjunctive particle ὅτι in Q 7:23 and 10:23. This differs from those in 6:20b-21 in which μακάριοι is followed by ὅτι to explain the reason for the blessing.

9. The Lucan text is preferred to the Matthean in this case. Cf. Jacobson, *First Gospel*, 157.

4

The Lord's Prayer and Its Application

A series of instructions about prayer is found in the third part of the second section of Q (11:2-4, 9-26; 12:4-12, 22-34; 17:3-4). Being composed of three redactions, they seem to convey various themes. However, when the texts of the second redaction are distinguished, they will show that the second redactor gave his audience an example of prayer and its application. They can be divided into eight paragraphs as follows: the Lord's Prayer (11:2-4), confidence in the prayer (11:9-10), confidence in God (11:11-13), the kingdom of God (11:14-15, 17-20), temptation (11:16, 29-30), fear of God (12:6-7), daily bread (12:22-31), and forgiveness of sin (17:3-4). This informs readers of the fact that the second redactor composed the main texts with theological intention.

A. THE LORD'S PRAYER (Q 11:2-4)

The example of prayer is described in Q 11:2-4 (Luke11: 2-4; Matt 6:9-13).[1] Although this text follows Q^3 10:21-24 by the theme of God the Father,

---

1. It is necessary to decide which version between the Lucan and the Matthean preserves the original wording of Q 11:2-4. While Matthew includes six elements of the prayer, Luke includes five of them. Both numbers have their own theological meaning. While the number six is the double of the number three, the number five reminds readers of the Pentateuch: Genesis, Exodus, Leviticus, Numbers, and Deuteronomy. In addition, Psalms is also composed of five books. Proverbs can be divided into five groups according to the authors. Among the intertestamental documents, 1 Enoch is also composed of five books. In this way, the Jews were fond of the number five. In addition, it is more reasonable to conclude that the Lucan version is more original than the Matthean from the fact that Matthew probably added the will of the Father into

it seems that they belonged to different redactions from each other.[2] The instruction about prayer appears for the first time at the second stage of redaction.

The Lord's Prayer begins with the vocative form of God. Jesus taught his followers to call God "Father" in Q 11:2a. Jesus already said that people would be the "sons of your Father [God]" if they observed what he had taught (Q^1 6:35), then he identified God as "your Father" in the first redaction (Q^1 6:36). Their filial relationship with God is mentioned for the first time there. As mentioned before, this kind of instruction is not strange to the Jews because they were considered to be the sons of God (Exod 4:22; Hos 11:1; Isa 63:16, etc.). On the other hand, in 11:2a, Jesus taught his followers to call God "Father" directly. The description about their filial relationship with God in the first redaction changed to the vocative form in 11:2. In this respect, the redactor of this text expressed a more intimate relationship of the followers of Jesus to God than the first redactor. In other words, the redactor of 11:2 understood the relationship of God and the followers of Jesus in a more advanced manner than the first redactor. This means that 11:2a was written later than the texts of the first redaction regarding the filial relationship with God. Then, it can be said that the heavenly aspect of God in Q^3 10:21–22 shows a more developed concept than the vocative form of God in 11:2a. It implies that 10:21–22 was written later and added to 11:2a by the third redactor. This could mean that 11:2a originated in the second redaction.

The first petition of the Lord's Prayer is written in Q 11:2b. Jesus taught his followers that God's name be kept holy. For this, the first aorist passive imperative verb ἁγιασθήτω is used. God is asked to make his name holy at once. It seems to be understood under the light of the third commandment that says not to "misuse the name of the Lord your God" (Exod 20:7; Deut 5:11). Especially, the first aorist imperative verb indicates that the being hollowed will be done only once in the indefinite future. In this respect, the redactor paid attention to consistent eschatology in comparison to the

---

the Lord's Prayer. It is well known that Matthew's emphasis on the will of the Father is frequently found in Matthew's special sources (Matt 7:21; 12:50; 18:14; 20:14–15; 21:31). In Matt 12:50, Matthew changed the Markan term "the will of God" to "the will of Father" (Mk 3:35). This strengthens the fact that Matthew concentrated on the heavenly aspect of God the Father. Thus, it can be said that the shorter Lucan version of the Lord's Prayer represents the original in Q.

2. An abundance of linking words are found between Q 10:23–24 and 11:2–4, 9–13. Thus, Jacobson believes that they belong to the same redaction and were added later (*First Gospel*, 153). However, the terminological approach does not explain everything about the redaction. Rather, the theological differences between them should be taken into consideration.

realized or ongoing one in the first redaction (Q¹ 3:7–8a, 9; 6:20b). This reflects that the expectation of the end time was delayed as time passed. This kind of tendency was already found with regard to the eschatological reward or judgment that will be given in the future (Q² 6:21; 10:12). This provides a stepping-stone to understanding the first petition as a part of the second redaction.

The second petition is found in Q 11:2c. Jesus taught his followers to pray for the coming of the kingdom of God. For this, the first aorist passive imperative verb ἐλθέτω is used again. The followers of Jesus had to ask God to bring the kingdom to the earth at once. Jesus was able to deliver this petition because he had commanded them to proclaim the coming of the kingdom with the perfect tense verb ἤγγικεν in Q² 10:9. In other words, both texts agree with the belief that the kingdom of God had begun to come to the world but had not yet been fulfilled. Its fulfillment belongs to the indefinite future (Q² 6:21). In this sense, this differs from the instruction about the kingdom of God in the first redaction in which its presence was promised (Q¹ 6:20b). The presence of the kingdom in the first redaction changed to its futuristic coming in 11:2c. It is, however, unknown to us how the kingdom of God would come to the world and be realized. In addition, its form and reality are not described either. Probably, the redactors shared a certain concept about the kingdom of God with the contemporary Jews. In this respect, 11:2c also originated in the second redaction of Q.

The third petition is introduced in Q 11:3. It is about the bread for existence that should be immediately given today. For this, the first aorist passive imperative verb δός is used.[3] However, the meaning of τόν ἀρτόν ἡμῶν τόν ἐπιούσιον is ambiguous to the modern reader. This indicates the wish that the food, which will be given once at the end of the world, be given today. In this respect, the moment of eschatological reward is expected to be soon. Then, the plea for the eschatological bread calls our attention to the instruction about the dietary satisfaction that was promised in the second beatitude (Q² 6:21a). While the food was promised to those who were hungry in the indefinite future (6:21a), the eschatological bread is supposed to be given to the followers of Jesus today (11:3). It is noteworthy that as the kingdom of God was followed by the matter of food in 6:20b–21a, so is it in 11:2–3. In other words, the eschatological food that will be given in the kingdom of God should be given today. By doing so, the redactor showed his wish to enjoy the kingdom of God as soon as possible in the world. This

---

3. While the Lucan version used the present imperative verb δίδου (Luke 11:3), the Matthean version adopted the first aorist imperative verb δός (Matt 6:11). The fact that the first and second petition used the first aorist imperative verbs makes it possible that the third petition also used the same form of verb.

interpretation leads us to the dietary service provided by the household who accepted the followers of Jesus (Q^2 10:7-8). Daily food was promised to the followers of Jesus who had worked for the kingdom of God (10:9). This aspect strengthens the interpretation that "the bread for existence" is closely related with the eschatological reward that will be given in the kingdom of God. These elements result in the conclusion that 11:3 belongs to the second redaction along with 6:21 and 10:7-9.

The fourth petition is described in Q 11:4a. Jesus taught his followers that God would forgive them their debts when they would forgive others the debts committed against them. It seems that the term "debt" was used as the substitute for "sin" in this context. The fact that the second aorist active imperative verb ἄφες is adopted for forgiveness implies its eschatological aspect in that the forgiveness will be made only once. In addition, this petition conveys instruction about reciprocal relationship. As treated before, the first redaction dealt with it by emphasizing the giving of more than what the opponent had wanted from the followers of Jesus (Q^1 6:27, 29-38). On the other hand, the second redactor applied the principle of reciprocal relationship to the followers of Jesus when they should announce "peace" to the household (Q^2 10:6). In the same manner, it was used in the fourth petition of the Lord's Prayer focusing on the benefit from God corresponding to what a person had done for his or her fellows (11:4a). In this respect, 11:4a seems to originate in the second redaction with 10:6.

The fifth petition is mentioned in Q 11:4b. According to Jesus, his disciples have to pray not to be led into temptation. For this, the first aorist active subjunctive verb εἰσενέγκῃς is used. This is the only petition that does not adopt the aorist imperative form with the negative particle. The subjunctive verbs were already used in the first redaction (Q^1 6:31-32, 34, 37) and in the second redaction (Q^2 10:5-6, 10). It is, however, noteworthy that the second aorist active subjunctive verb εἰσέλθητε is used for the action of the followers of Jesus (10:5, 10). They had the right to choose whether they would enter the house or not. This tendency is also found in the fifth petition of the Lord's Prayer. God has the right to lead them into temptation or not. This means that the followers of Jesus were not in temptation but wished God not to lead them into temptation. In this respect, 11:4b also originated from the second redaction with 10:5, 10. It is noteworthy that temptation is mentioned here for the first time. However, the kind of temptation in view here is not made clear. Probably, Jesus did not wish his followers to meet some situations that would seduce them during their mission. Food and material possessions especially could be matters of temptation and seduction.

The Lord's Prayer seems to be written against the backdrop of the garden of Eden. In other words, every petition alludes to the words or actions that happened there. The first petition, asking to keep the name of God holy, reminds readers of Adam and Eve dishonoring his name by disobeying the commandment (Gen 3:1–5). The second petition, asking for the coming of the kingdom of God, should be connected with the saying that it "has come" [ἤγγικεν] (Q² 10:9). As mentioned before, the kingdom of God had begun to come but had not yet been fulfilled. Then, it can refer to the garden of Eden from which Adam and Eve were expelled; however, access has been prohibited and concealed from the people of God in order to give them the fruit from the tree of life when it opens at another time (Gen 3:22–24). The third petition, which deals with the bread for existence, could refer to the abundant fruit in the garden of Eden provided for Adam and Eve for their daily food. On the other hand, aspiration for the fruit from the tree of life has continued throughout Jewish literature (Gen 3:22; Prov 3:18; 1 En 25:5; TLevi 18:10; Rev 22:2, etc.). The fourth petition, which mentions forgiving others as the basis for God's forgiveness, is in contrast with the reproach of Adam and Eve in front of God without forgiving each other in the garden of Eden (Gen 3:11–19). Finally, the fifth petition, which describes the theme of temptation, recalls the serpent's temptation of Eve in the garden of Eden (3:1–5). Although the above analysis is not entirely conclusive, it still shows the possibility that the second redactor regarded the garden of Eden as representative of the ideal condition, as hoped for in the five petitions of the Lord's Prayer. Allusion to the primordial situation was already found in the second beatitude (Q² 6:21a; Gen 1:11–12), located after the first one which deals with the kingdom of God (Q¹ 6:20b). Then, it can be said that the kingdom of God was understood in light of the garden of Eden in the second redaction. In this respect, the theological interpretation began to be applied to Jesus and his followers by the second redactor.

B. CONFIDENCE IN PRAYER (Q 11:9–10)

The instruction about confidence in prayer appears in Q 11:9–10 (Luke 11:9–10; Matt 7:7–9). This text follows Q² 11:2–4 by the linking word "give." This is located just after the Lord's Prayer in order to encourage the followers of Jesus to keep praying with confidence in God. It seems to be an exposition of the Lord's Prayer.[4] In this respect, 11:9–10 originated in the second redaction with 11:2–4.

---

4. Jacobson, *First Gospel*, 159.

The instruction is introduced with the introductory formula λέγω ὑμῖν in Q 11:9. This formula was already used in Q¹ 6:27 and Q² 10:12. While the former led a sapiential saying, the latter introduced a prophetic judgment saying. It seems that this formula leads a sapiential saying regarding confidence in prayer (11:9). Using this formula, the redactor heightened the authority of Jesus' words.

The principle of prayer is described in Q 11:9. For this, three sets of proverbial sayings appear. When the followers of Jesus ask for something, they will be given; when they search, they will find; and when they knock, it will be opened to them. For instruction, present imperative verbs are used; therefore, the followers have to keep praying to get what they want in the imminent future. In these proverbial sayings, the imperative is followed by the indicative. The combination of the imperative and indicative indicates the authority of Jesus, in that his promise will be fulfilled. That the proverbial sayings are located just after the Lord's Prayer shows that the followers of Jesus have to have confidence in prayer to God. This text shares common characteristics with some previous texts. First of all, this text calls our attention to the second and third beatitudes because the expected result is written in the form of the future passive verb (Q² 6:21). All of these refer to the eschatological reward that will be given in the indefinite future. Second, this text also shares a common theme with the fourth petition of the Lord's Prayer in that both convey instruction about relationship with God (Q² 11:4). When the followers of Jesus do something, they will be rewarded by God. In this respect, 11:9 seems to originate from the second redaction with 6:21 and 11:4.

The instruction of Q 11:9 is repeated in a different form in 11:10. Everyone who asks receives, the one who searches finds, and the door will be opened to the one who knocks. Its difference from the previous text is found in that the first and second sayings are written in the form of the indicative, not imperative; on the other hand, the third one is described in the form of the future passive. With regard to the reward, the present tense verb is used, not the future passive. However, these differences do not provide readers with any obstacle to say that 11:10 goes well with 11:9. In addition, the parallel between 11:9 and 11:10 reminds readers of Q² 6:21 in which two beatitudes are introduced in the form of parallelism. Then, it can be said that 11:10 also originated in the second redaction along with 6:21 and 11:9. The second redactor emphasized confidence in prayer by using the present active and future passive verbs. In conclusion, by conveying both the present and futuristic aspects of eschatological reward, this text summarizes the preceding instructions regarding it.

C. CONFIDENCE IN THE FATHER: THE VOCATIVE (Q 11:11–13)

Instruction about God the Father is written in Q 11:11–13 (Luke 11:11–13; Matt 7:9–11). This text follows Q^2 11:9–10 by the connecting words "ask" and "give." This is an explanation about God the Father that appears in the form of the vocative at the beginning of the Lord's Prayer (11:2). This is the first case that applies its element. It will be seen that this text originated in the second redaction.

The instruction about the love of the father is written in Q 11:11–13.[5] This text can be connected with the Lord's Prayer by the connecting words "bread" and "give" and the theme of filial relationship with God (Q^2 11:2–4). This indicates that the redactor intentionally narrated these texts in order to heighten the theme of the father's love for his son. In addition, as mentioned above, this text shares the theme of "giving" with Q^2 11:9–10. Moreover, God's paternal love of providing his children with bread and fish calls our attention to the divine promise of provision with food in the future (Q^2 6:21a). In this respect, the text of 11:11–13 seems to belong to the second redaction in which 6:21; 11:2–4 and 11:9–10 are also included.

The second redactor introduced two metaphors in order to describe the father's love for his son. Using a pair of metaphors, the second redactor maximized the message of paternal love. Metaphor is a literary device that can convey more things than the indicative does. If even an evil father gives no stone or snake to his son asking for bread or fish, how much more does God the heavenly Father give good things to his son? With this metaphor and rhetorical question, the second redactor used the antithesis which was already used at the beginning of the main texts of the second redaction (Q^2 9:57–58). In this way, the second redactor described the character of God; he is the heavenly Father who gives better than what a person wishes and asks. At any rate, this makes the followers of Jesus rely upon God the Father. In this way, the second redactor urged them to have confidence in God and keep praying to him. In this respect, this text can be considered to be an application of the vocative "Father" written at the beginning of the Lord's Prayer.[6]

---

5. Although there is a significant difference between the Lucan and the Matthean versions in terms of words, the latter is preferred to the former in this case. While Luke uses the words "egg" and "scorpion," Matthew adopts "bread" and "stone." It seems that the words "bread" and "stone" fit in the context of Q because "bread" was already used in the Lord's Prayer (11:3). Cf. Robinson et al., *Critical Edition*, 218–19.

6. Cf. Sato, *Q*, 39; and Sato, "Shape," 171. For the brief summary, see also Jacobson, *First Gospel*, 159.

D. THE KINGDOM OF GOD: THE SECOND PETITION
(Q 11:14-15, 17-26)

The instruction about the kingdom of God is described in Q 11:14-15, 17-26. Its composition seems to be accomplished through triple redaction. As a result, this text plays the role of explanation about the coming of the kingdom of God that is the second petition of the Lord's Prayer.

The Beelzebul Controversy

The Beelzebul Controversy is written in Q 11:14-15, 17-20 (Luke 11:14-15, 17-20; Matt 12:22-28). This text follows Q^2 11:11-13 by the theme of relationship between father and son (11:13, 19). It seems that this text was given as the application of the second petition of the Lord's Prayer regarding the kingdom of God. Then, it will be shown that this text also originated in the second redaction.

The Beelzebul Controversy begins by laying out the circumstances in Q 11:14-15. Jesus healed the mute by casting out the demon in front of crowds. As soon as the mute spoke, the crowds were amazed but criticized Jesus that he had cast out the demon by the power of Beelzebul. According to their accusation, Beelzebul is supposed to be the head of demons. This is the first healing miracle so far in the first and second stages of redaction. As Jesus had commanded his followers to heal the sick (Q^2 10:9), he cast out the demon and healed the mute. In this respect, 11:14-15 seems to originate in the second redaction. In addition, the term "demons" is mentioned for the first time in this redaction, too. This implies that the second redactor began to pay attention to the spiritual beings. Moreover, his exorcism brought about the critique of the crowds against him. They appeared as challengers for the first time. However, this is somewhat different from the description of John rebuking the crowds coming to him in the first redaction (Q^1 3:7). In addition, while the first redactor provided Jesus' instructions about the harsh relationship that could develop between ordinary and marginal people (Q^1 6:27, 29-38), the second redactor introduced their challenge against Jesus (Q^2 11:14-15). This difference implies that Jesus was not easily accepted by his people at the time of the writing of the second redaction.

The response of Jesus is written in Q 11:17-18. Knowing the thoughts of the crowds, he said that every kingdom divided against itself is left ruined and every household divided against itself will not stand firmly. First, it is noteworthy that the terms "kingdom" and "household" are used here for a certain group of people or social constitution. However, they are used from a neutral perspective, not yet a negative one. In this vein, the terms "kingdom" and "household" call our attention to those used in Q^2 10:5–9. Second, it is interesting that Jesus applied the idea of division to Satan, saying that if Satan is divided against himself, his kingdom will not stand. It is noteworthy that the kingdom of Satan was acknowledged and that it could be contrasted with the kingdom of God. Although it is not clear whether Satan is to be identified as Beelzebul, it seems that Satan is the most authoritative among the evil beings. At this point, the idea of division on account of their relationship with Jesus appears for the first time in here. While the first redactor mentioned the two different groups of people—namely, the evil and the good—in Q^1 6:35, without any challenge between them, the redactor focuses on the challenge of the ordinary people against Jesus (Q 11:17–18). In this way, this text shows the different groups of people regarding their relationship with God or Satan from a spiritual perspective. In this respect, 11:17–18 continues the story in the second redaction regarding the kingdom of God.

Then, the response of Jesus continued in Q 11:19–20. As a counterattack to the crowds, he raised the question, if he cast out demons by Beelzebul, then by whom did their sons cast them out? This indicates that ordinary people also performed exorcisms in the name of God. In other words, Jesus did not consider them to be his opponents yet. Thus, he said that their sons could be the judges in order to confirm the miraculous works of God performed by Jesus. Therefore, Jesus said further that if he cast out demons by the finger of God,[7] the kingdom of God has come [ἔφθασεν] upon them.[8] It is, however, noteworthy that the kingdom of God could be verified during the exorcism performed by the finger of God in the world. According to Jacobson, "Exorcism, whether by Jesus or other exorcists, is construed as evidence of the presence of the kingdom of God."[9] In this respect, the kingdom of God seemed to be a place experienced when a certain precondition is met. While the kingdom of God belonged to the poor according to the first redactor (Q^1 6:20b), it is no longer theirs according to the redactor of 11:19–20. In this respect, the realm of the kingdom is limited to a certain

---

7. The phrase "the finger of God" probably originates in Exod 9:15–16 (LXX) where the phrase "the hand of God" refers to the power of God or in 8:19 where "the finger of God" is spoken of through the Egyptian magicians as the means of miracle (Cf. Allison, *Intertextual Jesus*, x, 53–57). It is also to be noted that the phrase "finger of God" appears in Deut 9:10 as a method to write down the decree and law on the stone tablet.

8. It seems that the Lucan phrase "the finger of God" represents the original wording of Q. Cf. Kloppenborg, *Formation of Q*, 124.

9. Jacobson, *First Gospel*, 163–64.

group of people who experience the divine miracle.[10] The fact that the kingdom of God and healing the sick appear together calls our attention to Q^2 10:9 in which Jesus commanded his followers to heal the sick and to proclaim the kingdom of God. In addition, it is noteworthy that the kingdom of God is mentioned in the second petition of the Lord's Prayer (11:2). Then, it can be said that the Beelzebul Controversy is introduced as an application of the second petition of the Lord's Prayer. This is how the kingdom of God comes to the people as they prayed. In this respect, the Beelzebul Controversy seems to originate from the second redaction.

The Beelzebul Controversy reveals the social aspect at the stage of the second redaction. According to the second redactor, Jesus accepted exorcisms performed by other people.[11] In other words, the followers of Jesus were not the only group who performed divine miracles. Rather, they were one of the various groups who performed exorcisms at that time. This means that the followers of Jesus did not separate themselves from Jewish society at the time of the writing of the second redaction. The second redactor acknowledged that God was working among the followers of Jesus as well as ordinary people. It is to be agreed that the critique of a party against its competitors occurs frequently in their normal life from a sociological perspective. This kind of social aspect reminds readers of the guideline given by Jesus in Q^2 10:10–11.[12] Rejection and challenge could happen among people of the same society. This implies that there was no animosity between the followers of Jesus and their fellows from a socio-religious perspective at the stage of the second redaction.

Later Addition

The parable of the strong person is described in Q 11:21–23 (Luke 11:21–23; Matt 12:29–30). This follows Q^2 11:14–15, 17–20 by the theme of competition between two groups. Although the Beelzebul Controversy does not describe a hostile competition, this parable does.[13] In this way, the parable of the strong person seems to have been added to the Beelzebul Controversy later. As a result, this parable seems to deliver the instruction that Jesus is stronger than Beelzebul, who is Satan, when both stories are read together. The description about the stronger one reminds readers of the proclamation of John in Q^3 3:16–17 because he proclaimed the one who would come after

---

10. Jacobson "Literary Unity," 381n46.
11. Cf. Shireck, "Whose Exorcists," 46.
12. Cf. Jacobson, *First Gospel*, 163.
13. Cf. Kloppenborg, *Formation*, 125; and Jacobson, *First Gospel*, 163.

him being more powerful than him. In addition, the fact that the description about the relationship with Jesus is focused in 11:23 reminds readers of the same tendency written in Q^3 6:22–23b and 10:16. These imply that 11:21–23 was written by the third redaction along with 3:16–17; 6:22–23b; and 10:16.

The parable of the unclean spirit is introduced in Q 11:24–26 (Luke 11:24–26; Matt 12:43–45). This follows Q^3 11:21–23 by the linking word "house" and the theme of the stronger one. While the parable of the strong person deals with the stronger one, the parable of the unclean spirit mentions the worsened situation. This parable was probably added to the previous one in order to support the meaning of the Beelzebul Controversy by linking themes of spiritual beings and competition among them. It is, however, noteworthy that the parable of the unclean spirit shows different aspects from the Beelzebul Controversy and the parable of the strong person in various aspects. While the Beelzebul Controversy adopted terms such as "Beelzebul," "Satan," and "demons" for the spiritual beings, the parable of the unclean spirit uses the term "unclean spirit."[14] In addition, while the former describes the competition between the two parties, the latter deals with the situation of opposition. On the other hand, the parable of the unclean spirit also differs from the parable of the strong person. While the parable of the strong person described the forced seizure to expel the weaker, the parable of the unclean spirit mentions the voluntary fugitive.[15] These differences imply that the parable of the unclean spirit belongs to the redaction other than the second and third redactions. The parable of the unclean spirit reveals some elements found in the temptation story. First, the fugitive unclean spirit is reminiscent of the departure of the devil (Q^4 4:13). Second, the place where there was no water can be compared to the wilderness of temptation (4:2). Third, the theme of returning to the house he originally inhabited reminds readers of the devil who left Jesus for a while but is supposed to return. These elements seem to show that the parable of the unclean spirit originated in the fourth redaction to which the temptation story also belong (4:1–13; 11:24–26).

E. TEMPTATION: THE FIFTH PETITION (Q 11:16; 11:29—12:3)

Instruction about temptation is given in Q 11:16; 11:29—12:3. However, these texts also underwent a process of redaction showing different

---

14. Jacobson, *First Gospel*, 155.
15. Kloppenborg, *Formation*, 126.

characteristics. It seems that 11:16, 29–30 was written in order to explain the fifth petition of the Lord's Prayer in the second redaction.

Temptation about the Sign

For some, temptation regarding the heavenly sign is in view in Q 11:16, 29–30 (Luke 11:16, 29–30; Matt 12:38–40 [16:1–2a, 4]).[16] It seems that Q 11:16 was originally followed by 11:29–30 as reflected in Matthew.[17] In addition, it seems that 11:16, 29–30 originally followed the Beelzebul Controversy in the second redaction by a common theme of sign (Q^2 11:14–15, 17–20).

The temptation about the heavenly sign was on the agenda to some people (Q 11:16). It seems to be written in order to explain the fifth petition of the Lord's Prayer regarding temptation (Q^2 11:4). In addition, the term "seek" reminds readers of the same term used in Q^2 11:9–10. In this respect, 11:16 seems to have originated from the second redaction. This followed 11:14–15, 17–20 in the second redaction by the theme of sign that refers to the divine wonder and miracle before Q^3 11:21–26 was interpolated later between Q^2 11:14–15, 17–20 and 11:16, 29–30. The demand for a sign was usual for the contemporary Jews in order to verify whether a certain person was sent from God. It is, however, noteworthy that they asked for it in order to tempt Jesus (cf. Matt 16:1).[18] This means that Jesus was tested as to whether he was really a servant of God or not. This reflects the historical situation that the followers of Jesus were actually competing with the contemporary people from a religious perspective as shown in the Beelzebul Controversy (Q^2 11:19–20). Thus, they should not be led into temptation during their ministry.

The response of Jesus is described in Q 11:29–30. This text can be also related to Q^2 11:11–13 by the linking word "evil" and the theme of attention to heaven. In addition, 11:29–30 can be also related to 11:9–10 by the linking word "seek." It seems that the crowds were not satisfied with watching the healing miracle of the mute alone (11:14–15, 17–20); thus, they cannot help but ask Jesus for another sign. However, identifying the people as an evil generation, Jesus refused to show a heavenly sign. This means that even if Jesus or his followers could show the sign sometimes, they were not able

---

16. It seems that Matthew used Q 11:16, 29–30 once again in 16:1–2a, 4. This tendency appears in many places; for instance, 9:27–30 / 20:29–34 and 9:32–34 / 12:22–28 can be considered.

17. Vaage, "Son of Man," 115–17; and Schürmann, "QLk 11,14–36," 574–77.

18. Matthew does not use the term "tempt" in 12:38. On the contrary, he uses it in Matt 16:1.

to do it whenever the crowds asked for it.[19] In this respect, the followers of Jesus were not different from other people from a religious point of view at the stage of redaction of 11:29–30. When Jesus mentioned the sign of Jonah in response to the crowds' demand for the sign,[20] it could refer to his proclamation of repentance to the Ninevites.[21] Then, the importance of repentance in front of God comes to the fore again since it appeared in the first redaction (Q^1 3:8a). In addition, it is noteworthy that Jonah who worked in the Gentile area was mentioned for the first time. The Gentiles implicitly became the object of comparison with the contemporary people in a similar manner that Sodom did (Q^2 10:12). Jesus is compared with the minor prophet Jonah rather than the major ones such as Isaiah, Jeremiah, Ezekiel, etc. This reveals the redactor's intention to compare Jesus to the prophet Jonah. Although the title "Son of Man" was applied to Jesus in parallel with Jonah, he is not the messianic, eschatological, or apocalyptic figure yet.[22] It is, however, to be noted that the title "Son of Man" is used in connection with the sign of judgment upon the people. The title "Son of Man" could provide a basis to connect 11:30 with Q^2 9:58 with regard to its use as the substitute for the first person "I." Furthermore, the authority of Jesus is implied in that he did not respond as the people had wanted. Rather than showing a sign, Jesus referred to the sign of Jonah. This reminds readers of his response to the follower, because Jesus did not give an answer as he had wanted and expected (Q^2 9:57–58). Jesus is the one who answers what he wants to. In this respect, it can be concluded that 11:16, 29–30 belonged to the second redaction with 9:57–58; 11:2–4, 9–10, and 11:11–13.

Later Addition

The saying about the eschatological judgment by the Gentiles is written in Q 11:31–32 (Luke 11:31–32; Matt 12:41–42). This follows Q^2 11:16, 29–30 by the linking word "generation." However, this saying shows different

---

19. Jacobson, *First Gospel*, 169. Kloppenborg believes that the opponents of Jesus asked for a sign not a miracle (*Formation*, 132).

20. Matthew says that the sign refers to the staying of the Son of Man in the heart of the earth for three days and nights as Jonah did in the belly of a huge fish (Matt 12:40; cf. Jonah 1:17). However, it is not clear whether this text is a part of Q. It seems that it was a theological interpretation made by Matthew with a reference to the resurrection of Jesus. However, Q does not know about his resurrection.

21. Cf. Kloppenborg, *Formation*, 133; and Jacobson, *First Gospel*, 165. Kloppenborg believes that the sign of Jonah does not refer to the resurrection of Jesus described in Matthew 12:40 (Q, 71).

22. Cf. Jacobson, *First Gospel*, 166n44.

characteristics from it. The theme of judgment by the Gentiles—such as the Queen of the South and the Ninevites—is different from the sign of Jonah that is the proclamation of repentance to the Gentiles (Q^2 11:30). This implies that 11:31-32 belonged to a redaction other than the second one. Rather 11:31-32 conveys the theme of a positive attitude toward the Gentiles, as Q^3 7:1-10 and 10:13-15 did. In addition, this text deals with the eschatological judgment which was inaugurated in 3:16-17 and 6:47-49. Moreover, the comparative description was already implied in 3:16-17 and 11:21-23 with regard to the identity of Jesus. Furthermore, this text focuses on the status of Jesus; as is well known, this kind of tendency already appeared in 6:22-23b; 6:46; 7:6; 10:16. Finally, the judgment upon this generation was already seen in 7:31-32. All the elements listed above inform readers of the possibility that 11:31-32 originated in the third redaction, to which all the texts listed above belonged.

Metaphoric sayings are introduced in Q 11:33-35 (Luke 11:33-35; Matt 5:15; 6:22-23). As reflected in the Lucan version, this seems to follow Q^3 11:31-32 in order to urge the people to make a right decision.[23] The parable of the lamp (11:33) is connected to that of the eye (11:34) by the linking word "lamp."[24] The image of light is contrasted with the blind in 6:39-40, and the eyes are once mentioned in 6:41-42. The sharp contrast is found between "under a peck-measurer" and "on the lampstand" in 11:33 and then between "healthy" and "bad" in 11:34-35. This kind of contrast reminds readers of those described in 3:16-17; 6:41-42, 48-49 and 7:31-34. In this respect, it seems that 11:33-35 belonged to the third redaction, with the texts mentioned above.

A series of woes are listed in Q 11:39-52 (Luke 11:39-52; Matt 23:4, 6-7, 23, 25-28). Q introduces seven woes against the opponents.[25] The literary form "woe to you" recalls the woe in Q^3 10:13-15. However, a caution is necessary because of a slight difference among the seven woes. The first woe follows the parable of the lamp in terms of accordance between the inside and the outside of body (Q 11:39-41). While the parable of the lamp deals with the relationship with the eye and the body (Q^3 11:33-35), the first woe mentions the difference between the inside and the outside of body. In this way, the redactor criticized the hypocrisy of those who would not accept

---

23. It seems that Q 11:33-35 follows 11:31-32 as reflected in the Lucan order. Matthew divided this saying into two and used them in different places according to his own theological intention.

24. Kloppenborg, *Formation*, 135.

25. As for the sequence of the seven woes, refer to Jacobson, *First Gospel*, 174-76; and Kloppenborg, *Formation*, 139-40. The Matthean order is generally preferred to the Lucan one.

the instruction of Jesus (cf. Q^3 6:42). The critique against the opponents implies that they were in opposition to Jesus and his followers. This differs from the challenge reflected in the second redaction in that it turned into the opposition (Q^2 11:14–15, 17–20 and 11:16, 29–30). This means that the relationship with the surrounding people was getting worse as the redaction of Q progressed. The second woe is described in 11:42 regarding the tithe, the third one is mentioned in 11:43 regarding the social respect, the fourth one is introduced in 11:44 regarding the hidden personality, and the fifth one is written in 11:45–46 regarding the avoidance of one's duty. Then, it is possible that they originated in the third redaction with 10:13–15.

On the other hand, the sixth one needs a careful examination because it differs from the previous ones (Q 11:47–51).[26] Above all, the length of text increased rapidly in comparison to the preceding five woes. Then, the sixth woe suddenly deals with the persecution of disciples and their martyrdom in the temple. The theme of death at the temple already implied in Q^4 4:1–13; in addition, the theme of death is also written in 9:59–60a and 10:3. Especially, the death of prophets is treated with the background of the forefathers' persecution that reminds readers of the description in 6:23c.[27] Moreover, the wisdom can be connected with that in 7:35.[28] In this respect, 11:47–51 seems to originate in the fourth redaction to which 4:1–13; 6:23c; 7:35; 9:59–60a and 10:3 belong.

The seventh woe is written in Q 11:52. It deals with the one who holds the key but protects others from entering. This is not much different from the first five woes. In this respect, it seems to belong to the third redaction. So far, the third redactor introduced six woes against the opponents. This implies that their relationship with the neighboring people was getting worse at the stage of the third redaction.

Two proverbs are mentioned in Q 12:2–3 (Luke 12:2–3; Matt 10:26–27). They follow Q^3 11:52 by a linking word; while the noun "knowledge" is used in 11:52, the future passive verb "being known" is used in 12:2. On the other hand, this text reveals a pair of contrasts between being concealed and being revealed. This contrast recalls the contrast in Q^3 10:21–24. This contrast can be in parallel with that between light and darkness in 11:33–35. In this respect, 12:2–3 seems to originate in the third redaction with the texts 10:21–24; 11:33–35 and 11:39–46, 52.

26. Sato believes that Q 11:49–51 was interpolated between 11:47–48 and 11:52, and it belongs to Redaction C. Q, 40; and Kloppenborg, "Shape," 172. It is, however, noteworthy that 11:47–48 is to be connected with 11:49–51 together in the same redaction. Cf. Jacobson, "Literary Unity," 374; and Jacobson, *First Gospel*, 177–78.

27. Jacobson, *First Gospel*, 101; and Kloppenborg, *Formation*, 228.

28. Carlson, "Wisdom," 104–5.

The instruction about the fear of God is introduced in Q 12:4–5 (Luke 12:4–5; Matt 10:28). This text is located just after Q^3 12:2–3; however, no linking word or theme is found between them.[29] Rather, the theme of death embedded in this text reminds readers of Q^4 11:47–51, in which the martyrdom of Zechariah is mentioned. It is also expressed in the story of the follower in 9:59–60a. Since the theme of death was written in 4:1–13 for the first time, it can be concluded that 12:4–5 belonged to the fourth redaction along with 4:1–13; 9:59–60a; and 11:47–51.

F. THE FEAR OF GOD: THE FIRST PETITION (Q 12:6–12)

Instruction about the fear of God is found in Q 12:6–12. Its composition was simply accomplished through a series of supplements. In other words, three layers of redaction are found in it. Thus, it is necessary to isolate the texts of the second redaction. Then, it will be shown that it was written in order to explain the first petition of the Lord's Prayer—that is, the fear of God.

The Fear of God

The instruction about the fear of God is described in Q 12:6–7 (Luke 12:6–7; Matt 10:29–31). This follows Q^4 12:4–5 by the theme of "Do not fear." However, the difference is definite in that while the supernatural phenomenon is focused on in 12:4–5, the natural one is dealt with in 12:6–7. Another difference is found in that while 12:6–7 introduces the care of God as the reason to fear God, 12:4–5 points out the authority to kill both the body and soul as the reason to fear God. This implies that 12:4–5 reveals a more theologically developed aspect and was added later to 12:6–7. Then, it is necessary to identify the redactional stage of 12:6–7.

The instruction about the fear of God starts with the metaphor of a sparrow in Q 12:6. Although sparrows are sold according to their price, none of them will fall to the ground without the consent of God. This means that no matter how small and insignificant a creature they might be, God will not give up on them. It is noteworthy that the second redactor was fond of mentioning animals, such as fox, bird, fish, and snake (Q^2 9:57; 11:11). This is contrasted with the first redaction, which used the metaphor of a tree (Q^1 3:9). Why the second redactor adopted the image of animals rather than

---

29. Jacobson, *First Gospel*, 185.

plants has not been known; however, it can be surmised that the followers of Jesus were commissioned to move around for the proclamation of the kingdom of God and to treat the sick (Q^2 9:57–58; 10:9). In this respect, 12:6 also reveals the characteristic of the second redaction.

Another metaphoric saying is written in Q 12:7. God numbers even the hairs of the head. This means that God is very meticulous in taking care of people. Moreover, they are encouraged not to be afraid of being taken care of. This is the reason that they can rely upon God. Thus, Jesus concludes that his followers should not be afraid because they are worth more than the sparrows. The comparative form was used once in the second redaction (Q^2 10:12). This time, it is applied to the text which emphasizes God's care of the followers of Jesus (12:7). Thus, they have to fear and respect God. Then, it can be said that 12:6–7 seems to belong to the second redaction with 10:12.

As shown above, fear of and respect for God are written about in Q^2 12:6–7. They lead one to keep the name of God holy as the first petition of the Lord's Prayer instructs. A similar way was already found in 11:11–13, which is written as an application of the vocative form "Father" at the beginning of the Lord's Prayer (11:2). In this respect, 12:6–7 is also used as an application of the first petition of the Lord's Prayer. It is possible to say that the second redactor developed the application of each element of the Lord's Prayer one by one.

Later Addition

The role of the Son of Man is described in Q 12:8–9 (Luke 12:8–9; Matt 10:32–33). It seems that this text was located after Q^2 12:6–7 on account of the theme of divine care. However, the caretaking agents differs from each other; while it was God in 12:6–7, it is the Son of Man in 12:8–9.[30] This text concentrates on one's relationship with the Son of Man which already appeared in Q^3 6:22–23b and 7:23. In addition, the importance of one's attitude toward Jesus was also emphasized in 11:23. Jesus plays the role of mediator between God and people, which reminds readers of his role as described in 10:16. The fact that the Son of Man is described in parallel with the angels [messengers] reveals a slightly different aspect from the earthly figure described in Q^2 9:57 and 11:30. These aspects imply that 12:8–9 was

---

30. It is to be discussed whether Q 12:8–9 uses the title "Son of Man." While the Lucan text adopts the title, the Matthean uses the first person "I." The same tendency is reflected in Q 6:22–23b (Luke 6:22–23b; Matt 5:11–12b). It seems that Q contains the title "Son of Man" in Q 12:8–9.

added to 12:6-7 later and belonged to the third redaction with 6:22-23b and 11:21-23.

Then, the role of the Spirit is introduced in Q 12:10-12 (Luke 12:10-12; Matt 10:18-19; 12:32). First of all, this text follows Q^3 12:8-9 with the linking word "Son of Man."[31] However, a significant difference is found between them; while the Son of Man is focused on in 12:8-9, the Spirit plays the key role in 12:10. This shows a theological development in that the Son of Man is subordinate to the Spirit. This implies that 12:10 was added to 12:8-9 later. The same relationship is found in the story of temptation because Jesus was led to the wilderness by the Spirit (Q^4 4:1-13). In other words, Jesus the Son of Man is subordinate to the Spirit. Second, it seems that 12:11-12 follows Q^4 12:10 by the linking word "speak." When one does not speak against the Spirit (12:10), he or she will be instructed how to speak (12:11-12). Both texts emphasize how and what to say. It seems that 12:11-12 also originated from the same redaction to which 12:10 belonged. Then, persecution by authority is reminiscent of the martyrdom by authority in Q^4 12:4-5. This reminds readers of the serious persecution by the workers of the temple (11:47-51). Finally, 12:11-12 is to be interpreted in connection with the temptation story (4:1-13) because both texts convey the theme of persecution and the importance of words in common; however, Jesus defeated the devil by the words of God (4:1-13). Then, it can be concluded that 12:10-12 originated from the fourth redaction.

G. DAILY BREAD: THE THIRD PETITION (Q 12:22-34)

Instruction about daily bread is addressed in Q 12:22-34. This text seems to have been subjected to redaction two times. When the texts of the second redaction are distinguished from the other, they will be shown as an application of the third petition of the Lord's Prayer.

Daily Bread

Instruction about daily sustenance is described in Q 12:22-31 (Luke 12:22-31; Matt 6:25-33).[32] This text follows Q^4 12:10-12 by the common phrase "Do not worry." It is, however, to be noted that while 12:11-12 focuses on the case of persecution, 12:22-31 deals with the daily life. This suggests the

---

31. Kloppenborg, *Formation*, 213.

32. On the contrary, Jacobson argues that Q 12:22b-31 "is not as radical as Q 9:57a-60" (*First Gospel*, 191). It is, however, to be noted that the total dependence upon God regarding daily life is conveyed in both texts.

possibility that they belong to different redactions from each other. It seems to be placed in its present location in order to explain the third petition of the Lord's Prayer.

The instruction about the daily sustenance begins with the commandment "Do not worry about" (Q 12:22–23). The disciples should not worry about what to eat for life or what to put on for the body. This reminds readers of Jesus' instruction not to carry a purse, knapsack, or sandals (Q^2 10:4). They had no place to eat and sleep (10:5–8). It is natural for the followers of Jesus to worry about food for life and clothing for the body. However, Jesus told them not to worry about food and clothing because life is more worthy than food, and the body is more important than clothes. He was able to teach this instruction because he already mentioned the lifestyle of the Son of Man (9:57–58).[33] It was because Jesus believed that God would provide the food for life in advance as he had taught in the third petition of the Lord's Prayer (11:3). In addition, the comparative form used in 12:23 recalls the comparative found in previous texts such as Q^2 10:12 and 11:13. In these cases, it is adopted in connection with the objective matter, place, or person. Moreover, the parallel between life and body is reminiscent of that used in other texts of the second redaction regarding various topics (6:21; 9:58; 11:11–12). In this respect, 12:22–23 carries the characteristic of the second redaction.

Three examples are listed in order to show how important life is in Q 12:24–28. First, it is said that God raises the ravens in the sky even though they neither sow seed nor reap (12:24). Jesus then raised the question of how much more important human beings are than ravens. This means that God takes care of human beings, who are much more important than ravens. The appearance of raven recalls the use of animals in the second redaction (9:57–58; 11:11–12; 12:6–7). This makes us regard 12:24 as a part of the second redaction. Jesus used a comparative sentence that human beings are much more important than ravens. It seems that this is the fifth case of using the comparative sentence in the second redaction (Q^2 10:12; 11:13; 12:7, 23). Second, Jesus suggests another example for the instruction about "Do not worry about" in 12:25–26. Having pointed out the incapability of human beings to add a cubit to his or her stature, Jesus taught the necessity not to worry about food and clothing. Third, Jesus introduced the other example that the lilies do not work or spin (12:27). However, God makes them grow and put on clothes that are better than those of Solomon. It is noteworthy that Solomon appears as the object of comparison, as Sodom was in Q^2 10:12. Jesus used another comparative sentence, that human beings are

---

33. Jacobson, *First Gospel*, 191.

much more important than the flowers. In this way, the redactor delivered the instruction that God takes care of the followers of Jesus. Since the first redactor had already used the image of a tree (Q^1 3:9) the second redactor did not hesitate to use the image of a flower here in combination with ravens and human beings. It is noteworthy that the redactor used the combination of bird, stature, and flower here, as he used that of bird and hair in Q^2 12:6–7. Finally, Jesus concluded that there were some "persons of little faith" for the first time (12:28). Those who worry about food and clothes are those of little faith. On the contrary, those who do not worry about them and are dependent upon God are those of faith. In this respect, faith in God results in not worrying about material possessions. In this respect, 12:24–28 seems to be part of the second redaction.

The conclusion to the previous texts is written in Q 12:29–31. The followers of Jesus do not have to worry about what to eat and what to put on (12:29)—that is, their unstable situation from an economic perspective. The fact that 12:29 is a repetition of Q^2 12:22 indicates that it also originated from the second redaction. What they needed was the bread for existence—that is, the third petition of the Lord's Prayer (11:3). This supports the fact that 12:29 belongs to the second redaction. Therefore, the followers of Jesus were encouraged to be completely dependent upon God the Father who already knew their situation and would provide them with what they had needed (12:30). Once again, the followers of Jesus are described in a filial relationship with God, as they were taught in the vocative of the Lord's Prayer (Q^2 11:2). Then, the redactor delivered the conclusive instruction, that the followers of Jesus had to seek the kingdom of God first, then, God will provide them with what they needed (12:31). It is noteworthy that the kingdom of God is mentioned first and then material possessions later. This sequence recalls the order of the second and third petitions of the Lord's Prayer (11:2–3). In addition, the combination of imperative and indicative reminds readers of the combination used three times in 11:9. In this way, the redactor added authority to the saying of Jesus about the kingdom of God. In this respect, 12:31 also seems to originate from the second redaction. In conclusion, it can be said that 12:29–31 plays the role of conclusion to what has been discussed in 12:22–28 regarding worry about what to eat and what to put on.

The second redaction seems to convey a consistent eschatology in that the kingdom still belongs to the indefinite future. While the first redaction characterized the present aspect of the kingdom of God (Q^1 6:20b), the second redactor changed the perspective on the kingdom. Its coming is proclaimed in the perfect tense in Q^2 10:9. Next, the kingdom is described as being verified when a certain precondition is met ; for this, the kingdom is wished to come in 11:2. Moreover, it is confirmed when a certain condition is met (11:20). Finally, it is still to be sought to come in 12:31. As the redaction of Q progressed, the kingdom of God became the reality to wait and seek. It seems to exist but has not yet completely come according to the second redactor. The second redactor changed his temporal perspective on the kingdom of God because it did not come as the first redactor announced it would (Q^1 6:20b; cf. 7:29–30).

Later Addition

The instruction about material possessions is described in Q 12:33–34 (Luke 12:33–34; Matt 6:19–21). This follows Q^2 12:22–31 by the theme of material possessions. However, the difference is clear between them; while the matter of material possessions for life is mentioned in 12:22–31, attention to heavenly treasure is focused on in 12:33–34. This helps to build a foundation upon which readers can notice the difference in the redaction of Q. The emphasis on the heavenly aspect recalls the heavenly voice in Q^3 3:16–17 and the heavenly reward in 6:22–23b. In addition, the reference to the thieves alludes to the opponents with whom the followers of Jesus were in conflict as mentioned in 10:13–14 and 11:39–46, 52. This means that 12:33–34 seems to originate in the redaction to which 3:16–17; 6:22–23b; 10:13–14 and 11:39–46, 52 also belonged—that is, the third redaction.

H. FORGIVENESS: THE FOURTH PETITION (Q 17:3–4)

Instruction on repentance and forgiveness is written about in Q 17:3–4 (Luke 17:3–4; Matt 18:15, 21–22). This text seems to follow Q^2 12:22–31 in the second redaction, although many texts were interpolated between them by later redactors. The matter of repentance and forgiveness calls our attention to the fifth petition of the Lord's Prayer.

The instruction on repentance and forgiveness appears in Q 17:3. For this, the term "brother" is used for the followers of Jesus. The brotherhood indicates the constitution of a separate group. It is, however, unknown whether they lived together or not. In addition, its size has not been known, either. It is, however, definite that while they had a fellowship in the name of Jesus, some of them committed sins against each other. Thus, it was necessary to instruct them on how to solve conflicts among them. If a person committed sins and repented, the followers of Jesus must forgive his or her sins. The instruction about forgiveness reminds readers of the fourth petition of the Lord's Prayer (Q^2 11:4). Repentance and forgiveness between the two parties become the basis for the request of divine forgiveness expressed in the Lord's Prayer. Then, it can be said that 17:3 was given as an application of the fourth petition of the Lord's Prayer. In this respect, 17:3 seems to be part of the second redaction. While repentance was proclaimed by John in the first redaction (Q^1 3:8a), a reciprocal relationship is emphasized in that repentance must precede forgiveness in the second redaction. It is, however, noteworthy that the fruit worthy of repentance is not required in this case. In this respect, the strict and radical aspect of the instruction of Jesus diminished in the second redaction.

Instruction about complete forgiveness is found in Q 17:4. Jesus taught his followers to forgive sinners their sins seven times a day, if they repent their sins seven times.[34] The number "seven" is used here for the first time in the second redaction. When the number "seven" means the complete condition, then the disciples are asked to forgive those who repent completely. The second redactor seems to seek the completeness in their religious life. While the first redactor dealt with repentance in relationship with God (Q^1 3:7–8a, 9), the second redactor described the repentance and forgiveness performed between God and human beings (Q^2 11:4), and then among brothers—that is, the followers of Jesus (Q^2 17:3–4). This reflects that the occasion for writing was the social context of many people gathering together in the name of Jesus at the stage of the second redaction.

---

34. On the contrary, Matthew wrote that the disciples of Jesus must forgive the sinners seventy-seven times or seventy times seven depending upon the old manuscripts. The number used by Matthew reflects that in Gen 4:24. While the Masoretic Text (MT) adopted the number seventy-seven, LXX used the number seventy times seven. At any rate, Matthew shows a more developed theology regarding the theme of forgiveness.

5

Conclusion

The second section of Q also reveals the process of redaction. It seems that the second redactor inserted a pair of beatitudes into the main texts of the first redaction and then attached the main texts that are mostly found in the second section. More texts were collected in the second redaction than in the first redaction.

It is necessary to see how the second section of Q was subjected to redaction. The texts of the second section seem to consist of three redactions. First of all, the second redaction was composed of the texts such as Q 9:57–58; 10:4–12; 11:2–4, 9–10, 11–13, 14–20, 29–30; 12:6–7, 22–31; 17:3–4. Then, the third redactor interpolated some texts in the main texts of the second redaction such as 10:2, 13–16, 21–24; 11:21–23, 31–35, 39–46, 52; 12:2–3, 8–9, 33–34. Finally, the fourth redactor also interpolated some texts such as 9:59–60a; 10:3; 11:24–26, 47–51; 12:4–5, 10–12. While the texts of the second redaction show a well-organized structure in terms of thematic development and its theology regarding the mission of Jesus given to his followers, the texts of the third and fourth redactions do not show it yet.

The texts of the second redaction show that more sources were added to the first redaction by the second redactor. This implies that as time passed, more sources were collected and added for the description of Jesus and his followers. The second redactor focused on their ministry for the kingdom of God. When the second redaction was completed, the shape of Q was likely as follows:

I. John and Jesus

   A. The Ministry of John

Q^1 3:2–4 (Luke 3:2–4 / Matt 3:1–3, 5–6)

Q^1 3:7–8a (Luke 3:7–8a / Matt 3:7–9a)

Q^1 3:9 (Luke 3:9 / Matt 3:10)

B. The Ministry of Jesus

Q^1 6:20b (Luke 6:20b / Matt 5:2b–3)

Q^2 6:21 (Luke 6:21 / Matt 5:4, 6)

Q^1 6:27, 29–38 (Luke 6:27, 29–38 / Matt 5:39–40, 42, 44a, 45–48; 7:1–2, 12)

C. Jesus and John

Q^1 7:29–30 (Luke 7:29–30 / Matt 21:31–32)

II. Jesus' Followers and Their Missions

A. The Followers of Jesus

Q^2 9:57–58 (Luke 9:57–58 / Matt 8:19–20)

B. The Manual for Ministry

Q^2 10:4–12 (Luke 10:4–12 / Matt 10:7–15 (11:24))

C. The Lord's Prayer and Its Application

1. The Lord's Prayer

Q^2 11:2–4 (Luke 11:2–4 / Matt 6:9–13)

2. Confidence in Prayer

Q^2 11:9–10 (Luke 11:9–10 / Matt 7:7–8)

3. Confidence in the Father: The Vocative

Q^2 11:11–13 (Luke 11:11–13 / Matt 7:9–11)

4. The Kingdom of God: The Second Petition

Q^2 11:14–15, 17–20 (Luke 11:14–15, 17–20 / Matt 12:22–28)

5. Temptation: The Fifth Petition

Q^2 11:16, 29–30 (Luke 11:16, 29–30 / Matt 12:38–40)

6. Fear of God: The First Petition

Q^2 12:6–7 (Luke 12:6–7 / Matt 10:29–31)

7. Daily Bread: The Third Petition

Q^2 12:22–31 (Luke 12:22–31 / Matt 6:25–33)

8. Forgiveness: The Forth Petition

CONCLUSION

Q² 17:3–4 (Luke 17:3–4 / Matt 18:15, 21–22)

The texts listed above show how the texts of the second redaction were added to the main texts of the first redaction.

When the first and second redactions were complete, Q shows a significant development regarding its description of Jesus and his followers. At the stage of the second redaction, Jesus is described as the religious leader who gave his followers the mission to proclaim the kingdom of God to their neighbors and heal them. Jesus delivered the manual that they had to keep during their ministry. Moreover, he provided them with the Lord's Prayer and its application. In this respect, he does not seem to be different from other Jewish teachers who summoned disciples and sent them out to people in order to collect more followers. According to the second redactor, Jesus was a prophetic teacher who prepared his followers for the eschatological kingdom of God and provided them with instruction for their daily life. It is also noteworthy that the second redactor delivered a certain theology regarding the number "five." The Lord's Prayer consists of five petitions and each of them is explained in the following texts. Then, this implies that while the first redaction did not reveal any particular theological work on John and Jesus, the second redactor described Jesus and his followers with theological intention, with the Pentateuch as its background. Especially, it is to be noted that the Lord's Prayer was composed of five petitions reminding readers of the temptation of Adam and Eve by the serpent in the garden of Eden. It seems that the second redactor tried to form his or her own theology regarding the status and work of Jesus. In this respect, it is to be studied in more detail whether the texts of the second redaction originated in the historical Jesus or not.

Part 3

The Third Redaction and Later Addition

The third section of Q deals with the Son of Man and the kingdom of God in 12:39—22:30. The third section can be divided into three parts: preparation for the Son of Man (12:39–59), the kingdom of God (13:18—17:2), and the coming of the Son of Man (17:23—22:30). An *inclusio* is found among them regarding the Son of Man; thus, it indicates the indispensible relationship between the Son of Man and the kingdom of God. It is, however, noteworthy that this section was also accomplished through a process of redaction. When we apply form critical, redaction critical, composition critical, and socio-historical approaches to the third section, they will lead us to the conclusion that it consists of two layers of redaction. In other words, the main texts of the third redaction are found in it; in addition, the texts of the fourth redaction will be distinguished.

In part 3, the texts of the third redaction will be examined. The texts interpolated into the main texts of the first redaction will be discussed first; then, those added to the main texts of the second redaction will be treated. Finally, the main texts of the third redaction will be dealt with. Then, the third redaction will show its concentration on Jesus as the Son of God and the Son of Man in response to the opposition of the people in the urban region of Galilee. In addition, it will be seen that the third redactor was interested in the eschatological judgment upon the Galileans.

1

The Texts Added to the First Redaction

Q was expanded by the third redaction. For this, many texts were interpolated into the main texts of the first redaction found in the first section of Q. The third redactor described Jesus as the one commissioned by God. Jesus is defined as a better leader than John. This implies that more members followed Jesus than John at the time of the third redaction. However, the followers of Jesus faced the opposition of the people. It is noteworthy that the third redactor took into consideration the theology of the first redaction when he or she interpolated texts into the main texts of the first redaction. Although the third redactor did not change the previous texts, he or she attempted to change the image of Jesus by adding texts. The most peculiar aspect is that, as Q went on a process of redaction further, it was more focused on Jesus. In this way, the theology of Q changed and developed.

A. THE PROCLAMATION OF JOHN (Q 3:16-17)

The second proclamation of John is written in Q^3 3:16-17 (Luke 3:16-17; Matt 3:11-12). As mentioned before, this text was added to Q^1 3:7-8a, 9 by the linking word "baptism" and the theme of eschatological judgment. However, the difference is definite; while the first redactor dealt with what people should do facing the end time, the third redactor focused on the theological description of Jesus as the eschatological agent.

The status and role of Jesus is described in Q^3 3:16. The third redactor focused on Jesus more than John. According to the first redactor, John was the prophetic figure who prepared the path for the Lord God and baptized those who had repented in the region of the Jordan (Q^1 3:4, 7). He was independent from Jesus; in other words, he had nothing to do with Jesus in the first redaction. However, the third redactor changed the relationship describing John as the forerunner of Jesus. This is seen in the description that John introduced Jesus as the one coming after him with more power. This implies that Jesus is a more important figure than John. As the redaction of Q progressed, the one who had come to prepare the path for the Lord God changed to the one as the forerunner of Jesus. In this respect, Jesus comes to the fore in comparison to John in the third redaction.

The third redactor described the role of Jesus from a comparative perspective. This is seen in that Jesus was more powerful than John.[1] Although the comparative form was adopted by the second redactor, it was never used for the comparison of Jesus with someone else (Q^2 10:12; 11:13; 12:7, 23–24, 28). While Jesus was described as the one powerful enough to expel the demon by the finger of God in the second redaction (Q^2 11:14–15, 17–20), the comparative form was not directly applied to him. On the other hand, having succeeded the comparative form from the second redaction, the third redactor applied it to the relationship between John and Jesus. In order to show that Jesus was more powerful than John, the third redactor made a comparison between the baptism of John with "water" and that of Jesus with "spirit" and "fire." No one denies that the latter is a more powerful means than the former. According to the third redactor, Jesus was indeed superior to John with regard to religious power.[2] In this way, Jesus came to the fore in comparison to John again. Although John was not disregarded yet, Jesus began to be more focused on at the stage of the third redaction.[3]

The third redactor mentioned the lordship of Jesus over John. This is seen in the saying that John was not worthy to untie even the thongs of the sandals of the one coming after him. This is what a servant has to do for his master. Compared with the role of John who spoke of bearing the fruit worthy of repentance and the eschatological judgment in the first redaction (Q^1 3:7–8a, 9), his role is significantly diminished in the third redaction. John was no more a partner of Jesus for the mission of God. Since the second

---

1. Cf. Kloppenborg, *Formation*, 104; and Jacobson, *First Gospel*, 84.
2. Cf. Jacobson, *First Gospel*, 85.
3. Cf. Robinson, "Sayings," 362.

redactor had exclusively described the instruction of Jesus for the ministry of his followers, the third redactor enhanced his understanding of Jesus and described John as his servant. In this respect, Jesus is defined as the lord or master of John at the very beginning of the third redaction. In this way, the status of John changed from the worker of the Lord God to the servant of the Lord Jesus in the third redaction. This implies that the number of those who followed John reduced at the time of the writing of the third redaction compared to those at the time of the writing of the first redaction.

The Spirit appears for the first time in the third redaction. This is seen when John preached that Jesus would baptize with the Spirit and fire. The Greek word πνεῦμα, which means "wind," is used for the Spirit. The third redactor seemed to put the term "wind" in parallel with "fire" for his or her understanding of Jesus' baptism. The word πνεῦμα seems to be used for both "wind" and "Spirit."[4] Even if the Greek word πνεῦμα refers only to "wind," it could make sense because the image of harvest with wind and fire appears for the eschatological judgment in Q^3 3:17. When a farmer clears the threshing floor with a pitchfork, he uses the wind to separate the wheat from the chaff and uses fire to burn the chaff. According to the Jewish tradition, fire has been understood to be a means of divine judgment (Gen 19:24–25; Ezek 30:8; Joel 2:3, 30; Mal 4:1; Matt 22:7, etc.). At any rate, it is to be noted that "Spirit" was used for the first time with the word πνεῦμα in the third redaction.

The meaning of baptism was changed in the third redaction. For this, it is necessary to take a look at the Bible. I would argue that the baptism of John and Jesus calls our attention to the relationship between Elijah and Elisha because the elements of water, wind, fire, and the Spirit appear all together in both stories. Elisha asked for a double portion of Elijah's spirit before a chariot of fire separated the two of them and a whirlwind lifted Elijah up to heaven (2 Kgs 2:8–11). Especially, it happened after Elijah had struck the water of the Jordan River with his cloak. Then, it was possible for the third redactor of Q to understand John and Jesus in light of Elijah and Elisha. In addition, since Elijah had been taken into consideration as the eschatological agent coming before the day of YHWH (Mal 4:5), the third redactor was able to strengthen the eschatological role of John by the proclamation about the one coming after him. It is also noteworthy that the transmission of spiritual power from Elijah to Elisha could be the mirror for the relationship between John and the one coming after him—that is, Jesus. Then, it can be understood why the third redactor described the baptism

---

4. Jacobson prefers "wind" to "spirit" on account of parallelism with "fire" as the agents of judgment (*First Gospel*, 84).

of Jesus with the Spirit [wind] and fire as the more powerful one than the baptism of John with water. The baptism of Jesus is a liturgical ritual for the preparation of eschatological judgment in the third redaction. Then, it can be said that the meaning of baptism has been changed from a symbol of repentance to circumvent the impending wrath (Q^1 3:7) to a liturgical ritual for the preparation of eschatological judgment (Q^3 3:16–17). As time passed, more theological meaning was imposed to the baptism of Jesus with the Spirit and fire.

It seems that baptism became an important ritual among the followers of Jesus at the stage of the third redaction. The emphasis on the Spirit and fire seems to reflect the changed social environment among the followers of Jesus. In other words, they moved from the region of the Jordan where they accessed water without difficulty (Q^1 3:2) to a place where they could not use water easily. On the other hand, the emphasis on the Spirit shows that they focused on the spiritual realm of baptism. In this respect, the third redactor cannot help but develop the theology of baptism in connection with the Spirit. Probably, the mission of Jesus' followers to the neighbors was successful in various towns described in the second redaction (Q^2 10:8–10); thus, they extended their missionary boundary to the urban area beyond the region of the Jordan River. If this interpretation is acceptable, then the third redactor should be credited with a significant achievement with regard to the theology of baptism.

A metaphor appears for the description of eschatological judgment in Q^3 3:17. It is said that Jesus will clear the threshing floor, gather the wheat into the granary, and throw the chaff into the unquenchable fire. They depict the process of harvest at the time of the first century CE. The scene of harvest was usually used as a reference to the eschatological judgment in the Jewish tradition (Isa 18:3–6; 24:13; Jer 51:33; Joel 3:13; Mic 4:11–13, etc.).[5] In addition, fire was introduced as the means for the judgment (Gen 19:24–25; Ezek 30:8; Joel 2:3, 30; Mal 4:1, etc.) The image of eschatological judgment with fire was also adopted by the second redactor (Q^2 10:12). There is no doubt that when the image of harvest with fire was adopted by the third redactor, it conveyed the eschatological judgment figuratively. Then, it can be said that Jesus was defined as the agent of eschatological judgment. While John was depicted as the one who proclaimed the eschatological judgment by saying that an ax was lying on the root of the tree in the first redaction (Q^1 3:9), Jesus was defined as its agent by describing that he himself performs the eschatological judgment in the third redaction. In this

---

5. Cf. Jacobson, *First Gospel*, 147n57.

respect, the status and role of Jesus was getting more important than those of John at the stage of the third redaction.

The third redactor conveyed the futuristic aspect of eschatological judgment. For this, future tense verbs are used: διακαθαριεῖ, συνάξει, and κατακαύσει. This shows how the temporal aspect of eschatological judgment changed as time passed. For instance, the first redactor introduced the ongoing judgment with fire by using present tense verbs (Q^1 3:9), and the second redaction mentioned the future aspect of judgment by using the future tense verb (Q^2 10:12). On the other hand, the third redactor introduced the eschatological judgment with fire that would happen in the indefinite future by using the future tense verbs (Q^3 3:17). In other words, as Q underwent a progress of redaction, the moment of eschatological judgment was postponed to the indefinite future. This indicates that it did not happen as John proclaimed in the first redaction at the time of the writing of the third redaction.

The third redactor distinguished different origins. For instance, wheat and chaff are different in their origins.[6] While the first redactor mentioned that the same tree could bear different fruit, either good or bad (Q^1 3:9), the third redactor dealt with wheat and the chaff, which are different in their very origins. It is impossible for wheat to become chaff and vice versa. The third redactor seemed to say that the followers of Jesus were different from their opponents with regard to their origin. The third redactor distinguished the followers of Jesus from their opponents. In other words, it reflects the social aspect that there was a conflict between the two parties. It seems that as time passed, the number of those who refused the instruction of Jesus increased among the fellow Jews.

B. THE BAPTISM OF JESUS (Q 3:21–22)

The baptism of Jesus is described in Q^3 3:21–22 (Luke 3:21–22; Matt 3:16–17). As mentioned before, this text follows Q^3 3:16–17 with the linking word "spirit" and the theme of baptism in the third redaction. Jesus had been baptized with the Spirit and then heard the heavenly voice. In this respect, their sequence is natural from a literary point of view. On the other hand, Q^3 3:21–22 was added to Q^1 3:7–8a, 9 so as to define Jesus as the commissioned servant of God at the beginning of his ministry.

The third redactor described the process of Jesus' baptism in Q^3 3:21. It is, however, unknown who baptized him in the present context. Although it has been generally believed that Jesus was baptized by John, the third

---

6. Webb, "Activity," 104, 109. Cf. Bonnard, *Matthieu*, 38.

redactor did not clearly say so. It is simply said that Jesus was baptized. This implies that the status of John had significantly reduced by the time of the writing of the third redaction. In addition, where Jesus was baptized is not described, either. In other words, the third redactor did not describe that Jesus was baptized in the region of the Jordan. This also implies that the majority of his followers were not active there anymore; rather, their ministry was successful in the area of towns as they had been instructed in the second redaction (Q² 10:8, 10). If this interpretation is acceptable, then they advanced from wilderness to towns from a geographical perspective.

The third redactor mentioned heaven opening at the baptism of Jesus. It is a mysterious and supernatural phenomenon depicted for the first time in the third redaction. The opening of heaven seems to be mentioned under the light of the prophetic tradition of the Bible (Ezek 1:1). It is, however, noteworthy that the terms "open" and "heaven" were already used in the second redaction. For instance, the Greek term ἀνοίγω [open] was used in order to urge the followers of Jesus to keep praying to God the Father in the second redaction (Q² 11:9–10). It refers to communication with God. In addition, interest in heaven already appeared in Q² 11:13 immediately after the word ἀνοίγω was used. Heaven was a place where God the Father was believed to dwell. In other words, communication with God in heaven was already emphasized in connection with prayer in the second redaction. Having succeeded these texts, the third redactor could describe that heaven opened at the baptism of Jesus. This implies communication initiated by God to human beings represented by Jesus at the baptism. In this respect, the third redactor seemed to develop the previous tradition for his or her theological purpose.

The descent of the Spirit is mentioned in Q³ 3:22. According to the third redactor, the Spirit descended from heaven upon Jesus in the form of a dove. It seems that the descent of the Spirit upon Jesus was described against the background of the prophets who received the Spirit of God (Isa 61:1; Ezek 2:2; Joel 2:28–29, etc.). This means that Jesus was understood to be a prophet by the third redactor. It is, however, noteworthy that the Greek word περιστερά [dove] is a translation of the Hebrew word יונה [Jonah], whose literal meaning is "dove." Then, it is possible to assume that the Hebrew word יונה had been used in the original version of Q before it was translated into Greek περιστερά and used by the Synoptic Gospels. This reminds readers of the sign of Jonah mentioned by Jesus in response to the request of the crowds for a heavenly sign in the second redaction (Q^2 11:16, 29–30). As discussed before, the sign of Jonah could refer to his proclamation of judgment upon Nineveh. In this respect, Jonah was an icon for divine judgment upon the Gentiles. Having succeeded this tradition, the third redactor seemed to create the description of the Spirit descending upon Jesus in the form of dove [יונה, περιστερὰ, Jonah] from heaven at the baptism. It seems there was a wordplay between the Hebrew and the Greek term of "dove." In this way, the third redactor gave the reader a further-developed answer regarding the sign of Jonah—that is, the descent of the Spirit in the form of a dove [Jonah] from heaven. On the other hand, the sign of Jonah in Q^2 11:16, 29–30 referred to the mysterious and miraculous descent of the dove [Jonah] when the third redaction was complete. In other words, the meaning of the sign of Jonah changed from his proclamation of judgment upon Nineveh in the second redaction to the mysterious and miraculous descent of a dove in the third redaction. Thus, the descent of the Spirit in the form of a dove from heaven at the baptism of Jesus pretypifies the divine judgment that would be passed upon those who did not accept and follow Jesus.[7] In this respect, the third redactor seemed to reveal his ability to interpret the previous tradition in his or her own way.

The heavenly voice is mentioned at the baptism of Jesus. According to the third redactor, Jesus heard a voice from heaven, "You are my [God's] Son, whom I love; with you I am well pleased." Whereas the first redactor depicted John as the voice in the wilderness (Q^1 3:2–4), the third redactor introduced the voice from heaven addressed to Jesus at the baptism (Q^3 3:21–22). This refers to God's initiative for communication with his servant Jesus.[8] It has been generally agreed that the heavenly saying is a combination of allusions to Ps 2:7 and Isa 42:1. Their context talks about judgment upon the Gentiles. In this respect, they fit well with the "descent of the Spirit in the form of a dove [Jonah]" because he was a prophet for judgment upon the Gentiles. As a result, the third redactor informs readers of Jesus as the eschatological agent for the divine judgment upon the Gentiles. Interest in the Gentiles comes to the fore in the third redaction for the first time since the instruction about eschatological judgment mentioned in the first redaction (Q^1 3:7–8a, 9). Thus, it can be surmised that the third redactor started describing the salvation and punishment of the Gentiles.

Jesus was identified as the Son of God through the heavenly voice. Literally speaking, he is "my [God's] Son." The Son of God is the one coming

---

7. There are a certain number of scholars who interpret the baptism of Jesus against the background of Noah's story. Cf. Keck, "Spirit," 48–49; and Lewis, *Study*, 174–76.

8. Cf. del Agua, "Narrative," 346; and Dunn, *Baptism*, 26.

after John and is more powerful than him. Jesus' filial identity appears for the first time in the third redaction. The idea of a filial relationship of people with God already appeared when Jesus taught his audience to love their enemies so as to become sons of the Father in the first redaction (Q^1 6:35). In addition, according to the second redactor, Jesus taught his followers to call God "Father" (Q^2 11:2) and defined their filial relationship with God figuratively (11:11–12). However, Jesus did not identify himself as a son of God in the first two redactions. On the other hand, having received the tradition about the filial relationship, the third redactor directly applied the title "God's Son" to Jesus.[9] It is important to note that the third redactor concentrated on the status of Jesus. As seen above, this tendency began from the very beginning of the third redaction when he was identified as the one coming after John (Q^3 3:16–17). Since the first half of the heavenly voice, "You are my [God's] Son," alludes to Ps 2:7, Jesus the Son of God could be connected with the eschatological Davidic Messiah because it was a part of the divine announcement toward David. In a sense, Jesus is the enthroned Son of God. Then, it can be said that the third redactor began to show his belief in things that extend beyond the realm of probable historical fact. In this respect, the third redactor is presumed to be a well-trained scribe in interpreting the Bible and applying it to Jesus.

C. THE BEATITUDE (Q 6:22–23B)

The fourth beatitude is introduced in Q^3 6:22–23b (Luke 6:22–23b; Matt 5:11–12b). This text follows Q^1 6:20b and Q^2 6:21 by the form of beatitude. Thus, they show how the beneficiary and reward changed. On the other hand, 6:22–23b follows 3:21–22 in the third redaction in order to define the status of Jesus by connecting the Son of Man with the Son of God.

First of all, the third redactor introduced a different form of beatitude in Q^3 6:22. It was directly addressed to the followers of Jesus with the second person plural "you." This differs from the preceding three beatitudes of the first and second redactions in that their beneficiaries are addressed to some sort of people. The first three beneficiaries were expressed with the substantive function of adjective or participle such as "the poor" (Q^1 6:20b), "the hungry," and "the mourning" (Q^2 6:21). In the third redaction, the direct

---

9. The Jewish tradition regarded various beings as the son of God; for instance, angels or angelic beings, Israelites as individuals or as a whole, a king, a righteous person, and the eschatological Davidic Messiah in the context of 2 Sam 7:11–14 and Ps 2:7. In particular, the last one attracts our attention as reflected in 4QFlor. 1.10f; 4QpsDan A. Cf. Dunn, *Christology*, 12–22.

address to the followers of Jesus reminds readers of the heavenly voice announced directly to him in the form of the second person singular "you" (Q^3 3:22). In other words, Jesus was able to use the form of the second person plural directly to his followers because he heard the heavenly voice in the form of the second person singular directly. This implies the intimate relationship between Jesus and his followers. As the redaction of Q progressed, the relationship of Jesus with his followers was described as the intimate one as well as the authoritative one.

The third redactor wrote the beatitude in a different form. While the first and second redactors used the word ὅτι [because] in Q 6:20b–21, the third redactor adopted another one ὅταν [when] in 6:22–23b. This implies that the followers of Jesus must meet the precondition to be blessed. According to the first redactor, the poor are promised to be blessed because they are simply poor (Q^1 6:20b); in a similar manner, the second redactor described that the hungry and the mourner will be blessed because they are simply hungry and mourning (Q^2 6:21). The precondition for blessing has nothing to do with their relationship with Jesus in the first two redactions. On the other hand, the third redactor showed a difference in that only those who were insulted and hated on account of Jesus, the Son of Man, would be blessed (Q^3 6:22–23b). It is noteworthy that one's relationship with Jesus came to the fore as the criterion to be blessed or not in the third redaction. This is in accordance with the description that Jesus was highlighted at the baptism scene (Q^3 3:16–17, 21–22). As the redaction of Q progressed, the criterion for being blessed changed from one's situation itself to his or her relationship with Jesus.

The third redactor listed what the followers of Jesus experienced while they had been on their ministry. It is written that they were insulted, hated, and faced every kind of evil on account of Jesus the Son of Man (Q^3 6:22–23b). The list reflects the maltreatment that the followers of Jesus experienced during their ministry commanded by Jesus according to the second redaction (Q^2 10:4–12). It seems that they experienced opposition from their neighbors. When they proclaimed the coming of the kingdom of God and healed the sick (Q^2 10:9), their fellow people would not accept the proclamation. According to the second redactor, Jesus anticipated their being unwelcomed in a house and taught them to shake off the dust from their feet (Q^2 10:10–11). However, the opposition that the followers of Jesus experienced seems to be harsher than they had anticipated. The opponents were aggressive as reflected in the third redaction: insult, hatred, and evil doings (Q^3 6:22). Thus, the third redactor could not help but encourage them by saying that when they overcome the opposition, they would be blessed (6:23b).

It is necessary to take a look at the title "Son of Man" used in the fourth beatitude (Q^3 6:22). When the Son of Man appeared for the first time in the second redaction (Q^2 9:58; 11:30), it was used for Jesus as a substitute for the first person "I"; in addition, the Son of Man was a model for his followers. In the third redaction, however, one's faithful attitude toward him becomes the top priority, so that one might be blessed. In this way, Jesus the Son of Man comes to the fore as the central figure with regard to blessing in the third redaction. However, the Son of Man still conveys the human aspect of Jesus. As the redaction of Q progressed, the Son of Man was becoming more concentrated and more important. This is supported by the theological tendency of the third redactor. While he was called "God's Son" at the baptism, he is identified as "the Son of Man" in the beatitude. The third redactor imposed the human aspect to the Son of Man in 6:22 because it was interpolated before Q^2 9:57–58 in which Jesus was identified as the human Son of Man. In this way, the third redactor was eager to shed light on Jesus from a theological perspective.

Then, the reward that the followers of Jesus will receive is mentioned in Q^3 6:23ab. They can be glad because they will receive the great reward in heaven. Although the second redaction was concerned with heaven in connection with God and sign (Q^2 11:13, 16), the third redaction mentioned heavenly reward for the first time. This kind of description was possible because communication between heaven and earth was mentioned in the preceding text of the third redaction (Q^3 3:21–22). It is, however, noteworthy that the chance to be blessed was getting slim as the redaction of Q progressed. For example, the first redactor announced the present aspect of reward, saying, "The kingdom of God is yours [the poor's]" (Q^1 6:20b); on the other hand, the second redactor postponed the moment of being blessed to the indefinite future saying, "You [the hungry] will be satisfied" and "You [the mourner] will be consoled." On the contrary, the third redactor projected the hope of reward to heaven, saying, "Great is your reward in heaven." As time passed, the earthy aspect of reward changed to a heavenly one and the present to a futuristic one. In this respect, the more the redaction of Q progressed, the further the theology developed regarding reward.

D. THE REQUEST FOR PRAYER (Q 6:28)

Prayer for those who mistreated the followers of Jesus is instructed in Q^3 6:28 (Luke 6:28; Matt 5:44b). In this respect, love of the enemy is connected with the theme of prayer for the first time in the third redaction. It seems that the socio-historical situation was getting worse at the time of the writing of the third redaction.

Instruction about prayer for those who mistreated the followers of Jesus is found in Q^3 6:28. This text was interpolated in between Q^1 6:27 and 6:29–30 in order to strengthen the instruction about love of the enemy. The third redactor taught that prayer for those who mistreated the followers of Jesus is a way of loving the enemy. As shown before, the second redactor developed instructions about prayer with the Lord's Prayer (Q^2 11:2–4). Having received the tradition about prayer, the third redactor was able to teach the followers of Jesus to pray for those who mistreated them. Since the mistreatment was mentioned in Q^3 6:22, the instruction on the prayer for those mistreating the followers of Jesus reveals a circumstance of opposition between the two parties in the third redaction (Q^3 6:28). Those who mistreated the followers of Jesus supposed to be understood as the enemy introduced in the first redaction (Q^1 6:27). In this way, the beneficiary of prayer was changed from "one's own self" in the second redaction to "others" in the third redaction.

E. ACCUSATIONS AGAINST OPPONENTS (Q 6:39–42)

Accusations against opponents are described in Q^3 6:39–42 (Luke 6:39–42; Matt 7:3–5; 10:24–25; 15:14). This text follows Q^1 6:27, 29–38 with the theme of reciprocal relationship. In addition, this text follows Q^3 6:22–23b, 28 with the theme of opposition in the third redaction. This reflects the social situation of conflict at the stage of the third redaction.

Accusation against the leader and his follower is described in Q^3 6:39. For this, the third redactor used a metaphor; if a blind person leads another, then both will fall into a pit. Without doubt, this saying was addressed to the opponents who were in competition with the followers of Jesus. From a metaphoric perspective, the opponents are compared to the blind who do not know where to go and what to do. By using the term "blind," the third redactor accused them of misleading the people and of ignorance about Jesus. Then, the metaphor is the answer to the opponents who insulted and hated his followers; in addition, the opponents committed evil actions against them (Q^3 6:22–23b). A similar instruction already appeared in the Beelzebul Controversy: "If Satan is divided against himself, how can his kingdom stand?" (Q^2 11:18). Although no accusation was made against the crowds around Jesus, the second redactor showed that they had turned their backs on the followers of Jesus who proclaimed the kingdom of God and healed the sick. Having inherited this tradition, the third redactor applied the metaphor of the blind to the opponents because the relationship had been getting worse between the two groups: the followers of Jesus and the ordinary people. Since their challenge and opposition were getting stronger, the third redactor could not help but accuse them of their misleading.

The third redactor introduced a proverbial saying in Q^3 6:40. It is said, "A student is not above his teacher, but everyone who is fully trained will be like his teacher." For this, the term μαθητής [student, disciple] is used for the first time at last in the third redaction. This implies that a certain group of people gathered around Jesus; of course, their opponents were also accustomed to the relationship between teacher and disciple. This reflects the fact that the ministry of the followers of Jesus was successful in persuading some people to accept the instruction of Jesus (Q^2 10:4–12). Of course, some of them became disciples of Jesus at last. At any rate, a disciple is not superior to his or her teacher, but it is enough for the disciple if he or she grows up as much as the teacher. This instruction encourages the disciples of Jesus to be like their teacher Jesus. This reflects the situation that Jesus was considered a teacher by his disciples at the stage of the third redaction. This also reminds readers of the instruction that God was introduced as the model to be taken after in the first redaction (Q^1 6:36). It is, however, noteworthy that the top priority was changed from God to Jesus in the third redaction. This is in accordance with the fact that the third redactor kept describing Jesus as the central figure to be known (Q^3 3:16–17; 6:22–23b). In this way, as the redaction of Q progressed, Jesus was more focused on as the key figure that the disciples should follow and take after. In this way, the third redactor kept imposing theological meaning to Jesus.

A critique against the hypocrite is written in Q^3 6:41–42. It is said that a person with a beam in his or her eye sees a speck in the eye of "brother" and then says, "Let me take the speck out of your eye." Thus, according to the third redactor, Jesus said that the person should take the beam out of his or her eye first and then ask the brother to take the speck out of his or her eye. First, this text reflects the conflict between the disciples of Jesus and their opponents—that is, those who would not accept the instruction of Jesus. The latter attempted to teach the former; however, the disciples criticized the opponents against their ignorance of Jesus, the servant of God. The metaphor reflects that the reason for writing was the polemic situation between the two groups.[10] Second, the term "brother" is used here since it appeared for the first time in the second redaction (Q^2 17:3). The term "brother" is a

---

10. Jacobson, *First Gospel*, 104, 106.

technical term used for members of a certain group of people at the stage of the third redaction; thus, it seems that the disciples of Jesus constituted a certain group within their society. It seems, however, that they did not separate themselves from the social community yet in which they enjoyed normal life. Third, the opponents seemed to be those who had insulted and hated the disciples on account of Jesus the Son of Man (Q^3 6:22–23b). If this interpretation is correct, there seems to be a serious conflict between the two groups. In this respect, the third redactor characterized the opponents one by one as the story advanced.

The contrast between "brother" and "hypocrite" highlights the polemic situation. The term "hypocrites" appears for the first time in the third redaction (Q^3 6:42). It is, however, noteworthy that some of the brothers will be called hypocrites. This means that the third redactor regarded the opponents as hypocrites because they did not accept the instruction of Jesus and they rather took an aggressive attitude toward the disciples of Jesus. Thus, the term "hypocrite" presents a harsh critique against those who were compared to the people with the beam in their eyes. This implies that the disciples of Jesus are known for striving to outperform their competitors. The third redactor tried to show that the disciples of Jesus were on the right track regarding the faith.

F. DIFFERENCE OF ORIGIN (Q 6:43–45)

Instruction about the difference of origin is written in Q^3 6:43–45 (Luke 6:43–45; Matt 7:16–18; 12:33–35). This text follows Q^3 6:39–42 in order to strengthen the difference between the two groups. It was added to the first redaction (Q^1 6:27, 29–38) so that it might teach that a reciprocal relationship among human beings was no longer possible at the stage of the third redaction.

The third redactor introduced the metaphor of the two kinds of trees in Q^3 6:43–44. The good tree bears good fruit, while the bad tree bears bad fruit. The good tree cannot bear bad fruit and vice versa. The tree is known by its fruit. The trees are distinct from the very beginning. This reminds readers of the distinction between the wheat and the chaff (Q^3 3:17). In this respect, the third redactor strengthened the distinction between the disciples of Jesus and their opponents from their origin. The disciples distinguished themselves from the opponents who insulted and hated them; especially they committed "evil" [σαπρός] actions against them (Q^3 6:22–23b). This means that the third redactor defined the opponents as the evil group. At this moment, it is necessary to see how the concept of "good" and "bad" or "evil" changed and developed as the redaction of Q progressed. The first redactor was concerned with bearing "good" [καλός] fruit, so that the tree might not be chopped down and thrown into the fire (Q^1 3:9). The term "bad" does not appear in this text. Rather, the phrase "does not produce good fruit" is used there. On the other hand, the second redactor conveyed the terms "good" [ἀγαθός] and "evil" [πονηρός] in order to explain the nature of fatherhood (Q^2 11:13). In this context, there is a certain relationship between good and evil. However, the third redactor adopted a sharp contrast between "good" [καλός] and "bad" [σαπρός] (Q^3 6:43). Their origins differ. This shows readers that as time passed, the redaction of Q came to draw a sharper contrast between the two groups: the disciple of Jesus and their opponents. The discussion above informs readers of the possibility that the disciples began to distinguish themselves from the opponents who mistreated them (Q^3 6:22–23b, 28). Although it is unknown whether the disciples constituted a separate community outside their society, they seemed to keep traveling for their ministry.

Another contrast between the "good" [ἀγαθός] person and the "evil" [πονηρός] one appears in Q^3 6:45. This succeeds the contrast between "good" [καλός] and "bad" [σαπρός] written in 6:43. The good person "brings good things out of the good stored up in his (her) heart" and vice versa. The third redactor strengthened the distinction between the good and evil from their origin once again. This means that the opponents were identified as the evil ones from a religious perspective. The fact that the third redactor used the term "evil" right after the term "bad" reflects the worsened situation from a religio-ethical perspective. This indicates that the relationship of the disciples with their opponents was getting worse with regard to the polemic circumstances.[11] From a sociological perspective, it can be said that the disciples of Jesus were getting separated from their opponents in religious society.

The emphasis on what one says appears for the first time in the third redaction (Q^3 6:45b). It is said, "For out of the overflow of his heart his mouth speaks." Everyone speaks out of what he or she thinks in his or her mind. Then, according to the third redactor, what was spoken represents what was in one's mind. This means that a person can be known by what he or she says. It is important that one's outside match his or her inside. If one does not, the person would be considered as a hypocrite (6:42). Then those who insulted the disciples on account of Jesus the Son of Man become those who spoke out what is in their mind (6:22). Thus, from a sociological

---

11. Cf. Jacobson, *First Gospel*, 105.

perspective, it can be said that the disciples of Jesus distinguished and separated themselves from their opponents.

G. THE OBSERVANCE OF WORDS (Q 6:46-49)

Instruction about the observance of words is described in Q^3 6:46-49 (Luke 6:46-49; Matt 7:21, 24-27). This text follows Q^3 6:43-45 by the theme of observing what one has said in the third redaction. In addition, this text was interpolated into the main texts of the first redaction, so that it might show the importance of observing what the Lord Jesus told his disciples.

The third redactor depicted Jesus as the Lord in Q^3 6:46. It is seen in the description that Jesus was called "the Lord." His lordship was already implied by John in that he did not deserve to untie the thongs of the sandals of Jesus (Q^3 3:16-17). While God was the Lord in the first redaction (Q^1 3:2-4), the title "Lord" was not used in the second redaction. Then, lordship was suddenly applied to Jesus in the third redaction. It is important to observe that as the redaction of Q progressed, the status of Jesus was getting heightened. It is in accordance with the tendency to describe Jesus as the Son of God (Q^3 3:21-22) and then identify him as the Son of Man (6:22-23b). In this way, the third redactor informed readers of his status one by one. By doing so, the third redactor contributed to the description of Jesus as the leader and built a religious group around him.

The third redactor emphasized the observance of what Jesus the Lord had taught in Q^3 6:47. The disciples of Jesus must keep what he said. It is important that the form of plural is used for what Jesus said. This indicates that Jesus taught a lot of things. So far, Jesus delivered the preaching about reciprocal relationships among human beings in the first redaction (Q^1 6:20b, 27, 29-38) and gave the manual for ministry and the Lord's Prayer including its application in the second redaction (Q^2 9:57-58; 10:4-12; 11:2-4, etc.). In addition, he taught the disciple the nature of their opponents in the third redaction (Q^3 6:22-23b, 28, 39-45). The disciples are required to observe all of these instructions. This is how they grow to become more like Jesus, their teacher (6:40). In this way, Jesus was exalted as the giver of new commandments in the third redaction. The emphasis on the observance of what he taught is to be understood as the acknowledgment of his authority. This reminds readers of the importance of one's relationship with Jesus so as to be blessed (6:22-23b). In this way, the third redactor imposed more authority to Jesus as the central figure.

The parable of the two builders is introduced in Q^3 6:48–49. In this parable, the third redactor used the phrase ὁμοιός ἐστιν [it is like] for the first time. The literary form "simile" is adopted for the parabolic expression. This implies that as the redaction of Q progressed, diverse literary forms were used in order to convey the instruction of Jesus. For instance, no metaphor was used for Jesus in the first redaction; rather, John used it (Q^1 3:9). Then, the second redactor adopted it several times (Q^2 9:58; 11:11; 12:6, 24–28). It seems that a well-trained writer was in charge of writing the second redaction from a literary point of view. On the other hand, the third redactor began to use the simile for the first time (Q^3 6:48–49). This is a way of describing more directly than a metaphor the role of Jesus. This implies that the further the redaction of Q progressed, the more literary devices the redactor needed to explain directly Jesus' instruction.

Hereby, the contrast between the wise and the unwise is clear in that they chose different places to build houses. While the unwise selected sand, the wise chose bedrock for the foundation of the house. The wise builder refers to the one who heard the words of Jesus and observed them; on the contrary, the unwise builder refers to the one who heard the words of Jesus but did not observe them. In this respect, two kinds of people are sharply contrasted by their way of response to the words of the Lord Jesus. This reminds readers of the instructions in Q^3 3:16–17 and 6:43–45 which also draw a sharp contrast between the two groups from their origin. The third redactor seems to heighten the distinction of disciples from their opponents. It seems that the more Q was subjected to redaction, the more clearly the disciples of Jesus separated themselves from their opponents. In other words, the third redactor justified the instruction of Jesus more and more in comparison to the contemporary Jewish instruction.

Natural phenomena appear as tools for destruction in the parable of the two builders. Rain and flash floods could collapse the house on the sand. It is noteworthy that rain and flash floods are aquatic tools of nature. They are introduced in connection with "fire" as the means of eschatological judgment. As shown before, the unquenchable fire was mentioned by John as the means of eschatological judgment in the first redaction (Q^1 3:9). There, Jesus did not deal with it at all. In the second redaction, Jesus introduced the term "Sodom" as the only reference to the eschatological judgment that reminds readers of "burning sulfur" as its means (Q^2 10:12). It is, however, noteworthy that the meaning of eschatological judgment does not appear directly in this context. On the other hand, the third redactor introduced rain and flash floods as well as fire as the means of eschatological judgment (Q^3 3:17; 6:48–49). In this respect, the third redactor employed both fire and water as mutually comparative. As Q went through a process of redaction, sharply contrasted means were adopted for eschatological judgment.

The third redactor described the result of eschatological judgment. The house [οἶκός] built on bedrock will remain, but the house built on sand will be collapsed by the rain and flash floods. While the second redactor mentioned the division of a house (Q^2 11:17), the third redactor applied it to the contrasted fate of houses built on sand and bedrock. In addition, the eschatological contrast between the two is in coherence with the previous description about the fate of wheat and chaff (Q^3 3:17). In this respect, the third redactor seemed to be a well-trained scribe for theological writing. According to the third redactor, the disciples of Jesus were required to observe the words of the Lord Jesus in order to avoid the eschatological judgment.

H. INTEREST IN THE GENTILES (Q 7:1-10)

Interest in the Gentiles is found in Q^3 7:1-10 (Luke 7:1-10; Matt 8:5-10, 13). This text follows Q^3 6:46-49 by connecting words such as "Lord," "words," and "house," and the theme of obedience to the words. This text was added to the first redaction (Q^1 6:20b, 27, 29-38) in order to show the importance of observing the words of Jesus the Lord. Especially, this shows an interest in the Gentiles for the first time.

The third redactor described the ministry of Jesus at Capernaum (Q^3 7:1). It is to be noted that the name of a contemporary city is mentioned for the first time. Although Sodom was mentioned in the second redaction (Q^2 10:12), it was not a city that existed in the first century CE. Rather, it was a city in the past mentioned just for the comparison with the towns that turned their backs on the followers of Jesus who proclaimed the kingdom of God (Q^2 10:8-11). Therefore, the introduction of Capernaum implies that the disciples of Jesus were active there at the time of the writing of the third redaction. In other words, their ministry was successful enough to advance to an urban area like Capernaum, which was a city big enough to be mentioned in the third redaction.

A centurion is introduced in the third redaction (Q^3 7:3). He was supposed to be a Gentile. This informs readers of the fact that interest in the Gentiles appears for the first time in the third redaction. Although the Ninevites were mentioned in the second redaction (Q^2 11:29-30), they appeared simply as an example in connection with the sign of Jonah.[12] No activity was

---

12. While the Matthean text does not mention the Ninevites, the Lucan does. It seems that the Lucan text reflects the original wording of Q in the fact that as Sodom was mentioned in the second redaction (Q^2 10:12), the Ninevites was too. Moreover,

mentioned with regard to their role. This is not much different from the negative perspective on the Gentiles in the second redaction (Q² 12:30). It does not mean that the followers of Jesus proclaimed his instruction to the Gentiles at the stage of the second redaction. On the other hand, the third redactor mentioned the Gentile centurion as the key figure in the story. It is, however, noteworthy that the interest in the Gentiles appears within the region of Galilee. This does not mean that the disciples were active in the Gentile region.

The first set of dialogue between Jesus and the centurion is written in Q³ 7:3-6. The centurion came to Jesus and reported the sickness of his servant [παῖς]. The reason that the Gentile centurion suddenly came to the fore is not known to readers; in addition, the nature of the sickness has not been told, either. In response to his report, Jesus said that he would visit his house and treat the servant. The reason that Jesus responded to his request without hesitation was because he already commanded his followers to treat the sick; in addition, he also healed the mute possessed by the demon in the second redaction (Q² 10:9; 11:14-15, 17-20). The difference is found in that the sickness was not related to the demon in the story of the Gentile centurion. In addition, while the second redactor acknowledged the ability of the contemporary people to perform healing miracles, the third redactor seems to exclusively emphasize the authority of Jesus to perform them. The third redactor emphasized the healing power of Jesus, in contrast to the reluctance to show another sign in the second redaction (Q² 11:16, 29-30). Although Jesus taught the audience to do more than what others wanted in the first redaction (Q¹ 6:27, 29-38), his decision to do something voluntarily for others appears for the first time here in the third redaction. In this respect, the third redactor taught the disciples to do something good for others voluntarily and immediately.

The second set of dialogue is written in Q³ 7:7-9. It starts with the response of the centurion calling Jesus "my Lord." The title "Lord" recalls its use in 6:46. As already shown, the Lordship of Jesus began to be mentioned when John proclaimed about the one coming after him (3:16-17). In this vein, the third redactor described that the centurion applied this title to Jesus.[13] In other words, Jesus was identified as the Lord of both the disciples and the centurion; in other words, he was the Lord of the Jews and the Gentiles. Then the centurion told Jesus that he was not worthy to invite him to his house. From the fact that the term "worthy" [ἱκανός] is also used in 3:16,

---

the text 11:31-32 follows 11:16, 29-30 by the linking word "the Ninevites."

13. There is an opinion that the centurion cannot be regarded as a Gentile. Probably, he could be a mercenary hired in the region of Galilee. Cf. Catchpole, "Centurion's Faith," 519, 527, 539.

it can be said that the centurion is parallel to John regarding unworthiness in front of Jesus. Then, he asked Jesus for a word to heal his servant. In order to show his faith in Jesus, the centurion introduced an example that when he commanded his soldiers to come, they obeyed and came to him. In this way, he showed his readiness to obey the words of Jesus. Responding to his readiness, Jesus shouted that he did not see anyone like him in Israel. This means that the Gentiles could be better than the Israelites with regard to faith in Jesus. Thus, when Jesus told him to go to his house, the centurion obeyed his word and found his servant recovered from illness. In this way, the third redactor depicted the Lordship of Jesus over the people.

Two sets of dialogue appear for the first time in the third redaction. It is, however, necessary to see how the description of dialogue developed in Q. The first redactor did not describe dialogue at all. Only unilateral instruction and proclamation of John and Jesus appear in the first redaction. On the other hand, the second redactor introduced a set of dialogue in Q^2 9:57–58; 11:14–15, 17–20; and 11:16, 29–30. In response to the request of a certain person, Jesus answered with his own instruction. Having succeeded these texts, the third redactor developed the story of the centurion adding one more set of dialogue. In this way, the literary form of pericope significantly developed in the third redaction. The third redactor should be credited with an achievement in developing the pericope.

The story of the centurion shows readers his obedience to the words of Jesus the Lord. This is supported by the fact that the centurion obeyed the word of the Lord Jesus as instructed in Q^3 6:46–49.[14] In addition, it seems that the story begins with the term "words" as reflected in 7:1.[15] In this respect, the story of the centurion is in keeping with the instruction of observing the words of the Lord Jesus described in 6:46–49. The third redactor focused on the obedience of the centurion to Jesus in contrast to the disobedience of the opponents.[16] This reflects the polemic situation at the time of the writing of the third redaction.

The story of the centurion reveals the extended ministry to the Gentiles. At the stage of the third redaction, the disciples of Jesus extended their mission to the Gentiles within the region of Galilee. This is in accordance with the voice heard from heaven at the baptism of Jesus because it was written with a background of Ps 2:7 and Isa 42:1, which alluded to judgment upon the Gentiles (Q^3 3:22). However, the third redactor did not describe

---

14. Catchpole, "Centurion," 537.

15. While Luke took the word "sayings" [ῥήματα] in Luke 7:1, Matthew adopted the term "words" [λόγους] in Matt 7:28a. If the Lucan version represents the original wording of Q, it supports the relationship between Q^3 6:46–49 and 7:1–10.

16. Cf. Jacobson, *First Gospel*, 110–11.

Jesus working in the Gentile region yet.[17] Although the disciples of Jesus did not actively work in the Gentile area, the third redactor reflected interest in the Gentiles. Therefore, it is important to observe that the Gentiles appear in the third redaction of Q so as to highlight the reluctance of the opponents to accept the instruction of Jesus. In this respect, the ministry to the Gentiles is contrasted with the opposition of the people in the Galilean region.

I. JOHN'S DOUBT ABOUT JESUS (Q 7:18–23)

John's doubt about Jesus is described in Q^3 7:18–23 (Luke 7:18–23; Matt 11:2–6). This text follows Q^3 7:1–10 with a theme of faith in Jesus; while the centurion had faith in him, John did not. On the other hand, this text was interpolated into the main texts of the first redaction in order to adjust the status of John. As a result, John is described as one inferior to Jesus.

According to the third redactor, John sent his disciples to Jesus since he heard about what Jesus had done (Q^3 7:18–20). This shows that there were some people who followed John. It is clear that the followers of John were a group who had kept the relationship of teacher and disciples (6:40). At any rate, the disciples of John asked Jesus whether he was the one promised to come after John. This reminds readers of the proclamation of John in 3:16–17. He proclaimed that the more powerful one would come after him and baptize with the Spirit and fire. The reason why John was suspicious of Jesus is not known; however, it was probably because Jesus did not perform baptism with the Spirit and fire as John had proclaimed and expected. At any rate, his question about the person whom the crowds had to wait for indicates that John did not think Jesus was the one promised to come after him anymore. In the eyes of John, Jesus was not the agent of God who would pass eschatological judgment with the unquenchable fire. In this manner, the third redactor described that John lost his confidence in Jesus. It seems that the third redactor made a contrast between John and the centurion regarding faith in Jesus the Lord (7:1–10). While the centurion was obedient to Jesus, John did not obey him. The centurion asked Jesus to heal his servant, but John sent his disciple to raise a question about the status of Jesus. While the centurion was complemented by Jesus, John lost his confidence in Jesus. The sharp contrast between John and the centurion heightens the superiority of Gentiles to the Jews regarding faith in the Lord Jesus. The third redactor provided glimpses of John who was described as being

---

17. Jacobson, *First Gospel*, 110. On the other hand, Kloppenborg insists that the Q community was active in the mission to the Gentiles on the basis of Q 7:1–10 (*Formation*, 119).

inferior to Jesus; strictly speaking, the number of disciples of Jesus increased more than those of John at the time of the writing of the third redaction.[18] This reflects the contemporary situation that the hegemony moved from the disciples of John to those of Jesus. As the redaction of Q progressed, the status of Jesus was getting more authoritative. In this way, the subordination of John to Jesus was acknowledged at the stage of the third redaction.[19] John was disregarded as the one being suspicious of Jesus.

Jesus' answer to the disciples of John is written in Q^3 7:21–23. He said to them that they should go to John and tell what they had heard and seen about Jesus. Then, according to the third redactor, Jesus listed what they had to report, "alluding to the implied fulfillment of various Isaianic texts (Isa 29:18f; 35:5f; 61:1)":[20] the blind can see again, the lame can walk around, the leprous are cleansed, the deaf can hear again, the dead are revitalized, and the poor are proclaimed the good news.[21] However, Q does not describe all of what Jesus listed above; rather, the third redactor simply presumed that Jesus did all of these. If we can list some of them, they are the beatitude about the blessing to the poor (Q^1 6:20b), the command to heal the sick (Q^2 10:9), the expulsion of the demon from the mute (11:14–15, 17–20), and the healing of the servant of the centurion (Q^3 7:1–10).[22] These are what Jesus had done with the Spirit and fire. Therefore, the third redactor seems likely to say that the activities listed above are abundant enough to prove that Jesus was the one promised to come after John.[23] In addition, the motive of hearing and seeing was already alluded to in the description of the baptism of Jesus (3:21–22). In this respect, the answer of Jesus to the question of John was in the middle of the theological development of the third redaction.

The third redactor seems to be one of the Pharisees. The mentioning of revitalization of the dead implies that the third redactor believed in the general resurrection of people. If the third redactor had not been from the Pharisees, he or she would not have mentioned it. In addition, the allusion

---

18. Kloppenborg argues that Q 7:18–23 was created to invite the followers of John to the community after the resurrection of Jesus (*Formation*, 107). To my judgment, his argument lacks objective evidence to prove that kind of historical possibility.

19. Cf. Jacobson, *First Gospel*, 113–14. On the other hand, Tuckett opposes this kind of interpretation (*Q*, 126–27).

20. Tuckett, *Q*, 126.

21. A similar text is found in 4Q521. Cf. Kloppenborg, *Q*, 81.

22. Jacobson insists that Q^2 11:14–15, 17–20 is the miracle of expulsion of the demon and that this has nothing to do with the miracle listed in Q^3 7:22–23 (*First Gospel*, 112). However, when we consider the stages of redaction, Q^3 7:22–23 contains the experience of the healing of the mute described in Q^2 11:14–15, 17–20.

23. Cf. Robinson, "Sayings," 365; and Kloppenborg, *Q*, 70.

to various verses of the Bible informs us of the possibility that the third redactor was a well-trained scribe from the Pharisees. Inheriting the Pharisaic tradition, the third redactor seemed to interpret the ministry of Jesus with allusions to the Bible. It is, however, noteworthy that the third redactor did not show the Pharisaic characteristic much in other texts so far.

The third redactor introduced a beatitude in Q^3 7:23. It is announced that those who are not offended by Jesus are blessed. In the third redaction, the beatitude was once used in 6:22–23b; however, the difference is clear between them. While μακάριοί ἐστε ὅταν is used in 6:22–23b, μακάριός ἐστιν ὃς ἐὰν appears in 7:23. Beyond the difference with regard to the number used for persons, a common element is found in that a certain precondition should be met to be blessed. While insult and hatred on account of the Son of Man are listed as the precondition to be blessed in 6:22–23b, everyone who is not offended by Jesus is promised to be blessed in 7:23. In other words, one's relationship with Jesus the Son of Man is suggested as the precondition for being blessed. This is a different aspect from the beatitudes in the first and second redactions, which focus on the situation of the one who will be blessed (Q^1 6:20b; Q^2 6:21). In this way, the third redactor kept focusing on describing the status and role of Jesus. Jesus was being regarded more as the important criterion for the blessing of God. This shows how the third redactor theologically interpreted Jesus the Son of Man.

J. JESUS' EVALUATION OF JOHN (Q 7:24–27)

Jesus' evaluation of John is described in Q^3 7:24–27 (Luke 7:24–27; Matt 11:7–10). This text follows Q^3 7:18–23 by the description of John. On the other hand, this text was interpolated into the main texts of the first redaction in order to reestablish the status of John inferior to Jesus.

The third redactor described Jesus' evaluation of John in Q^3 7:24–26. For this, three sets of question are written. According to the third redactor, Jesus raised the first question "What did you go out into the desert [wilderness] to see? A reed swayed by the wind?" Although nobody gave an answer, the expected one was "No." It seems that the phrase "swaying reed" was used on purpose. As was well known, Herod Antipas was surnamed "the swaying reed."[24] He was the Tetrarch ruling the region of Galilee and Peraea from 4 BCE to 39 CE. The third redactor mentioned the phrase in order to show that John was not a man of indecision. If this text was created by the third redactor, the third redaction was probably completed in the region of Galilee and Peraea by 39 CE. Then, the second question follows: "If not, what

24. Theissen, *Gospels in Context*, 26–42.

did you go out to see? A man dressed in fine clothes?" As for this, Jesus answered, "No, those who wear expensive clothes and indulge in luxury are in palaces." In this way, having mentioned the royal family, the third redactor told that John was not a man of royal family. Finally, the third question is written, saying, "But what did you go out to see? A prophet?"[25] As for this, Jesus himself answered, saying, "Yes, I tell you, and more than a prophet." In this way, John was identified as the one more than a prophet. While the first redactor described John as a prophet who had prepared the way for the Lord God in the wilderness (Q^1 3:2-4), the third redactor defined him as the one more than a prophet. While the first redactor described John as a prophet like the one foretold by Isaiah, the third redactor defined him as the one more than a prophet whom the crowds wanted to see in the wilderness. In consequence, the third redactor described Jesus' evaluation of John from a prophetic perspective, so as to imply the status of Jesus superior to John.

The third redactor also added the prophetic aspect to Jesus. It is indirectly shown by the phrase ναὶ λέγω ὑμῖν [Yes, I tell you]. The phrase λέγω ὑμῖν was already used in order to reveal the sage aspect of Jesus in the first redaction (Q^1 6:27). Then, the second redactor used the phrase for the description of Jesus' prophetic and sage aspect; it introduced the prophecy about the Galilean cities (Q^2 10:12) and the sapiential saying regarding the way of life (12:22). In addition, the third redactor pronounced the prophetic content through the mouth of Jesus with this phrase (Q^3 7:9). As mentioned before, the phrase λέγω ὑμῖν is reminiscent of the prophetic introduction which used to say "YHWH says" in the Hebrew Bible. Thus, the third redactor once again used the phrase in order to characterize Jesus as a prophet when he identified the status of John as the one who was more than a prophet. In consequence, Jesus defined himself as the one who exceeds John with regard to their prophetic status and role. In this respect, Jesus was also seen from a prophetic perspective in the third redaction.

Finally, John was identified as the forerunner of Jesus in Q^3 7:27. For this, the third redactor cited verses partially from Exod 23:20 and Mal 3:1.[26] First, the quotation formula γέγραπται [as it is written] is used for the first

---

25. As mentioned before, the first redactor listed three instructions about the reciprocal relationship in parallel in Q^1 6:29-30. In a similar manner, the second redactor listed three sets of imperatives in Q^2 11:9-10 and then used the phrase "Do not worry about" three times in 12:24-28. Having inherited the use of the number three, the third redactor also used the phrase "What did you go out to see?" three times. It seems that the number three indicates completeness. Thus, the third redactor would like to point out the importance of what they saw in the wilderness. "Seeing" is an important theme in the third redaction as it already appeared in the preceding text (Q^3 7:22).

26. It has been argued that the first half of the quotation is from Exod 23:20 (LXX) and the second half from Mal 3:1b (MT). Cf. Allison, *Intertextual Jesus*, 39.

time. This quotation cast John in the light of the Hebrew Bible. Although a quotation was already made in connection with John in the first redaction (Q^1 3:4), its formula was not adopted there. Second, while the phrase "you" referred to the Israelites in the Bible, the third redactor pointed to Jesus with it. Whereas the role of John changed from the forerunner of God in the first redaction to the one for Jesus in the third redaction,[27] Jesus is understood to be the antitype of the Israelites. The Israelites/Moses typology seems to be adopted here. The quotation was applied to the relationship between John and Jesus in order to "recapitulate the foundational events of the exodus."[28] With this quotation, therefore, the third redactor reestablished the relationship between Jesus and John in that John is downgraded.[29] Third, the partial quotation from Mal 3:1 adds the image of Elijah to John in that he was supposed to come before the day of YHWH arrives (Mal 4:5). Then, the third redactor described him as an eschatological prophet better than any other prophets written about in the Bible.[30] In consequence, Jesus is defined as the eschatological agent for whom John played the role of forerunner. In this respect, the third redactor heightened the prophetic aspect of Jesus as much as he could. This indicates that the third redactor was possibly one of the Pharisees, who had their own way of training in interpreting the prophecies of the Bible.

The social aspect at the time of the writing of the third redaction can be detected in Q^3 7:24–27. It is seen in the description that the further the redaction of Q progressed, the more negatively John was described. While the first redactor described John as a prophetic figure preparing the path for the Lord God (Q^1 3:2–4), the second redactor did not deal with him at all. On the other hand, the third redactor made a comparison between John and Jesus, and described John's proclamation about the one coming after him with more power (Q^3 3:16–17). Then, John was depicted as the one who cast a doubt about Jesus (7:18–23). Finally, although John was described as the one sent by God, he came to prepare the way for Jesus (7:24–27). In this respect, the third redactor downgraded John in comparison to Jesus. In other words, John was subordinate to Jesus.[31] This reflects that as the redaction of Q progressed, more people followed Jesus than John.[32] In other

---

27. Cf. Jacobson, *First Gospel*, 81; and Catchpole, "Beginning," 211.

28. Allison, *Intertextual Jesus*, 39.

29. Tuckett would not agree with the opinion that John was downgraded in Q 3:16 and 7:27. Rather, he argues that his relationship to Jesus "simply serves to highlight the positive significance of Jesus." Cf. Tuckett, Q, 128–29.

30. Cf. Catchpole, "Beginning," 208–9.

31. Vassiliadis, "Function," 407.

32. Cf. Catchpole, "Beginning," 210.

words, the instruction of Jesus was favored more than that of John at the stage of the third redaction.

K. THE CRITIQUE AGAINST THIS GENERATION (Q 7:31-34)

Jesus' critique of this generation is described in Q^3 7:31–34 (Luke 7:31–34; Matt 11:16–19). This text follows Q^1 7:29–30 in order to adjust the role of John. On the other hand, Q^3 7:31–34 was added to 7:24–27 in order to reestablish the relationship between John and Jesus in the third redaction.

The introductory formulas τίνι... ὁμοιώσω [to what... compare] and ὁμοία ἐστίν [it is like] appear for the description of "this generation" (Q^3 7:31–32). Especially, the latter recalls the phrase ὅμοιός ἐστιν used for the parable of the two builders (6:48). Once again, the third redactor adopted a simile in order to explain something beyond what can be described with the indicative form. A simile is a literary device more suitable than a metaphor in explaining the situation which the disciples of Jesus faced. It makes it possible to compare allegorically one thing to another.

The term "this generation" is used for the first time (Q^3 7:31). It appears in the question of Jesus about the comparison of "this generation." While "evil generation" was used in the second redaction (Q^2 11:29–30), "this generation" was adopted for the first time by the third redactor. It seems that the third redactor inherited the term "evil generation" and changed it to "this generation" for a theological purpose. In a sense, "this generation" becomes a technical term for the opponents in the third redaction. This calls our attention to the opposition and animosity of people—especially, those in Capernaum—against the disciples of Jesus. This was already implied in Q^3 6:39 with regard to the blind, in 6:41–42 in terms of eyes which had a speck or beam, and in 7:1–10 regarding the contrast between the centurion and the Israelites. As the story of the third redaction advances, the intensity of opposition gets stronger. Thus, the third redactor used the term "this generation" in order to heighten their evil attitude.

The parable of the children in the marketplace is introduced in Q^3 7:32. According to the third redactor, this generation was "like children [παῖδες] sitting in the marketplace and calling out to each other: 'We played the flute for you, and you did not dance; we sang a dirge, and you did not cry.'" A sharp contrast between the two parties has been drawn in the parable: we and you, playing a flute and singing a dirge, and dancing and crying. While playing the flute and dancing allude to a festive event, singing a dirge and crying remind readers of a funeral. A sharp contrast is used in the third redaction: the wheat and the chaff, the good and the evil, and the wise and the unwise (Q³ 3:17; 6:43–44, 48–49). In addition, it is noteworthy that the story of the centurion already adopted the term παῖς [servant] and made a sharp contrast between the faithful centurion and the unfaithful Israelites (7:1–10). The third redactor frequently drew a sharp contrast in order to distinguish the disciples of Jesus from their opponents. The contrast was used to strengthen their identities and make their unity stronger.

A critique of this generation against John is introduced in Q³ 7:33. When John did not eat and drink, this generation said that he was possessed by a demon. It is noteworthy that a demon was already mentioned when the crowds accused Jesus of healing the mute in the second redaction (Q² 11:14–15, 17–20); in addition, the matter of eating and drinking was also mentioned (Q² 12:29). Thus, the third redactor could use the demon for the critique of this generation against John on account of his ascetic life. Why this generation considered John's ascetic lifestyle to be demonic has not been known. It seems like there was no other reason than that the third redactor wanted to downgrade the status of John by describing him as possessed by a demon. This means that John was denied his status as the third redaction advanced.

In a similar manner, the critique of "this generation" against Jesus is described in Q³ 7:34. This generation accused Jesus of eating and drinking, called him a glutton, a drunkard, and a friend of tax collectors and sinners. It is noteworthy that the tax collectors were introduced as at least having common sense (Q¹ 6:32; cf. Matt 5:46) and described as those who positively responded to the righteousness related with John in the first redaction (Q¹ 7:29; cf. Matt 21:32). The fact that the tax collectors appear again in relationship with Jesus in the third redaction indicates that they joined the group of disciples continuously. In addition, Jesus was able to eat and drink because he had taught his disciples not to worry about what to eat and drink in the second redaction (Q² 12:22–34). At any rate, the reason that this generation accused Jesus of his lifestyle as a glutton, drunkard, and the friend of tax collectors and sinners has also not been known. As the opponents did to John, so they did to Jesus without rational reason. They did not like John and Jesus because John and Jesus gathered people around them and many people followed them. In this respect, a conflict was brought out between the disciples of Jesus and John and those of their opponents from a religio-ethical perspective. In other words, the boundary of controversy was expanded as the redaction of Q progressed further.

The third redactor drew a contrast between John and Jesus regarding the matter of eating and drinking. While John took the ascetic life, Jesus enjoyed the normal life. It is, however, noteworthy that John and Jesus took different lifestyles although they were the objects of accusation by their opponents. While John was criticized as the one being possessed by a demon, Jesus was rebuked as a glutton, drunkard, and friend of tax collectors and sinners. The accusation against John is harsher than that against Jesus. Although both John and Jesus were accused for their lifestyles, a difference is found between them from a comparative point of view. In this respect, it can be said that John was downgraded more than Jesus in the third redaction.[33] This tendency began with the proclamation of John about Jesus in Q^3 3:16–17 and continued in 7:18–27. As the third redaction progressed, Jesus was described more favorably than John.[34] From a sociological perspective, this reflects that the occasion for writing was that the number of those who followed Jesus increased more than those who followed John at the stage of the third redaction.[35] Or the disciples of John left the instruction of Jesus at last; in other words, they separated themselves from the Q community.

The title "Son of Man" is used a second time in the third redaction (Q^3 7:34). The Son of Man takes the role of medium for the connection of Q^3 7:31–34 to Q^2 9:57–58. On the other hand, the Son of Man is put in contrast with "this generation." As mentioned above, the people of this generation criticized him as a glutton, drunkard, and friend of tax collectors and sinners. In a sense, the Son of Man still carries the human aspect. The third redactor could not but help impose the human aspect to the Son of Man in 7:34 as well as 6:22 written ahead of Q^2 9:57-58 which conveys the human aspect of the Son of Man for the first time in the second redaction.[36] While the insult and hatred of the people against Jesus' disciples on account of the Son of Man were treated in 6:22–23b, the accusation against the Son of Man is mentioned in 7:34. While the title "Son of Man" did not appear in the first redaction, it was used in the context of someone's plea in the second redaction (Q^2 9:58; 11:30). On the other hand, the title appears in the context of opposition and accusation in the third redaction (Q^3 6:22–23b; 7:34). This shows that as Q went through a process of redaction, the Son of Man stood at the center of opposition and accusation. In this respect, the Son of Man

---

33. In this respect, Kloppenborg insists on their partnership (*Formation*, 112). However, I do not agree with his opinion because Q progressively downgraded the status of John.

34. Jacobson, *First Gospel*, 123.

35. On the contrary, Tuckett argues for a relationship of cooperation between John and Jesus because they "appear alongside each other as preachers facing this generation" (*Q*, 131–32). It this, however, to be noted the difference about their companions such as demons and tax collectors. See also Catchpole, *Quest*, 69.

36. Jacobson insists that the Son of Man does not reveal the apocalyptic aspect in Q 7:34 (*First Gospel*, 123).

came to the fore in connection with the context of opposition at the stage of the third redaction.

The text of Q^3 7:31–34 shows the economic environment at the time of the writing of the third redaction. The mentioning of a marketplace provides a clue for it (7:32). It is undeniable that the marketplace was in a place that was bigger than the town mentioned in the second redaction (Q^2 10:8). The mentioning of a marketplace indicates that the disciples of Jesus advanced to an urban area. For instance, Capernaum could be an economically stable city (Q^3 7:1). In addition, the mentioning of musical instrument and amusing dance at the marketplace also implies that the disciples of Jesus were exposed to an economically stable environment.[37] Moreover, the mentioning of eating bread and drinking wine also refers to an economically stabilized environment (7:34). This is different from the wilderness mentioned in the first redaction (Q^1 3:2–4) and the towns that appeared in the second redaction (Q^2 10:8, 11). This reflects that the disciples extended their boundary of ministry to urban areas such as Capernaum at the stage of the third redaction.

The third redactor revealed the social situation at that time. It can be characterized as one of opposition. This is well reflected in the description that this generation did not respond to the instruction of Jesus; although they heard the musical instrument they did not dance, and although they heard a dirge they did not cry. Without doubt, "this generation" refers to those who would not listen to the instruction of Jesus delivered by his disciples. In particular, they had a fellowship with the tax collectors and the sinners. This might have annoyed the people in Capernaum who regarded themselves as Israelites (Q^3 7:9); in addition, this makes them insult and hate the disciples of Jesus (6:22–23b, 28). Of course, they did not like that the disciples of Jesus were acquainted with the Gentiles (7:1–10). In this respect, the opponents are contrasted with the centurion in that they heard the words of the Lord Jesus but did not obey.[38] The disciples of Jesus faced a serious opposition from their surrounding people since they accepted those who were regarded as unclean, such as the tax collectors and the sinners. The further the redaction of Q progressed, the bigger the gap formed between the disciples of Jesus and their opponents from a socio-religious perspective.

---

37. It has been generally acknowledged that the marketplace (ἀγορά) was the place where a court was held. Cotter, "Parable," 302.

38. Cf. Kloppenborg, *Formation*, 119.

2

The Texts Added to the Second Redaction

As the third redactor had interpolated some texts into the main texts of the first redaction, he also added some texts to those of the second redaction. By doing so, the third redactor strengthened the theology which he tried to deliver. The third redactor maintained a consistent theological position. For instance, Jesus is more focused on as the mediator between God and the disciples. The social aspect of the disciples is revealed more clearly in that they were in conflict with their opponents. As a result, the third redactor turned his eyes toward mission to the Gentiles more than he did in the previous work. In this manner, the third redactor kept describing the theology found in the texts of the third redaction interpolated into the main texts of the first redaction.

A. THE ESCHATOLOGICAL WORKER (Q 10:2)

The request for eschatological workers is mentioned in Q^3 10:2 (Luke 10:2; Matt 9:37–38). This text was added to Q^2 9:57–58 with a theme of workers for the mission at the stage of the third redaction. On the other hand, this text follows Q^3 7:31–34 in the third redaction; however, no particular connection is found between them except the contrast between the nonresponse of "this generation" and the request for eschatological workers.

The third redactor described the request for eschatological workers. According to the redactor, Jesus taught his disciples to ask the Lord of harvest for workers because the harvest was plentiful but the workers were few.

First, the third redactor paid attention to the form of prayer to God. It seems that the third redactor was influenced by the Lord's Prayer (Q^2 11:2-4) and its application written in the second redaction (11:9-20, 29-30; 12:6-7, 22-31; 17:3-4). In addition, the third redactor mentioned prayer for those who mistreated the disciples of Jesus (Q^3 6:28). In this vein, according to the third redactor, Jesus could address his wish to God in the form of prayer in 10:2. In other words, this reflects that the occasion for writing was the fact that the disciples of Jesus considered prayer an important element of their religious life. Furthermore, this text provides reason to pray before the Lord's Prayer, because when the third redaction was complete, Q^3 10:2 comes ahead of Q^2 11:2-4.

The third redactor imposed the image of harvest to the first text of the third redaction in the second section (Q^3 10:2). The request for workers reminds readers of the image of harvest described in Q^3 3:17, where Jesus was understood to be the agent of harvest. As shown before, the Jewish tradition related the harvest with the eschatological judgment.[1] Having planted the texts about the image of harvest at the beginning of the first and second sections (Q^3 3:17; 10:2), the third redactor put emphasis on the theme of eschatological judgment. This implies that the disciples of Jesus felt a sense of crisis in their relationship with their opponents. Thus, it will be seen that the theme of eschatological judgment dominates the rest of the third redaction.

The third redactor defined Jesus as the agent of eschatological judgment. According to the redactor, Jesus told his disciples to ask the Lord of harvest for more workers. However, it is difficult to define the identity of the Lord of harvest. Is the Lord of harvest either God or Jesus? On the one hand, it seems that the Lord of harvest refers to God in this context. The Lord of harvest appears as the one higher than Jesus, who asked him for the workers. In addition, the first redactor already applied the title to God (Q^1 3:4). On the other hand, the Lord could refer to Jesus in the third redaction because Jesus is described as the Lord a few times (Q^3 3:16-17; 6:46; 7:6). In addition, the third redactor identified Jesus as the agent of eschatological judgment (3:16-17). This makes it difficult for the agent of eschatological judgment to be identified with the Lord of harvest. It is, therefore, more reasonable to consider God to be the Lord of harvest than Jesus in this context.

The third redactor attributed the identity of the workers for the harvest to the disciples of Jesus. They are the workers for the eschatological judgment. Their identity changed from itinerant workers for the kingdom of God in the second redaction (Q^2 10:9) to eschatological workers in the third

---

1. Cf. Kloppenborg, *Formation*, 103. For instances, Isa 24:13; Hos 6:11; Mic 4:11-13; Joel 4:1-21; Rev 14:15; 4 Ezra 9:1-25, 29-37, etc., convey the theme of eschatological judgment. See also Jacobson, *First Gospel*, 147, esp. 147n57.

redaction. In this respect, the status and role of the disciples were enhanced as the redaction of Q progressed. Jesus was the head of his disciples with regard to the eschatological role. While the third redactor focused on the status and role of Jesus in the texts interpolated into the main texts of the first redaction, he paid attention to the disciples of Jesus from the first text interpolated into the main texts of the second redaction.

B. ESCHATOLOGICAL WOE (Q 10:13-15)

A number of woes are listed in Q^3 10:13-15 (Luke 10:13-15; Matt 11:21-24). This text was added to Q^2 10:4-12 by the linking phrase ἀνεκτότερον ἔσται [will be more bearable than]. On the other hand, this text was added to Q^3 10:2 by the theme of eschatological judgment in the third redaction.

The third redactor used the literary device "woe" in Q^3 10:13. This appears for the first time in the third redaction. The third redactor condemned Chorazin and Bethsaida through the mouth of Jesus. The reason that woe was announced was because the people of Chorazin and Bethsaida would not repent even though they saw the wonders performed in the name Jesus. If these had been done in Tyre and Sidon, they would have repented their sins long ago in sackcloth on ashes. This means that Chorazin and Bethsaida were more sinful than Tyre and Sidon because they did not accept Jesus and his instruction. The wonders were understood to be divine signs according to the Jewish tradition. Although no wonder or miracle is mentioned in connection with Chorazin and Bethsaida, the third redactor simply presumed that these were performed there. Probably, the third redactor had in mind the healing miracle of the servant of the Gentile centurion in Capernaum, which was not far from Chorazin and Bethsaida (Q^3 7:1-10). Therefore, it means that Chorazin and Bethsaida rejected Jesus and God by not accepting the divine signs. This is why woe was addressed to them in the third redaction.

The third redactor dealt with the theme of repentance. This was already mentioned in the first redaction when John proclaimed that the people had to bear the fruit worthy of repentance (Q^1 3:8a). The second redactor mentioned the matter of forgiveness in the Lord's Prayer (Q^2 11:4) and that of repentance and forgiveness in its application (17:3-4).[2] On the other hand, the third redactor connected repentance with the wonders per-

---

2. Whereas Luke mentions the word "repent," Matthew does not (Luke 17:3; Matt 18:15). It is difficult to decide which version represents the original wording of Q because there is no related evidence to support one of them. To my judgment, the Lucan version is preferred to the Matthean because repentance is one of the major themes.

formed among the people. There was a reason that the third redactor connected the wonders with repentance in sackcloth and ashes. As the second redactor described, Jesus refused to show another sign to the crowds; rather, he mentioned the sign of Jonah (Q^2 11:16, 29–30) that made the Ninevites repent their sins dressed in sackcloth sitting on ashes (Jonah 3:5–6). Having inherited this tradition, the third redactor was able to describe that Chorazin and Bethsaida did not repent dressed in sackcloth on ashes. It seems that as Q underwent a process of redaction, the theme of repentance was getting more emphasized in connection with the eschatological judgment.

The attention to the Gentiles appears again in Q^3 10:13–14. It is seen in the description that Tyre and Sidon will be more bearable than Chorazin and Bethsaida at the eschatological judgment. It is, however, noteworthy that Jesus or his disciples did not actually or actively worked there. They appear just for the sake of comparison with Chorazin and Bethsaida.[3] The interest in the Gentiles was already alluded to in the heavenly voice at the baptism of Jesus (Q^3 3:21–22). Then, it was specifically shown in the story of the centurion in Capernaum (7:1–10). Then, the third redactor showed interest in the Gentiles by mentioning the names of Tyre and Sidon (11:13–14). The further the story advanced in the third redaction, the more attention was paid to the Gentiles. This indicates that the third redactor was concerned with the Gentiles in order to highlight the unfaithfulness of the people of Chorazin and Bethsaida.

The critique against Capernaum is mentioned in Q^3 10:15. For this, however, the literary device "woe" was not used. It is said that Capernaum would go down to hades since people exalted themselves up to heaven. First, the interest in heaven appears here as it was already mentioned at the beginning of the third redaction (Q^3 3:21–22; 6:22–23b). From a typological perspective, Capernaum can be compared to the tower of Babel regarding self-exaltation. As is well known, the people of Shinar said, "Come, let us build ourselves a city, with a tower that reaches to the heavens, so that we may make a name for ourselves" (Gen 11:4). Responding to their activity, God said to them, "Come, let us go down and confuse their languages so they will not understand each other" (11:7). If the tower of Babel event is the mirror for the critique against Capernaum, the Gentiles become the object of comparison. Second, the third redactor mentioned hades as a transcendental realm because it is in contrast with heaven. It was possible for the third redactor to describe hades on the basis of previous redactions. Although the first redactor implied an eschatological place when he or she mentioned

---

3. A certain number of scholars insist that Q 10:13–15 reveals the repentance of the Gentiles. Cf. Kloppenborg, *Formation*, 196.

the fire at the time of the impending wrath, its shape and location was not explained (Q^1 3:7, 9). Then, although the kingdom of Satan is mentioned in the second redaction, it was not clear whether the kingdom belongs to the transcendental realm or not (Q^2 11:17–18). On the other hand, the third redactor alluded to the place of unquenchable fire as the transcendental realm that one goes to after eschatological judgment (Q^3 3:17). It seems that based on this description, the third redactor could mention hades in the same way. This means that the disciples of Jesus were interested in the transcendental realm contrasted to heaven at the stage of the third redaction.

The third redactor provided glimpses of people who were active in the urban area of Galilee. The mentioning of Chorazin, Bethsaida, and Capernaum implies that the disciples of Jesus advanced to the cities and were active there for the mission at the stage of the third redaction. This is in accordance with the description of the "swaying reed" representing Herod the Tetrarch in the previous text of the third redaction (Q 7:24–25). At any rate, the disciples of Jesus probably caused the religious authorities to be jealous of their success in ministry and activity. Thus, the people of the Galilean cities refused to accept the instruction of Jesus and rather hated his disciples.[4] Responding their refusal, the disciples of Jesus probably shook off the dust from their feet according to the instruction taught in the second redaction (Q^2 10:11) and pronounced the woes that Tyre and Sidon would be more bearable at the eschatological judgment (Q^3 10:13–14). The third redactor aggressively accused their opposition by announcing the woes. In this vein, the third redactor condemned Capernaum figuratively (10:15). Then, this means that the relationship between the disciples of Jesus and the religious authorities of the Galilean cities was getting worse as time passed by. In this respect, the disciples of Jesus were successful in the Galilean region at the time of the third redaction.

C. THE ONLY CHANNEL BETWEEN GOD AND PEOPLE (Q 10:16)

A series of relationships among the disciples, Jesus, and God is described in Q^3 10:16 (Luke 10:16; Matt 10:40). This text follows Q^3 10:13–15 in order to provide the reason that Jesus could condemn the people of the Galilean cities. On the other hand, this text was added to Q^2 10:4–12 of the second redaction in order to strengthen the reason to hear the instruction delivered by the disciples of Jesus.

---

4. Kloppenborg, *Formation*, 195.

The third redactor introduced the relationship of Jesus between God and people in Q^3 10:16. It is said that those who receive the words of the disciples are those who receive the words of Jesus, and that those who receive Jesus are those who receive God. First, the third redactor defined Jesus as the mediator between God and the disciples of Jesus. In this way, the third redactor introduced another role of Jesus after describing him as the one coming after John (Q^3 3:16-17), the Son of God (3:21-22), the Son of Man (6:22-23b), the Lord (6:46-47; 7:6), the servant of God whose path was prepared by John the messenger of God (7:26-27), and the mediator who asked for eschatological workers (10:2).[5] In addition to the intermediary request of Jesus for the eschatological workers in 10:2, the mediatory role of Jesus between God and the disciples is described in 10:16. This means that Jesus is the only channel between God and his disciples. There is no other way that people can have a fellowship with God if they are not connected through Jesus. In other words, Jesus represents God as his messenger. This is in accordance with the instruction that one's relationship with the Son of Man is the criterion to be blessed in the third redaction (Q^3 6:22-23b; 7:23). It seems that as the redaction of Q progressed, the mediatory role of Jesus was becoming more significant.

The third redactor revealed the origin of the disciples. It is described in their relationship with God through Jesus. Whereas the second redactor described the followers as those sent by Jesus (Q^2 10:4-12), the third redactor surrounded Q^2 10:4-12 with Q^3 10:2 and Q^3 10:16 to heighten the importance of Jesus' mediatory role between God and his disciples. By doing so, the disciples are identified as those ultimately sent by God, the Lord of eschatological harvest, through the mediatory request of Jesus. In this way, the status of the disciples of Jesus was upgraded in the third redaction. This is in contrast with John whose status was getting downgraded as the third redaction of Q progressed.

D. THE PRAYER OF JESUS AS THE MEDIATOR

The mediatory role of Jesus is described in Q^3 10:21-24. This text follows Q^3 10:16 with the theme of mediator between God and people in the third redaction. On the other hand, this text was interpolated into the main texts of the second redaction in order to strengthen the identity of the disciples.

---

5. Cf. Kloppenborg, *Formation*, 196.

The Mediator Jesus (Q 10:21–22)

The third redactor described the mediatory prayer of Jesus in Q^3 10:21–22 (Luke 10:21–22; Matt 11:25–27). The thanksgiving of Jesus to God appears for the first time in the third redaction. While the second redactor taught the disciples how to pray suggesting the Lord's Prayer and its application (Q^2 11:2–4, 9–20, 29–46; 12:4–7, 22–31; 17:3–4), the third redactor mentioned prayer for those who had mistreated the disciples (Q^3 6:28) and then introduced the thanksgiving of Jesus to God (10:21–22). It seems that as the redaction of Q progressed, the more attention was paid to the instruction on prayer.

First of all, it is noteworthy that the third redactor put the thanksgiving of Jesus to God in front of the Lord's Prayer (Q^3 10:21–22; Q^2 11:2–4). By doing so, the third redactor delivered the instruction that Jesus had been praying to God before he taught his disciples the Lord's Prayer. In other words, the literary flow is natural in that Jesus had once prayed to God and then gave his disciples an example of prayer. In this way, the thanksgiving of Jesus to God plays as an introduction to the Lord's Prayer when the third redaction was complete. This shows that the third redactor kept paying attention to the prayer emphasizing the role of Jesus for the disciples.

The third redactor emphasized the filial relationship of Jesus with God in Q^3 10:21. God was called "Father, the Lord of heaven and earth" by Jesus. The filial relationship has been developed as the redaction of Q progressed. As mentioned before, the first redactor defined the audience of Jesus as the sons of "your Father" (Q^1 6:35–36). This implies that they considered God their "Father" as the Jews regarded themselves the sons of God. Then, according to the second redactor, Jesus had his disciples call God "Father" in the Lord's Prayer (Q^2 11:2) and depicted God as the heavenly Father (11:13). It is noteworthy that the disciples were taught to call God "Father" directly. Having inherited this tradition, the third redactor defined Jesus as a "Son of God" at the baptism (Q^3 3:21–22) and then depicted God as "Father, Lord of heaven and earth" by adding the element of "lordship," "heaven," and "earth" to "Father" (10:21). This is the first case where Jesus identified God as his "Father" in the third redaction. As a result, the third redactor strengthened the filial relationship of Jesus with God the Father.[6] In addition, he or she enhanced the fatherhood of God in his relationship with Jesus starting in the story of baptism.

The heavenly aspect was strengthened in connection with God the Father. As shown above, the term "heaven" is a favorite of the third redactor

---

6. Jacobson, *First Gospel*, 149–50.

(Q^3 3:21–22; 6:22–23b; and 10:15). As is well known, "the Lord of heaven and earth" reminds readers of God who created the heaven and earth (Q^3 10:21; Gen 1:1; 2:4). The third redactor succeeded all the traditions from the first and second redactors in order to extend the concept of God. As mentioned in the first redaction, God is depicted as the one who gives sunlight to both good and evil, and rain to both righteous and unrighteous (Q^1 6:35). The first redactor heightened the general grace of God who manages the weather. In a similar manner, the second redactor also described God as the one who provides a hole for foxes and a nest for birds (Q^2 9:57–58), takes care of even sparrows of the sky so they might not fall to the earth (12:6), and raises the ravens, the wild grasses, and even human beings (12:24–28). God is defined as the one who takes care of the living things that he created in the second redaction. On the other hand, the third redactor mentioned the matter of bearing fruit according to the tree's nature (Q^3 6:43–44) and the natural phenomena such as rain and flash floods (6:48–49). All of them were under the control of God. In this way, the third redactor contributed to the identification of God as the Lord of heaven and earth—that is, God the Creator who is the most authoritative being in the universe. This shows that as the redaction of Q progressed, a connection with primordial time was getting strengthened.

The third redactor provided readers with the reason why Jesus thanked God (Q^3 10:21b). It is because God had hidden "these things from the wise and learned, and revealed them to little children." It is not easy to interpret the word ταῦτα [these things] because its antecedent is not clear. From its context, it could mean what Jesus had taught his disciples in the previous texts of the third redaction. If it is correct, then "these things" refer to the instruction about Jesus' and the disciples' status and role in relationship with God (10:2, 13–16). On the other hand, the term "these things" could mean that the disciples are the coworkers of Jesus for the eschatological judgment. It is, however, important to be reminded that the term ταῦτα is the neutral plural pronoun. In other words, it can refer to everything that is beyond our interpretation in this context.

The third redactor put the little children in sharp contrast to the wise and learned. These titles appear for the first time in the third redaction. This means that there were those who regarded themselves as the wise and learned outside of the disciples of Jesus. On the other hand, the third redactor also introduced the term νήπιος [child] for the first time. It seems that the term was used with a different meaning from the term παῖς [child, servant] used in Q^3 7:3 and 7:32. The fact that the term νήπιος is used in contrast with the worldly wise and learned tells people about its positive meaning from a religious and spiritual point of view. Although the third redactor did not explain their identity, they are supposed to be the disciples of Jesus who were in contrast with the religious authorities of the Galilean cities. In other words, the disciples of Jesus were those who were like children from a spiritual perspective. Thus, they could not help but rely upon God.

The second reason why Jesus thanked God is introduced in Q^3 10:21c. This is introduced by the conjunctive particle ὅτι [because]. It is said, "for this was your good pleasure"; literally speaking, "because it became a pleasure in front of you" [ἔμπροσθέν σου] (cf. 7:27). According to the third redactor, Jesus thanked God because "these things" were done according to the will of God. Then, it is necessary to know what was done according to the will of God. It probably refers to the eschatological judgment upon the Galilean cities which did not accept the instruction of Jesus (10:13–15) and did not receive the disciples of Jesus sent by God (10:16). In this respect, the characteristic of God has been changed as the redaction of Q progressed; while God was the one who gives sunlight to both good and evil in the first redaction (Q^1 6:35) and the one who takes care of his people in the second redaction (Q^2 11:11–13; 12:22–31), God is described as the one who passes eschatological judgment upon those who would not receive the disciples of Jesus sent by God in the third redaction (Q^3 10:13–16). Thus, it can be said that the third redactor emphasized obedience to the will of God.

The third redactor described Jesus as the mediator in Q^3 10:22. His mediatory role is described well in the thanksgiving of Jesus to God. First of all, it is natural that Jesus called God "my Father" because he already heard "my [God's] son" in the heavenly voice (3:22). In addition, "my Father" appears in the form of the vocative that is more intimate than "Father, the Lord of heaven and earth" used in 10:21. In this respect, the filial relationship of Jesus with God is solidified; at the same time, the fatherhood of God in relationship to Jesus is also strengthened. Moreover, it is noteworthy that the filial relationship with God is applied only to Jesus in the third redaction. Then, it can be concluded that as the redaction of Q progressed, his filial relationship with God was getting strengthened. Second, πάντα [everything] that was entrusted to Jesus should be discussed. It seems to include ταῦτα mentioned in 10:21 in that both are used in the form of the neutral plural. Then, it means that Jesus was entrusted with eschatological judgment by God the Father. This is in accordance with the description that Jesus announced eschatological judgment to the Galilean cities such as Chorazin, Bethsaida, and Capernaum (10:13–15). The third redactor described that Jesus had the authority to pass eschatological judgment upon those who regarded themselves as wise and learned.

An instruction is described in Q³ 10:22 regarding the role of Jesus as the unique mediator. It is said, "No one knows who the Son is except the Father, and no one knows who the Father is except the Son and those to whom the Son chooses to reveal him." This describes Jesus as the Son of God and the unique channel through which people can know God. Only those whom Jesus chose to reveal God know him. Jesus is the recipient of revelation as well as its transmitter. While the third redactor taught a devoted attitude toward Jesus in the texts interpolated into the main texts of the first redaction (Q³ 6:22–23b, 46–47; 7:1–10), he emphasized Jesus' authority to reveal God to the disciples in the text interpolated into the main texts of the second redaction (10:21–22). In this manner, the third redactor assigned the authority to reveal God to Jesus. The third redactor's reason for this is that only Jesus heard the heavenly voice (3:21–22). In addition, Jesus was once described as the mediator between God the Lord of harvest and its workers (10:2). Moreover, the role of channel between God and people was already mentioned in 10:16. In this respect, the third redactor concentrated on the role of Jesus as the unique mediator between God and the chosen people—that is, the disciples of Jesus.

The third redactor mentioned the authority of Jesus to choose people (Q³ 10:22). This is found in that only those to whom Jesus revealed God knew him. This is contrasted with the descriptions of the previous two redactions. The first redactor told nothing about whether Jesus chose his disciples or not. It seems that Jesus spoke to the same general audience in the wilderness as John did. On the other hand, the second redactor talked about a person who would like to follow Jesus (Q² 9:57–58). Jesus did not command him to follow; rather, he seemed to follow him voluntarily. From the fact that Jesus gave the manual for ministry, it can be surmised that some people joined and followed Jesus (Q² 10:4–12). Then, many people responded to the proclamation of the disciples about the kingdom of God. On the other hand, after the third redactor used the term "teacher" and "disciple [student]" for the first time in Q³ 6:39, he or she described that Jesus had the authority to choose some people to whom he wanted to reveal God. This implies that Jesus took the initiative to make his disciples. This suggests the occasion for writing was the fact that the followers of Jesus were successful in recruiting some people during their ministry. While the second redactor described the right that people could decide to follow Jesus or not (Q² 9:57–58), they were deprived of it in the third redaction. As the story of the third redaction advanced, the role of Jesus was getting more authoritative in his relationship with the disciples. It seems that the disciples of Jesus were formed relatively later than we generally thought.

The third redactor depicted Jesus as the mediator with an allusion to Moses (Q³ 10:22). Referring to Exod 33:11-23, Num 12:6-8, and Deut 34:10, Allison argues that the prayer of Jesus "recapitulates the experience of Moses on Sinai, the revealer who uniquely knew and was known by God and was entrusted with the fullness of the divine paradosis."[7] The third redactor was able to use the Moses typology on the basis of previous descriptions. For instance, while the instruction of Jesus alludes to the commandments written in Lev 19 in the first redaction (Q¹ 6:27, 29-38), the Lord's Prayer consists of five petitions reminding readers of the Pentateuch (Q² 11:2-4). On the other hand, the baptism of Jesus alludes to the crossing of the Red Sea (Q³ 3:21-22) and the sending of messengers refers to the angels during the exodus/Moses in the third redaction (7:27). In this sequence, the third redactor applied the Moses typology to Jesus as the mediator in 10:21-22. As Q went through a process of redaction, the Moses typology came to the fore.

The Beatitude (Q 10:23-24)

The third redactor introduced the beatitude in Q³ 10:23-24 (Luke 10:23-24; Matt 13:16-17). It says, "Blessed are the eyes that see what you see." The literary form is somewhat different from other beatitudes in the third redaction (Q³ 6:22-23b; 7:23). At any rate, the third redactor suggested a certain precondition through the mouth of Jesus in order to be blessed—that is, seeing what the disciples saw. No particular precondition was required except being poor in the first redaction (Q¹ 6:20b) and being hungry and mourning in the second redaction (Q² 6:21). On the other hand, the third redactor suggested a certain precondition such as being insulted and hated on account of the Son of Man and not being offended by Jesus (Q³ 6:22-23b; 7:23). Then, the third redactor introduced another precondition, that only those who saw what the disciples had seen deserve to be blessed (10:23). The disciples of Jesus were introduced as exemplars of those who had met the criteria for blessing because they had already received the revelation of God probably through vision (10:22). Their position was getting heightened with regard to their relationship with Jesus. The third redactor made the disciples of Jesus the model for others as reflected in 10:16. The further the redaction of Q progressed, the more specific the preconditions became for receiving blessing.

The motive of seeing is mentioned in the third redaction (Q³ 10:23). The disciples of Jesus were those who saw what others wanted to see but

7. Allison, *Intertextual Jesus*, 51. See also 41-51.

could not. It is important to observe that the third redactor emphasized the motive of seeing a couple of times before. First, the vision of a descending dove was introduced at the second text of the third redaction (3:21–22). Then, after the metaphor of the blind was described (6:39), a contrast was drawn between the eyes with beams and with specks (6:41–42). In addition, Jesus said to the disciples of John, "Go back and report to John what you have seen and heard" (7:22). In this case, the matter of seeing appears significant with regard to the miraculous events. Moreover, Jesus told the crowds, "What did you go out to see?" three times (7:24–27). Of course, it was the prophet that they wanted to see in the wilderness. Finally, the third redactor said, "Blessed are the eyes that see what you see" (10:23). In this way, as the story of the third redaction advanced, the third redactor mentioned what the disciples of Jesus had seen, as the model for what people had to see. Although the third redactor did not describe what they saw, it seems to refer to the events that happened during the ministry of the disciples. They could be the sign of God for the disciples of Jesus. In this respect, the third redactor put emphasis on seeing what Jesus had performed. This means that the situation has changed and that the third redactor could not help but emphasize the theme of seeing.

The third redactor introduced what people had said about the identity of the disciples in Q^3 10:24. It is said that many prophets and kings wanted to see what the disciples saw but failed. In the same manner, they wanted to hear what the disciples heard but failed to hear. While the matter of seeing was treated above, that of hearing should be examined.[8] The third redactor once dealt with the matter of hearing when Jesus heard the voice announced from heaven at his baptism (3:21–22). Then, the matter of hearing is written in connection with the disciples of Jesus in 6:46–47. One should observe what he or she heard from Jesus. It probably includes the good news proclaimed to the poor. It seems that the third redactor thought the theme of hearing from Jesus was important to the disciples. Without hearing from Jesus, no one could understand his instruction. It is noteworthy that the third redactor used the theme of seeing and hearing in combination. They already appeared in Q^3 7:22, and then are used again in 10:24. At this moment, the baptism of Jesus comes to our mind as the background for the theme of seeing and hearing. When Jesus was baptized, he saw the Spirit descending from heaven and heard the heavenly voice. It was a mysterious but spiritual scene for readers of the third redaction. In addition, the third redactor described the story of the centurion in which the disciples

---

8. Jacobson believes that Q conveys only the text about seeing (*First Gospel*, 157). It is, however, to be noted that hearing is also an important theme in Q.

heard what Jesus told the centurion and saw how the servant was healed (7:1–10). Then, the themes of seeing and hearing reached its culmination in 10:23–24. In this respect, the third redactor developed the element of faith in Jesus by introducing the theme of seeing and hearing.

The status of the disciples is in comparison to the prophet and king in Q^3 10:24. They are described as those who saw what the prophet and the king would like to see and heard what they would like to hear but failed. The third redactor informed the readers that the disciples were superior to the prophet and king from a religious and spiritual perspective. While the second redactor had already mentioned Jonah the prophet and Solomon the king (Q^2 11:29–30; 12:27), the third redactor introduced the prophet and the king in order to describe the status and role of John (Q^3 7:25–26) and the disciples of Jesus (10:24). As John was defined as the one more than a prophet, the disciples of Jesus were identified as those more than the prophet and the king. In this respect, the disciples of Jesus were understood as those who were superior to John in the third redaction. It seems that the third redactor defined the disciples of Jesus greater than Jonah, representing the prophet, and Solomon, representing the king. In this way, their status was upgraded to a new level by the third redactor.

E. THE STRONGER ONE (Q 11:21–23)

The parable of the stronger one is introduced in Q^3 11:21–23 (Luke 11:21–23; Matt 12:29–30).[9] This text was added to Q^2 11:14–15, 17–20 in order to show that Jesus was the stronger one in comparison to Beelzebul and Satan. On the other hand, this text follows Q^3 10:21–24 in the third redaction, so that it might verify the identity of the disciples of Jesus as the stronger one—that is, greater than the prophet and king.

The third redactor mentioned the strong person in Q^3 11:21. It is said that when a strong person keeps the house, his material possessions are safe because no one can loot his house. The image of looting appears for the first time. It is, however, unclear to whom the strong one refers in this context. In the immediate context, the strong one could refer to the crowds, demon, Beelzebul, or Satan(Q^2 11:14–15, 17–20). On the other hand, it could refer to the prophet and king in the third redaction (Q^3 10:23–24). It seems,

---

9. The Lucan version is a little bit longer than the Matthean (Luke 11:21–23; Matt 12:29–30). In addition, the former adopts the comparative form, the latter simply mentions the strong person. To my judgment, the Lucan version reflects the original text of Q because it accords well with other texts in the third redaction (Robinson et al., *Critical Edition*, 234–35).

however, that the third redactor intended to convey both when he added the parable of the strong one in its present place.

Then, the third redactor used the term "stronger" in Q^3 11:22. It is said that when a stronger person attacks and overpowers the strong one, he will plunder the house and distribute the spoils. The theme of "stronger" already appeared in the proclamation of John (Q^3 3:16–17). In addition, while the comparative form was used in the second redaction (Q^2 10:12; 12:23–24), the third redactor inherited and applied it to John and Jesus (Q^3 3:16; 7:26; 10:14). This implies that the third redactor compared the stronger one to Jesus, the one coming after John. Moreover, the image of "stronger" is found in the story about the centurion (7:1–10). Jesus is defined as the stronger one than the centurion in that he called Jesus "Lord" and obeyed his words. The fact that the third redactor used the comparative form more frequently than any other redactors reflects the underlying social situation that the disciples of Jesus were in conflict and competition with their opponents. As shown above, the stronger one is usually applied to the servant of God in the third redaction and Jesus should be acknowledged as the stronger person. Then, the third redactor urged the disciples of Jesus to be active and aggressive in their ministry because they are stronger than their opponents.

A proverbial saying appears in Q^3 11:23. It is said that the one who is not with Jesus is against him, and the one who does not gather with him is scattering. This emphasizes one's exclusive relationship with Jesus. One's identity is determined by his or her relationship with Jesus. This theme was already used in 6:22–23b; 7:23 and 10:16. In particular, Jesus was described as the only mediator between God and the disciples in 10:22. Thus, 11:23 can be in sequence of this trend of theology in the third redaction. In this sense, the third redactor urged the disciples to be loyal and faithful to Jesus. It was necessary for the third redactor to ask for solidarity among the disciples. The matter of being with Jesus is an important element to the disciples because they had to be connected with God through him as instructed in 10:16 and 10:22. In addition, the third redactor used terms such as "gather" and "scatter" because the term "gather" was already used in order to describe the image of eschatological judgment in connection with the harvest of wheat (3:17). On the other hand, the term "scatter" was added in order to heighten the contrast with gathering. It seems that the matter of gathering and scattering was important to the disciples at the time of the writing of the third redaction. This reflects that there was an aggressive attempt to scatter the disciples of Jesus. In this respect, at the stage of the third redaction, solidarity came to the fore as an important issue.

F. ESCHATOLOGICAL JUDGMENT (Q 11:31-32)

Interest in the Gentiles is written about in Q³ 11:31-32 (Luke 11:31-32; Matt 12:41-42). They appear as the agent for eschatological judgment upon "this generation." This text follows Q³ 11:21-24 in the third redaction, so that the Gentiles might be considered stronger from a religious perspective. This text was added to Q² 11:16, 29-30 of the second redaction in order to strengthen the theme of Jonah's sign.

The third redactor focused on the eschatological judgment upon "this generation" (Q³ 11:31-32). While the second redactor used the phrase ἐν τῇ ἡμέρα [on that day] for the eschatological judgment (Q² 10:12), the third redactor adopted the phrase ἐν τῇ κρίσει [at the judgment] for the first time. In a sense, it becomes a technical term for the eschatological judgment. The third redactor seems to think it will come at a specific time, although the specific time cannot be decided. Interest in the eschatological judgment kept developing in the third redaction (Q³ 3:16-17; 6:46-49; 10:13-15, etc.). In addition, the phrase "this generation" is used for the second time since it was mentioned for the first time in Q³ 7:31, where it referred to those who opposed John and Jesus. On the other hand, it refers to those who opposed Jesus and his disciples in 11:31-32. This implies that the animosity of the opponents increased against the disciples of Jesus. In this respect, the third redactor was sure that eschatological judgment upon this generation would occur in the indefinite future.

The third redactor introduced the agent of eschatological judgment (Q³ 11:31-32). For instance, it would be the Queen of the South and the Ninevites. The Queen of the South is the one who came to Solomon the king in order to listen to his wisdom, and the Ninevites were those who heard the announcement of Jonah the prophet about repentance. The positive perspective on the Gentiles reminds readers of the centurion at Capernaum who obeyed the words of the Lord Jesus (7:1-10) and the Gentile cities Tyre and Sidon which were mentioned in comparison to the unfaithful Chorazin and Bethsaida (10:13-14). In this vein, the third redactor introduced the Queen and the Ninevites who were Gentiles; while the Queen was a woman of the highest class, the Ninevites were people of the strongest country at that time. As the story of the third redaction advances, the more highly ranked Gentiles are introduced as the agent for the eschatological judgment. However, it does not mean that the Gentiles will replace the status and role of the Israelites from a religious perspective.[10] They are used in order to draw out the contrast with the unfaithful Israelites in front of God.

---

10. Cf. Horsley, "Questions," 187.

The third redactor used the term "condemn" for the first time (Q³ 11:31–32). This appears in connection with the eschatological judgment upon this generation by the Gentiles. For the Israelites, it was unacceptable that they would be condemned by the Gentiles. In this way, the third redactor applied an extremely negative perspective to the Israelites in the region of Galilee after he or she had mentioned it for the first time in 7:9. This recalls the woes against Chorazin, Bethsaida, and Capernaum (10:13–15). Hereby, the third redactor revealed his theological strategy in that after the term "woe" had been used against the Galilean cities in comparison to the Gentile ones, then the term "condemn" was directly applied to the Israelites in contrast with the Gentiles. In this way, the third redactor increased the intensity of criticism against the opponents.

A man and woman pair appears between "the Queen of the South" [βασίλισσα νότου] and "the Ninevites" [ἄνδρες Νινευῖται] for the first time in the third redaction (Q³ 11:31–32). It seems that the third redactor placed men and women on equal ground regarding roles at the eschatological judgment. The fact that a woman was mentioned implies that the female disciples had a crucial role or that the redactor attributed theological meaning to the role of women.[11] It has not been known why the third redactor introduced a male-female pair. It can be surmised, however, that the creation story was in his or her mind. As shown before, the second redactor already made allusions to the garden of Eden with the five petitions of the Lord's Prayer (Q² 11:2–4). Then, the third redactor adopted the phrase "the Lord of heaven and earth" which recalls Gen 1:1 and 2:4 (Q³ 10:21–22). Finally, a male-female pair is introduced in order to point to the first pair, Adam and Eve, created according to the image of God (Gen 1:27). If this interpretation is acceptable, it can be said that the third redactor paid attention to the beginning of the world as the theological basis for the description of the eschatological judgment. In this respect, the end of the world was described in connection with its beginning at the stage of the third redaction.

The third redactor introduced the theme of resurrection. It means that the Gentiles will really rise up to pass judgment upon the Israelites at the end of the world. The description that the Queen of the South and the Ninevites will arise and pass judgment upon "this generation" at the end of the world reflects the general resurrection.[12] The general resurrection was already mentioned when Jesus responded to the disciples of John with the

---

11. Batten argues that Q "provides glimpses of a group of people who offered a more inclusive environment for women. By no means was such a community unique, as examples from such groups as the *Therapeutae* and the Cynics indicate" ("More Queries," 49).

12. Cf. Kloppenborg, *Q*, 81–82.

present passive verb ἐγείρονται (Q³ 7:22). The other is found in his teaching about the eschatological judgment with the future verbs ἐγερθήσεται and ἀναστήσονται (11:31–32).[13] It is noteworthy that a passive verb is used in 7:22 and 11:31, while a middle voice verb is adopted for the active meaning in 11:32. The third redactor seemed to convey that God is the agent for the general resurrection. It seems that Q mentions both the miracle of revitalization (7:22) and the general resurrection of the dead at the end of time (11:31–32). In this way, the third redactor revealed interest in the resurrection. The descriptions make it possible to surmise that the third redactor was a Pharisaic scribe because the Pharisees believed the general resurrection of people at the end of the world. In this respect, the third redactor showed his Pharisaic characteristic.

The third redactor introduced Solomon the king and Jonah the prophet in order to identify the status of Jesus. Solomon was once mentioned when the beauty of wild grasses was compared with his clothes (Q² 12:27) and Jonah was also mentioned in connection with the sign in the second redaction (11:16, 29–30). In this vein, the third redactor mentioned Solomon the king and Jonah the prophet (Q³ 11:31–32). After mentioning the prophet and the king (Q³ 7:24–26), the third redactor defined the disciples of Jesus as those more than the prophet and king (10:23–24). Then, Jesus is identified as the one more than Solomon and Jonah (11:31). Whereas Solomon represents the wise and Jonah represents the prophet, Jesus is the one more than the wise and the prophet. His words are something more than the wise sayings of Solomon and the prophetic proclamations of Jonah.[14] In this respect, the third redactor kept concentrating on defining Jesus' status. It is, however, noteworthy that the priest does not appear in this context. The third redactor was probably not in favor with the ritual system of the Jerusalem temple in the region of Galilee at that time.

G. PARABLES OF LIGHT

Two parables of light are introduced in Q³ 11:33–35. They are connected with a word "lamp." It is difficult to know why they are located here; however, it seems that light is related to the eschatological judgment in its context.

---

13. Quotations are from Robinson et al., *Critical Edition*, 124, 252–53.
14. Cf. Jacobson, *First Gospel*, 168.

The Parable of the Lamp (Q 11:33)

The parable of the lamp is written in Q^3 11:33 (Luke 11:33; Matt 5:15). This text follows Q^3 11:31–32 in the third redaction and was interpolated into the main texts of the second redaction by the third redactor. It is, however, difficult to see why this text is located in its present place because no linking word or theme is found with its preceding text.

The third redactor introduced the parable of the lamp. It is said that no one lights the lamp and puts it under a peck-measurer but on the lampstand, so that it can give light to everyone in the house. It is not clear what the lamp symbolizes because it is used for the first time; however, from the context, the light could refer to the instruction of Jesus. The light is definitely in contrast with the blind (Q^3 6:39). In addition, "giving the light" reminds readers of "these thing" that had been hidden from the wise and the learned but revealed to the little children (10:21). In other words, the third redactor tried to teach that the instruction of Jesus should be known to as many people as possible. By adopting the image of light and lamp, the third redactor provided readers with the message of God's revelation. This implies that the disciples of Jesus actively spread the instruction of Jesus as the divine revelation.

The third redactor mentioned the house in which the light be shed. It is noteworthy that this term was already used in the second redaction as an object the followers of Jesus had to look for (Q^2 10:5, 7). On the other hand, the third redactor dealt with the matter of building up a house on sand or bedrock (Q^3 6:47–49). It probably signified constituting a community of those who have heard the words of Jesus the Lord and followed him. In addition, the third redactor mentioned the house as a place to be filled with light; probably, this means that the disciples of Jesus made a community which was constituted by those who followed his instruction. Then, it can be said, the term "house" was used as a technical term referring to the disciples in the third redaction. It seems that as time passed by, the disciples of Jesus were concerned with how to observe his instruction sincerely and faithfully.

The Parable of the Light (Q 11:34–35)

The parable of the light is described in Q^3 11:34–35 (Luke 11:34–35; Matt 6:22–23). This text follows Q^3 11:33 by the connecting word "lamp" in the third redaction, so that it could support the instruction conveyed in the parable of the lamp. On the other hand, this text was interpolated into the main texts of the second redaction, just after Q^2 11:16, 29–30, in order to teach that the disciples of Jesus should overcome the temptation with his instruction symbolized by the light.

The third redactor described the parable of the light in Q³ 11:34–35. It is said that the eye is the lamp of the body. The third redactor conveyed instruction about the relationship between the eye and the body. It is, however, difficult to know what this parable means because the eye does not give light itself to the body. Rather, it receives light from the outside. Then, it could mean the intelligent and spiritual ability to recognize the truth of God delivered by Jesus and his disciples.[15] The third redactor seemed to have self-understanding that he was able to discern the divine truth; he is compared to the little children to whom Jesus revealed "these thing" (Q³ 10:21). One's eye must be healthy without something symbolized as speck or beam (6:41-42) and the whole body must be radiant. On the contrary, one's bad eye makes the body dark reminding readers of the blind (6:39). Hereby, two sets of contrast are drawn between the healthy eye and the bad one, and radiant and dark. This kind of sharp contrast was already used in Q³ 3:17; 6:43–44; 7:31–34; and 10:21. The third redactor kept using the instruction regarding the relationship between the eye and the body. This means that one who has the intelligent and spiritual ability to recognize the truth of God will find the mind or spirit full of light; on the contrary, the one who does not have the ability to discern the truth of God will find the mind or spirit full of darkness.[16]

The third redactor talked about the darkness of one's body in Q³ 11:35. It seems to criticize either some of the disciples of Jesus for their lack of faith or the opponents who would not accept the instruction of Jesus. If the term "dark" refers to the latter, then it can be a critique against the people who insulted and hated the disciples on account of Jesus the Son of Man (6:22–23b). Then, it can be explained why this text is located in its present place. It was for the critique against the outsiders who will be condemned by the Gentiles at the eschatological judgment (11:31–32).

H. SIX WOES AGAINST THE PHARISEES

Six more woes are listed in Q³ 11:39–45, 52. After the third redactor used the literary device "woe" once in 10:13, he or she introduced six more woes

---

15. Allison insists on the relationship of vision with the eye ("Eye," 79).

16. Kloppenborg argues that the body full of light means the ethical life (*Formation*, 136). On the contrary, studying the theme of light and eye in Greek and Jewish literature, Allison concludes that when the body is full of light, the eye gets healthy ("Eye," 74–77).

here. It is noteworthy that they are composed of three sets of pairs. The first two woes are about the matter of observing the law, the next two woes are related to ethical matters, and the last two woes are against the lawyers. The text of Q³ 11:39-45, 52 was interpolated into the main texts of the second redaction in order to support the matter of temptation described in Q² 11:16, 29-30.

The First Woe (Q 11:39-41)

The first woe is introduced in Q³ 11:39-41 (Luke 11:39-41; Matt 23:25-26).[17] This text follows Q³ 11:33-35 by the theme of critique against the opponents who were characterized with the term "dark." In this respect, it is natural that the woe follows the parable of the light from a thematic perspective.

The third redactor introduced the first woe against the Pharisees on account of their hypocritical discordance (Q³ 11:39-41). It is said that they cleansed the outside of the cup and dish, but their inside was full of greed and wickedness. Accordance between the inside and the outside carries a similar theme to the parable of the light in that if the eye is healthy, then the body is full of light (11:34-35). Then, the same instruction is found in that a person speaks "out of the overflow of his heart" (6:45). This shows that the theme of accordance between inside and outside was an important issue to the third redactor.

The Pharisees are introduced for the first time in Q³ 11:39. Cleansing was an important matter to the Pharisees. As shown above, the third redactor revealed his identity as a Pharisee in the description of general resurrection (7:22; 11:31-32). Then, the matter of cleansing is mentioned in connection with the title "Pharisees." In this way, the identity of the third redactor as a Pharisee is revealed from a literary and theological perspective. It is natural that the third redactor put an emphasis on observing the nature of the law. It seems that he or she did not segregate himself or herself from the Pharisaic group in the region of Galilee, yet. Rather, it seems that he or she was in conflict with the Pharisees. At any rate, the third redactor was a man of Pharisaic tradition who had been well trained enough to write the instruction through the mouth of Jesus. Thus, third redactor applied to Jesus the way of theological interpretation that he learned as a Pharisee.

The first woe reveals various aspects of the disciples of Jesus at the stage of the third redaction. First of all, they seemed to observe the law or

---

17. The Lucan version does not use the term "woe" in 11:39. However, using it, the Matthean version indicates that this belongs to the woe in Q (Robinson et al., *Critical Edition*, 268).

the Pharisaic tradition from a religious perspective.[18] This is seen in the way that the third redactor dealt with the cleansing ritual. However, the ritual itself was not denied or criticized. The third redactor criticized those who do not observe it in a right manner. The law or the Jewish tradition was important to the disciples of Jesus at the time of the writing of the third redaction. Second, from a sociological perspective, there was a conflict with the Pharisees regarding the matter of the cleansing ritual. It is seen in that the text mentions the term "clean" twice. Then, it is to be noted that the verb καθαρίζω [cleanse] was already used for the cleansing of leprosy in Q^3 7:22. This implies that the third redactor was concerned with the matter of cleansing. Thus, the critique against the matter of cleansing was critical enough to make the Pharisees annoyed. This indicates that the third redactor got involved in the conflict with the Pharisees with regard to their tradition and the law. This indicates that the disciples of Jesus were not refrained from the Jewish society yet which respect the true virtue of the law at the time of the writing of the third redaction.

The Second Woe (Q 11:42)

The second woe is found in Q^3 11:42 (Luke 11:42; Matt 23:23). This text follows Q^3 11:39–41 by the theme of accordance between the inside and the outside regarding the religious life. Especially, this text deals with the matter of tithe.

The third redactor criticized the Pharisees on account of their religious life.[19] They tithed mint, dill, and cumin, but they gave up justice, mercy, and faithfulness (Num 18:21–28; Deut 12:6–17; 14:22–29; 26:12). The third redactor put the first three elements in sharp contrast with the following three. As already shown, the sharp contrast between the two is a typical characteristic found in the third redaction (Q^3 3:17; 6:43–45, 48–49; 7:31–34; 10:24; 11:23, 31–32, etc.). The third redactor emphasized accordance between the outside and the inside regarding the religious life and described Jesus' acknowledgment of observing both of them. It seems that the second woe delivers how to emphasize what the third redactor would like to do in order that the disciples follow his instruction. It seems that the third redactor "accepted a legal perspective characteristic of Pharisees but then went on in prophetic fashion to condemn any sort of myopic understanding of

---

18. Cf. Jacobson, *First Gospel*, 176.

19. It has been known that the Pharisees and scribes were serving under the authority of Jerusalem in the region of Galilee prior to 70 CE (Sadarini, "Roles," 200–209; and Horsley, *Jesus*, 28–29).

what the law truly required."[20] In this way, the third redactor got involved in the matter of observing the law rightly again. What the third redactor criticized was the attitude of the Pharisees who insisted on one side of the commandments but neglected the other side.[21] This indicates that the disciples of Jesus observed the law in the region of Galilee at the stage of the third redaction.

The second woe reveals the economic environment at the time of the writing of the third redaction. There were some who were wealthy enough to tithe mint, dill, and cumin. While the second redactor had mentioned worry about the daily bread (Q^2 11:3; 12:22–31), the third redaction dealt with an economic situation stable enough to tithe mint, dill, and cumin (Q^3 11:42). As shown above, the economically stable situation is implied in various places in the third redaction. For instance, the image of the wheat gathered into the granary (3:17), the festive aspect of eating and drinking (7:32–34), the request for workers of the harvest (10:2), the reference to the material possessions to protect (11:21–23), etc. Although these instances do not assure readers of the wealth of the disciples of Jesus, it could mean that they were exposed to a stable enough economic situation at the time of the writing of the third redaction.

The Third Woe (Q 11:43)

The third woe is introduced in Q^3 11:43 (Luke 11:43; Matt 23:6–7). The third redactor dealt with the ethical behavior of the Pharisees. In this respect, this shows a different matter from the previous two woes.

The third redactor described a critique against the Pharisees regarding their behavior. It is described that they liked places of honor such as the front seat in the synagogue and being greeted at the marketplace. According to the second redactor, Jesus instructed his followers not to greet on the road but say, "Peace to the house," whenever they looked for a place to stay (Q^2 10:4–5). On the other hand, the third redactor depicted Jesus' critique against Capernaum on account of her tendency to lift herself up to heaven (Q^3 10:15). In the same manner, the Pharisees were criticized because they lifted themselves up by loving the honored place at the banquet and enjoyed being greeted at the marketplace. This is opposite to the instruction that a person must do to others first in the way he or she wants to be treated by others, which is written in the first redaction (Q^1 6:31). In this respect, the third woe criticized the lifestyle of Pharisees from an ethical perspective.

20. Wild, "Encounter," 115.
21. Kloppenborg, Q, 69.

The third redactor revealed the social situation of the disciples of Jesus. For example, the mentioning of banquet refers to an economically stable situation. The image of banquet was already used in the description of eating and drinking (Q 7:33–34). Although it is not clear whether the disciples of Jesus used to take part in the banquet or not, the third redactor was at least familiar enough with the circumstances to have been exposed to banquets. Then, synagogue is mentioned for the first time. Synagogue was a place for the Jews and Gentile God-fearers to worship God outside Jerusalem. This means that the third redactor did not completely separate himself from the Jewish religious system. Rather, the third redactor was in competition or conflict with the Pharisees within the Jewish religion and society. It is, however, noteworthy that the temple and the priests are not mentioned yet. Once again, this means that the disciples of Jesus were active in cities such as Capernaum, Chorazin, and Bethsaida, not in Jerusalem, at the time of the writing of the third redaction. In addition, the third redactor introduced the marketplace once again (Q^3 7:32). The marketplace was not a place just for commercial business; rather, it could be a place for all kinds of business including legal, administrative, intellectual, etc.[22] It seems that the Pharisees were involved in various activities there. Then, the third redactor was actively involved in the urban life of the Jews as known from the fact that he criticized the Pharisees at the marketplace.

The Fourth Woe (Q 11:44)

The fourth woe is written in Q^3 11:44 (Luke 11:44; Matt 23:27–28).[23] Unawareness of one's nature is mentioned in this woe. It seems to be related to the ethical matter written about in the third woe (Q^3 11:43).

The third redactor paid attention to the comparison of opponents with indistinct tombs. On this, the term ὡς [be like] is used. When the term ὡς [as] was used for the expression of reciprocal relationship between God and human beings in the second redaction (Q^2 11:4), it delivers a common ground between them with regard to the paternal affection. However, when it was adopted for the object of comparison between master/teacher and servants/disciples in the third redaction (Q^3 6:40), it acknowledges

---

22. Cf. Cotter, "Parable," 302.

23. Although the Lucan and Matthean versions are different from each other, there are a couple of common elements between them (Luke 11:44; Matt 23:27–28). First of all, both share the literary device "woe." Second, they mention the tomb. Third, they describe that ordinary people were not aware of their situation standing on an indistinct tomb. In this respect, the fourth woe was in Q as part of the third redaction (Robinson et al., *Critical Edition*, 276–77).

a difference between them in terms of social class. In this vein, the third redactor pointed out the discordance between the inside and the outside of the Pharisee using the term ὡς in connection with the indistinct tomb. However, it is noteworthy that the term "tomb" appears for the first time. Tomb is a place where a dead body is buried. This reminds readers of Q^3 7:32 and 10:15 in which the allusion to death appears. As the dirge and hades are related with the matter of death, the indistinct tomb is also to be understood in connection with it. However it is irrelevant to a forced death. It seems that the image of tomb was adopted for the lifeless aspect of the Pharisees from a religious perspective. Especially, the indistinct tomb refers to the origin of uncleanness and corruption.[24] In this respect, the third redactor criticized the Pharisees on account of their hypocrisy.

The third redactor compared the opponents with those who were standing on the indistinct tomb. It is, however, noteworthy that they were not aware of it. This means that the opponents were criticized for ignorance of their behavior. In a sense, this reminds the reader of Q^3 6:41-42 which also deals with ignorance of one's serious situation. It also recalls 6:43-44 in that the third redactor wished to define the Pharisees as bad trees bearing bad fruit though pretending to be good trees bearing good fruit. In this vein, the fourth woe was written in order to show the discordance between the inside and the outside of the Pharisees. When the fourth woe is connected with the third, it can be also interpreted as hypocrisy from an ethical point of view.

The Fifth Woe (Q 11:46)

The third redactor introduced the fifth woe in Q^3 11:46 (Luke 11:46; Matt 23:4). It deals with the ethical behavior of the lawyer with regard to his relationship with others. The lawyer was criticized because he did not do what he had taught people to do. In this respect, the fifth woe carries the same theme as the first, second, and fourth ones.

The fifth woe describes the hypocrisy of the lawyer (Q^3 11:46). According to the third redactor, Jesus said, "You load people down with burdens they can hardly carry, and you yourselves will not lift one finger to help them." This saying was addressed to the lawyers who taught people what they had to do. They taught people what was too difficult to observe; however, they did not help them to observe it. It is noteworthy that the third redactor mentioned the finger. While the second redactor used the term "finger of God" as the device for the spiritual power to expel the demon (Q^2

---

24. Eilberg-Schwartz, *Savage*, 184.

11:20), the third redactor adopted the term "finger" for the human labor. The third redactor did not explain much about the identity of lawyer, and it is not known what the burden was. They were criticized for not doing according to what they had taught. This implies that their inside is different from the outside (Q^3 11:39). Rather, they were the evil people who cast up evil things from their evil mind (6:45). In this respect, this woe is consistent with the instruction written in the third redaction regarding the nature of the opponents.

The burden could refer to the instruction related with the law or the Jewish tradition. The lawyer taught people how to live according to it; however, they did not observe what they had taught. This implies that the third redactor criticized those who had taught the Jewish law. It is, however, important to observe that the third redactor did not criticize the law or the Jewish tradition itself, but those who taught and did not observe it. This indicates the possibility that the disciples of Jesus also observed the law and the Jewish tradition but that their interpretation was different from the lawyer's at the time of the writing of the third redaction in the region of Galilee.

The Sixth Woe (Q 11:52)

The sixth woe is found in Q^3 11:52 (Luke 11:52; Matt 23:13). Although there are differences between the Lucan and Matthean versions, they share common elements.[25] This woe was located last in order to show the aspiration for entering the eschatological place, although it is not explicitly explained.

The sixth woe reveals the social situation of the disciples of Jesus at the time of the writing of the third redaction. It seems that there was a conflict between the disciples of Jesus and their opponents regarding entrance into the eschatological realm. The third redactor announced that the lawyers were responsible for the fact that people could not enter it because they prevented people from entering it. This calls our attention to Q^3 6:39 in that the blind leader leads people to a pit. Then, the lawyer is to be identified as the blind leader who did not lead people to the right place. It is clear that the third redactor attributed the responsibility to the lawyer who did not enter the eschatological place and rather prevented people from entering it. In this respect, the disciples of Jesus and the lawyer were in competition and conflict.

---

25. At least three common elements are found between the Lucan and the Matthean versions: keeping one's vested rights, the matter of entering, and preventing people from entering.

It is necessary to discuss the eschatological place. While Luke did not specify the place from which the lawyer prevented the people (Luke 11:52), Matthew clearly mentioned it as the kingdom of heaven (Matt 23:13).[26] However, the third redactor already mentioned "heaven" in contrast with "hades" (Q^3 10:15). Probably, the eschatological place was mentioned with "heaven" and "hades" in the background in the sixth woe. It seems that the eschatological place was defined as a transcendental one where people should make an effort to enter. However, it is the first case in which the eschatological place was described as the one where people should try to enter. As shown before, the kingdom of God was regarded as the place to come to the disciples in this world in the second redaction (Q^2 10:9; 11:2); in addition, it was a place that people must seek (12:31). Inheriting this tradition, the third redactor seems to develop the kingdom of God into a place that people should try to enter.

I. ESCHATOLOGICAL DISCLOSURE (Q 12:2–3)

Instruction about the eschatological disclosure is written in Q^3 12:2–3 (Luke 12:2–3; Matt 10:26–27). This text follows the six woes (Q^3 11:39–46, 52); therefore, this text plays the role of conclusion to the woes in that the nature of the criticized opponents will be disclosed at last. On the other hand, this text was ultimately added to the texts of the second redaction about the temptation that is the application of the fifth petition of the Lord's Prayer (Q^2 11:16, 29–30). In this way, this text supplements the theme of temptation when the third redaction was finally completed.

The third redactor treated the fate of concealed things with a proverbial saying in Q^3 12:2. It is said, "There is nothing concealed that will not be disclosed." The term κρυπτὸν [concealed] and ἀποκαλυφθήσεται [will be disclosed] reminds readers of ἔκρυψας [hid] and ἀπεκάλυψας [disclosed] in Q^3 10:21. The third redactor conveyed the instruction that something is hidden but will be disclosed at last. The disclosure is necessarily related to the eschatological judgment as written in 11:31–32 and the image of light expressed in 11:33–35. The light will make people see everything hidden in darkness. In this respect, the fact that everything will be finally disclosed is emphasized in the third redaction. Then, it can be said that 12:2 was planted

---

26. While the Lucan version uses the term "the key to knowledge," the Matthean version adopts "the kingdom of heaven." Some scholars regard the Matthean version as the original of Q (Robinson et al., *Critical Edition*, 280). On the other hand, some believe that the Lucan version represents the original wording of Q (Jacobson, *First Gospel*, 185).

in its present place in order to emphasize the fact that the hypocrisy of the Pharisees described in the six woes will be also disclosed at the end.

A pair of metaphoric sayings about the disclosure is found in Q³ 12:3. What is said in the dark will be told in the light, and what is whispered in the ear will be proclaimed on top of the house. Two sets of contrast emphasize the fact that there is nothing that will be hidden permanently. As shown before, the sharp contrast is a typical characteristic of the third redaction (Q³ 3:17; 6:43–44; 7:32–34; 11:39–41, etc.). This is usually used to describe the difference of their origin. Sharp contrast in the context of opposition indicates competition and conflict between the disciples of Jesus and their opponents. For this sharp contrast, the third redactor used the literary form of metaphor. While the first redactor used metaphor in Q¹ 3:9, the second redactor adopted it in Q² 12:24, 27. In this vein, using metaphor, the third redactor delivered a message of the inevitability that hidden things will be disclosed (Q³ 12:2–3). In other words, the hypocrisy of the Pharisees must be finally known to the public. In this way, the third redactor continued using metaphor in order to criticize the unfairness of the opponents. Therefore, it can be said that as the redaction of Q progressed, the third redactor revealed the social aspect of the disciples of Jesus more in connection with the Pharisees.

J. ESCHATOLOGICAL TESTIMONY (Q 12:8–9)

Eschatological testimony is described in Q³ 12:8–9 (Luke 12:8–9; Matt 10:32–33). This text follows Q³ 12:2–3 regarding the eschatological manifestation in the third redaction. On the other hand, Q³ 12:8–9 follows Q² 12:6–7 and it played the role of supplementary explanation for the application of the first petition of the Lord's Prayer.

The third redactor focused on one's relationship with the Son of Man in Q³ 12:8–9. It is said, "I tell you, whoever acknowledges me before men, the Son of Man will also acknowledge him before the angels of God." If a person acknowledges/disowns the Son of Man in front of people, then the Son of Man will acknowledge/disown the person in front of the messengers or angels [ἄγγελοι] of God. As shown several times before, the sharp contrast between the two carries the typical characteristic of the third redaction. In addition, the eschatological testimony was already implied in Q³ 11:31–32. The aspect of testimony is strengthened by the term ἔμπροθεν [in front of] which was already used by the third redactor (Q³ 7:27; 10:21). It will not be done in a hidden environment; rather, it will be done in public, so that it will be known to everybody (12:2–3). In this respect, the third redactor emphasized the disclosure of one's behavior and sayings at the end of the world.

The principle of reciprocity appears again in Q^3 12:8-9. It was once used regarding human relationship in the first redaction (Q^1 6:27, 29-38). It can be said that it was used from a social perspective. Then, it was applied to the relationship between God and human beings regarding the forgiveness in the second redaction (Q^2 11:4). In a sense, it was dealt from a religious perspective. However, the third redactor applied it to the relationship between Jesus the Son of Man and his disciples in front of the messengers or angels of God.[27] In other words, the eschatological aspect was added to the principle of reciprocity in the third redaction. One's relationship with Jesus the Son of Man will affect the result at the eschatological judgment. It means that as the redaction of Q progressed, the principle of reciprocity added its importance.

A number of theological emphasis are found in Q^3 12:8-9. First, one's relationship with Jesus the Son of Man comes to the fore again. It was already dealt with in connection to the Son of Man (6:22-23b; 7:34). This is somewhat related to the attitude of obedience toward Jesus the Lord (6:46-47; 7:6; 10:16, etc.). All these inform that one's relationship with Jesus results in one's eschatological fate. The reason that the Son of Man becomes the criterion of one's fate is because Jesus was given everything by God and he is the unique channel between God and people (10:16, 21-22). In this way, the identity of Jesus was getting more important. Second, the term ἄγγελος [angel or messenger] appears. While it was used for the messenger in 7:27, it is not clear in 12:8.[28] When the title was used in the text added to the main texts of the second redaction, his features were ambivalent (12:8-9); in other words, his role is interpreted differently depending on what ἄγγελοι identified. If the term ἄγγελοι refers to "the angels," the Son of Man would also be a transcendental figure. On the other hand, if it refers to "the messengers," he would be an earthly figure. To my judgment, the third redactor used it for a transitional role in this context for the next step. Third, the title "Son of Man" calls our attention to his nature. As shown before, the human feature was attributed to the Son of Man in the second redaction (Q^2 9:58; 11:30). Thus, the human aspect was applied to the Son of Man

---

27. Jacobson would not identify the Son of Man as Jesus (*First Gospel*, 188). There is, however, no reason to deny their identity because in the previous texts Jesus has been identified as the Son of Man.

28. Allison believes that in both places, the term ἄγγελος refers to the angels because it was already used in that sense in Q 4:1-13 (*Intertextual Jesus*, 40). It is, however, to be noted that in my view, the temptation story was added to Q later than 7:27 and 12:8-9. In this respect, Allison's interpretation is to be reconsidered.

when the third redactor added his or her texts in the middle of the main texts of the first redaction (Q^3 6:22; 7:34). On the other hand, using the title "Son of Man" in the text that comes later than Q^2 11:30, the third redactor would like to impose an aspect more than the earthly one to the Son of Man by putting it in parallel with the angels or messengers of God in the main texts of the second redaction (Q^3 12:8-9). It seems that the third redactor seemed to present the transcendental aspect to the Son of Man in order to strengthen his eschatological role.[29] At any rate, as the redaction of Q progressed further, the role of the Son of Man was getting more important. Fourth, no one is free from the eschatological judgment. For this, the third redactor used the term πᾶς [everyone]. No one is exempted from it in his or her relationship with Jesus the Son of Man. This type of tendency was already found in Q^3 7:23; 10:16 and 11:23 in that one's decision inevitably results in his or her fate. In this way, the third redactor emphasized one's responsibility for the eschatological judgment in his or her relationship with Jesus.

K. HEAVENLY TREASURE (Q 12:33-34)

Heavenly treasure is mentioned in Q^3 12:33-34 (Luke 12:33-34; Matt 6:19-21). This text follows Q^3 12:8-9 by the theme of the result that will be given after the eschatological testimony in the third redaction. On the other hand, this text was attached to Q^2 12:22-31 by the third redactor in order to strengthen the instruction about the daily bread for existence that is the application of the third petition of the Lord's Prayer in the second redaction. In other words, the heavenly treasure is more valuable than the daily bread.

The third redactor mentioned the treasure in Q^3 12:33. This reflects the social environment that some of the disciples were wealthy enough to mention treasure at the time of the writing of the third redaction. While they were instructed not to have any wallet, pouch, or sandals for their ministry in the second redaction (Q^2 9:58; 10:4), the third redactor showed their stable situation in that they had to pay attention to the matter of treasure. This is in accordance with the economic situation reflected in other texts in the third redaction such as Q^3 3:17; 6:48-49; 7:31-34; 10:2 and 11:21-23. All of them reflect the occasion for writing about the life of the middle class from an economic perspective. As the redaction of Q progressed, the third redactor revealed the economically stable environment of the disciples of Jesus.

---

29. Jacobson insists on the heavenly feature of the Son of Man in Q 12:8-9 (*First Gospel*, 188). To my judgment, however, it is not decisive to interpret that way yet.

The third redactor turned eyes to the theme of heaven. It is said that the disciples of Jesus should store the treasure in heaven by almsgiving.[30] The image of storing the treasure reminds readers of the granary for wheat in Q^3 3:17. The third redactor seemed to emphasize something heavenly at the baptism of Jesus (3:21-22). In addition, it also recalls the heavenly reward mentioned in 6:23b. The third redactor emphasized the heavenly aspect of God as the one who could give the hidden thing to the little children in 10:21. In this vein, 12:33-34 conveys the typical theology of the third redaction in that it pays attention to the heavenly matter. Emphasis on the heavenly aspect is one of the theological themes in the third redaction. In this respect, the third redactor imposed the religious characteristic to his or her teaching delivered through the mouth of Jesus with special emphasis on heaven.

The third redactor mentioned the moth and thief as the means of larceny in Q^3 12:33. In the fact that both of them are living beings, they are aggressive in their activity. It is noteworthy that the third redactor used the image of forfeit. While the image of looting was once used in the third redaction (Q^3 11:21-23), the image of robbery is adopted for the first time here. Without doubt, the third redactor wished to apply this image to the opponents—that is, especially the Pharisees. The further the redaction of Q progressed, the more negative the imagery applied to the opponents who insulted and hated the disciples of Jesus (6:22). In other words, the relationship between the two was getting worse as time passed by.

The third redactor introduced the conclusion in Q^3 12:34. It is said with a proverbial saying that where one's treasure is, there will be his or her mind. In this way, the third redactor urged the disciples of Jesus to look for heavenly things rather than earthly. It is, however, to be noted that the nature of treasure is not defined in this context. It could mean justice, mercy, and faithfulness beyond the tithe (11:42). These cannot be deprived by the moth or robber. Religious value is more than material possessions. The third redactor looked for heavenly things because the instruction of Jesus was not accepted by the Galilean people anymore led by the Pharisees. The opposition was increasing as time passed by.

---

30. Jacobson points out that "the association of alms with the heavenly treasure was a traditional theme" in the Jewish writings. For example, Sir 29:11-13; Tob 4:8-11; 12:8-9; TLevi 13:5-9; 2ApocBar 14:12; 24:1, etc. Cf. Jacobson, *First Gospel*, 192.

3

The Main Texts of the Third Redaction

The main texts of the third redaction are found in the third section (Q 12:39—22:30). After the interpolation of some texts into the main texts of the first and second redactions, the third redactor attached the main texts. Without doubt, some texts were interpolated into the main texts of the third redaction later by the fourth redactor. The third redactor kept writing his own theology and developed further in the main texts. In this section, the third redactor focused on the Son of Man and the kingdom of God. They are described in connection with the eschatological judgment that will happen at the end of the world. This section can be divided into three parts: preparation for the Son of Man (12:39-59), the kingdom of God (13:18—17:2), and the coming of the Son of Man (17:23—22:30). It seems that the third redactor adopted the literary pattern of *inclusio* in order to strengthen the kingdom of God surrounded by the theme of the Son of Man.

A. PREPARATION FOR THE SON OF MAN

Preparation for the Son of Man is described in Q 12:39-59. The Son of Man is understood to be the eschatological figure who will come at the end of the world. It is, however, to be noted that some texts were also interpolated into the main texts of the third redaction. Thus, the main texts of the third redaction should be separated and then it will show how the preparation for the Son of Man is maintained.

The Parable of the Thief (Q 12:39–40)

The sudden coming of the Son of Man is described in Q 12:39–40 (Luke 12:39–40; Matt 24:43–44). This follows Q³ 12:33–34 by the linking words κλέπτης [thief] and διορύσσω [break in].[1] This is the first text of the main texts of the third redaction; therefore, no linking word or theme is found with those of the second redaction.

The parable of the thief seems to be a part of the third redaction (Q 12:39–40). It is said that if the householder had known the time when the thief comes, he would not have let his house be broken into. As mentioned before, the term "thief" reminds readers of that in Q³ 12:33–34. In addition, the instruction about the coming of the Son of Man recalls the proclamation of John about the one coming after him (3:16–17; 7:18–27). Moreover, the theme "preparation" makes readers think of the parable of the two builders (6:48–49). Since the eschatological role was given to the Son of Man in 12:8–9, the third redactor was able to depict it again here. The elements listed above lead us to the conclusion that 12:39–40 originated in the third redaction to which 3:16–17; 6:48–49; 7:18–27 and 12:8–9, 33–34 also belong.

The sudden coming of the Son of Man is compared to a thief (Q³ 12:39–40). The thief does not give a warning to the householder before he intrudes. The unexpected coming is the main point between the thief and the Son of Man. At any rate, the sudden coming of the Son of Man refers to the end times, according to the Jewish tradition. It is, however, noteworthy that the third redactor did not talk about the place from which the Son of Man will come. In this respect, his origin is to be dealt with later. Since the transcendental role of the Son of Man was implied in 12:8–9, the third redactor could also imply his eschatological coming from the messengers [angels] of God here.

The third redactor emphasized the importance of keeping one's property. It is said that the householder should protect his house from being stolen and looted. This image was already found in the parable of the strong person (Q³ 11:21–23). While the parable of the strong person focused on being looted by the stronger one, the parable of the thief pays more attention to the unexpected coming of a thief than being stolen from. In this respect, the third redactor showed the economic environment of the disciples at the time of the writing of the third redaction; in other words, some of them were probably affluent enough to protect their property from a thief.

---

1. Jacobson, *First Gospel*, 196. Cf. Sato, *Q*, 41; and Jacobson, "Shape," 173.

The characterization of the "Son of Man" underwent a process of development as the redaction of Q progressed. As already shown, the second redactor used it for the earthly Jesus in Q^2 9:58; 11:30, and the third redactor mentioned the earthly aspect of the Son of Man in the texts interpolated into the main texts of the first redaction as well in Q^3 6:22–23b; 7:34. Then, the third redactor mentioned the intermediary role of the Son of Man between the messengers [angels] of God and people in the text interpolated into the main texts of the second redaction (12:8–9). Finally, the Son of Man is defined as the one who will come suddenly at the end of the world in the main texts of the third redaction (12:39–40). In this respect, as the redaction of Q progressed further, the more eschatological and transcendental aspect was given to the Son of Man. Although the Son of Man refers to Jesus, his identity is not clearly defined in this context.[2] The third redactor did not deal with the origin of the Son of Man yet. It is, however, to be noted that the third redactor wished to use the title "Son of Man" other than the substitute for the first person "I" used by the second redactor.

The Parable of the Manager (Q 12:42–46)

The parable of the manager is described in Q 12:42–46 (Luke 12:42–46; Matt 24:45–51). This text follows Q^3 12:39–40 by the theme of "unexpected coming." This makes the literary flow from 12:39–40 to 12:42–46 natural. The parable of the manager also originated from the third redaction.

The parable of the manager repeats the theological instruction already expressed in the previous texts of the third redaction. The relationship between the householder and the manager reminds readers of that between the Lord and the followers described in the third redaction (Q^3 3:16; 6:46; 7:6; 10:2, etc.). In addition, the beatitude with a precondition also recalls the relationship between Jesus and his disciples in the third redaction (6:22–23b; 7:23). The sharp contrast between the wise and unwise managers reminds readers of the parable of the two builders (6:48–49) because it also introduced the wise and unwise builders. In this respect, the parable of the manager can be regarded as another version of the parable of the two builders. In this respect, 12:42–46 shares the typical theology with its previous texts of the third redaction.

The third redactor said once again that the coming of the Son of Man was not known to the disciples. The description that the moment of the coming of the household is not known even to the manager refers to the sudden and unexpected coming of the Son of Man. The manager could be

---

2. Fleddermann, "Householder," 25–26.

compared to the leaders among the followers of Jesus. Then, it could mean that when he comes, there will be eschatological judgment between the wise and unwise disciples of Jesus; in addition, the parable can be applied to the eschatological distinction between the disciples of Jesus and their opponents. This kind of eschatological judgment reminds readers of the distinction between the wheat and the chaff (Q^3 3:16–17), between the wise and the unwise (6:48–49), and between those who acknowledged and who disowned (12:8–9). From an eschatological perspective, the third redactor focused on the suddenness and unexpectedness of the coming of the Son of Man in the main texts.[3]

The parable of the manager conveys a beatitude (Q^3 12:43). Its form "μακάριος ὁ δοῦλος . . ." recalls the beatitudes written in Q^1 6:20b and Q^2 6:21. However, the difference is clear in that while the first and second redactors referred to the group of people as the beneficiary of blessing, the third redactor designated an individual person as the beneficiary (Q^3 6:22–23b; 7:23; 12:43). In addition, while the first and second redactors acknowledged the contemporary situation of the beneficiary as the precondition for blessing, the third redactor introduced it in the relationship with Jesus. In this way, the third redactor narrowed down the boundary of beneficiary to the specific person. This indicates that the instruction of Jesus was addressed to a limited number of people rather than to the public at the stage of the third redaction. Only those who followed Jesus could be the beneficiaries of blessing.

The parable of the manager shows the social environment of the disciples of Jesus at the time of the writing of the third redaction. The economic situation was greatly improved in that there were some who ran a large household that must be entrusted to a manager and servants. The affluent situation is reflected in the description that the manager was in charge of distributing food to his servants on time. While the second redactor had mentioned worry about food and clothing (Q^2 12:22–31), the third redactor did not reveal such anxiety anymore. Rather, the matter of eating and drinking is described as part of a daily life in the third redaction (Q^3 7:34). The bigger economic situation is reflected in the parable of the manager. In this respect, the parable of the manager reflects the improved economic environment of the disciples of Jesus at the time of the writing of the third redaction.

The parable of the manager shows a well-balanced structure from a literary point of view. The master puts the manager in charge of distributing

---

3. There were some who would believe the delayed coming of the Son of Man (Fleddermann, "Householder," 26).

food to his servants on time. If the manager carries out his duty well, when the lord comes back, he will be blessed by the lord; on the contrary, if the manager does not commit his duty well, he will be punished. The thesis appears first, and then its explanation is narrated in the form of contrast. This type of balanced structure is one of the typical characteristics found in the third redaction; for instance, it is found in the parable of the two builders (Q^3 6:46-49) and the critique against "this generation (7:31-34). This informs readers of the fact that the third redactor was a well-trained writer with regard to literary skill. It made it possible that as Q underwent a process of redaction, it developed more from a literary perspective.

Later Addition

Some texts were added to the third redaction in Q 12:49, 51-56, 58-59 (Luke 12:49, 51-59; Matt 5:25-26; 10:34-36; 16:2-3). They seem to be added by a later redactor in order to show what the disciples have to do when the Son of Man comes. It is, however, noteworthy that they are loosely connected in terms of word and theme.

The text Q 12:49, 51-53 suddenly talks about division on account of Jesus.[4] In this respect, this text does not keep the natural flow from Q^3 12:39-40, 42-46. Rather, this saying is in accordance with Q^4 9:59-60a in that they deal with instruction about the relationship among family members in the case of following Jesus. This helps build a foundation upon which readers can recognize differences regarding the redactions. In this respect, 12:49, 51-53 seem to belong to the fourth redaction with 9:59-60a.

The text Q 12:54-56 deals with the sign of the time. This text follows Q^4 12:49, 51-53 by the connecting word πῦρ [fire][5] and the theme of sign.[6] The sign written in 12:54-56 is somewhat different from the sign asked for

---

4. The Matthean version describes that Jesus came to the world to hurl the "sword" (Matt 10:34), while the Lucan version uses the terms "fire" and "division" (Luke 12:49, 51). Although it is not easy to decide which represents the original wording of Q, there is a scholarly consensus that they were originated in Q. For example, Jacobson believes that Luke 12:49 was in Q, while Luke 12:51 was created (*First Gospel*, 198). Valantasis also thinks that the term "fire" was a part of Q 12:49 because it was used in 3:16-17 (*New Q*, 171-72). On the other hand, Robinson et al. believe that both "fire" in Q 12:49 and "sword" in 12:51 were in Q (*Critical Edition*, 376, 380).

5. The term πῦρ [fire] could be a connecting word between Q^4 12:49, 51-53 and 12:54-55. As reflected in the Matthean version (Matt 16:2-3), the description that the sky is flame red [πυρράζει] was in Q. In other words, while the redactor used πῦρ in 12:49, 51-53, he adopted πυρράζει in 12:54-55. Then, it can be said that the activity of Jesus throwing the fire was the sign for the end of the world.

6. Tuckett, *Q*, 158.

by the crowds in the second redaction, in which the divine miracle was regarded as the sign (Q^2 11:16, 29–30). On the other hand, the sign mentioned in 12:54–56 refers to what was learned from the changing times. This shows a difference regarding the nature of sign. In this respect, 12:54–56 seems to belong to the fourth redaction with 12:49, 51–53.

The text Q 12:58–59 introduces instruction about reconciliation. This text follows 12:54–56 by the theme of "rebuke for failure to understand what is going on."[7] And this is also connected with 12:49, 51–53 by the linking word βάλλω [throw]. This deals with the case that since the disciples of Jesus were charged with debt, they had to look for reconciliation with the creditor. Although 12:58–59 reveals a reciprocal relationship between the creditor and the debtor, this differs from what is written in Q^1 6:27, 29–30 and Q^2 11:4. In addition, the intervention of a judge also shows a different aspect from the unilateral judgment of the lord [master] on the manager in Q^3 12:39–46. This means that 12:58–59 seems to belong to a redaction later than the third one—that is, the fourth redaction. In conclusion, Q 12:58–59 could be a part of the fourth redaction in which 12:49, 51–56 is also included.

B. THE KINGDOM OF GOD

The kingdom of God is described in Q 13:18—17:2. Of course, this part is also composed of two redactions. It is then necessary to distinguish the third redaction and to study its theology. The third redactor focused on the description of the kingdom of God with parables.

The Parables of the Mustard Seed and Leaven (Q 13:18–21)

Two parables are introduced in order to describe the kingdom of God in Q 13:18–21 (Luke 13:18–21; Matt 13:31–33). They are connected to Q^4 12:58–59 by the linking word βάλλω [throw]. It is, however, to be noticed that 13:18–21 seem to belong to the third redaction.

Above all, the introductory formula τίνι ὁμοία ἐστιν [what it is like] is used in Q 13:18. It calls our attention to τίνι ἐστὶν ὁμοία used in the third redaction (Q^3 7:31). In addition, it also calls attention to the introductory formula ὁμοιός ἐστιν [it is like] used for the parable of the two builders (Q^3 6:48). Moreover, a well-developed form of parable is reminiscent of the parables in 6:48–49 and 11:21–22. While the parable of the mustard

---

7. Jacobson, *First Gospel*, 202.

introduces a male farmer who sowed mustard seed in the garden, the parable of the leaven introduces a female housewife who put leaven in the dough of flour. The male and female pair in the parables reminds readers of that of the Queen of the South and the Ninevites who will arise to pass judgment upon the people at the end of the world (Q^3 11:31–32). This indicates that 13:18–21 shares the typical aspects of the third redaction with the texts mentioned above.

The third redactor adopted the parable in order to describe the kingdom of God for the first time. Simile is a literary device that conveys characteristics of the kingdom of God. The parables of the mustard seed and leaven convey several common elements regarding the kingdom of God: hiddenness, growth, the act of placing, exaggerated amounts, etc.[8] First, the kingdom of God has been hidden. The hidden aspect is embedded in the description that while the mustard seed was sown into the soil, the leaven is put in the dough of flour. The third redactor conveyed that the kingdom of God is not seen by the eyes of people because it has been hidden.[9] Whereas the first redactor announced its presence among the poor (Q^1 6:20b), the second redactor described its presence when the finger of God expels the demon (Q^2 11:20). On the other hand, the third redactor pointed out its hidden aspect (Q^3 13:18–21). As the redaction of Q progressed, its acknowledgement was getting more difficult. In this way, its shape and reality do not appear in the parables of the third redaction.

Second, the kingdom of God has enlarged its size. This is seen in that the mustard seed grows as big as a tree on which the birds put their nests and that the leaven makes the dough bigger in size. The image of growth appears in both parables. The first and second redactors did not mention its size. On the other hand, the third redactor tried to say that the kingdom of God has been enlarged enough to accommodate as many people as possible. This seems to reflect that the occasion for writing was that the number of the disciples of Jesus increased at the time of the writing of the third redaction. Without doubt, this resulted from the successful mission to the neighbors in the region of Galilee as commanded in the second redaction (Q^2 10:4–12).

Third, the moment of its fulfillment seems to be postponed as the redaction of Q progressed. The first redactor mentioned the present aspect of the kingdom of God by using the present tense verb (Q^1 6:20b); however, the second redactor postponed its fulfillment to the indefinite future by pointing out that it should come (Q^2 10:9; 11:2; 12:31). On the other hand, the third redactor did not mention the moment of its coming and fulfillment;

---

8. Ibid., 203.
9. Ibid., 204.

rather, it is active but had not yet completely come (Q³ 13:18–21). Although the third redactor did not mention the time of its fulfillment, he or she was not sure of its presence in the world. This shows that as the redaction progressed, the moment of its fulfillment was getting postponed. The kingdom of God was not accomplished according to the third redaction as the historical Jesus had announced to the crowds as reflected in the first redaction.

Fourth, the kingdom of God has an aspect totally different from what the people generally have expected. While the Jews were accustomed to comparing the kingdom to a cedar tree (Ezek 17:22–24; 31:3–9), the mustard is a shabby plant that cannot be regarded as a tree.[10] It should not be planted in the garden (Mishnah Kilayim 3:2). In addition, the leaven was considered too unclean to be used for the bread offered to God at the temple (Lev 2:5; 6:16; 10:12). "In the view of all antiquity, Semitic and non-Semitic, panary fermentation represented a process of corruption and putrifaction in the mass of the dough."[11] On the other hand, the third redactor adopted leaven to describe the kingdom of God. It is explained with objects found in normal daily life. The comparison of the kingdom of God to the mustard seed and leaven is preposterous in the third redaction. In this respect, the third redactor delivered the instruction that the kingdom of God was not likely what the people generally expected.

Fifth, the kingdom of God is the place of rest. The image of a nest in a tree provides an image of peaceful rest. According to the Jewish tradition, the kingdom of God has been represented by big trees that provide rest.[12] On the other hand, the third redactor mentioned the nest on the mustard tree [shabby plant] in order to depict birds resting. It is not told how rest will be given to the disciples of Jesus. From the description of the third redactor looking for rest given by God, it can be induced that the primordial Sabbath could be the mirror for the rest in the kingdom of God (Gen 2:2–3). As shown before, the second redactor mentioned the kingdom of God in the context of the primordial creation and the garden of Eden (Q² 6:21a; 11:2–4) and the third redactor was interested in describing God against the backdrop of creation (Q³ 10:21). In this vein, the reference to rest given

---

10. According to Nils A. Dahl, "The figure of the great tree giving shelter to the birds of the air is a traditional picture of a great kingdom." "Parables of Growth," *Studia Theologica* 5 (1951) 147; quoted from Jacobson, *First Gospel*, 204. He lists scriptural verses such as Dan 4:11, 18; Ezek 17:22–24; 31:6; Judg 9:15; Lam 4:20; Eccl 14:26; Bar 1:12 and Sir 14:26.

11. Scott, "Jesus," 410. Cf. It is quoted from A. R. S. Kennedy, "Leaven," in *Encyclopaedia Bible*, edited by T. K. Cheyne and J. S. Black, (London: Black, 1902), 3:2754.

12. Jacobson, *First Gospel*, 204.

after the creation of the universe is used as the background to describe the characteristic of the kingdom of God in the third redaction.

Sixth, a male and female pair is used in order to describe the kingdom of God. The pair of male and female was already adopted between the Queen of the South and the Ninevites for the eschatological judgment (Q^3 11:31–32). The reason why the third redactor used it frequently was because they refer to the first man-woman pair made in the image of God (Gen 1:27)—that is, Adam and Eve (2:18—4:1). This inference can be supported by the interpretation that the kingdom of God was described against the backdrop of the garden of Eden by the second redactor while listing five petitions of the Lord's Prayer (Q^2 11:2–4). It seems that as the redaction of Q progressed, the redactors attempted to describe the kingdom of God in light of the primordial time of creation, especially the garden of Eden.

The Metaphor about the Door (Q 13:24–27)

The metaphor about the door appears in Q 13:24–27 (Luke 13:24–27; Matt 7:13–14, 22–23; 25:10–12). This text follows the parables of the mustard seed and leaven in terms of metaphoric sayings (Q^3 13:18–21). The theme of "entering" recalls the lawyer holding the key but hindering others from entering the eschatological place (11:52). In addition, the matter of eating and drinking reminds readers of John and Jesus who showed contrasting attitudes toward this matter (7:33–34). From the fact that 13:24–27 shares common elements with 7:33–34; 11:52; and 13:18–21, it can be said that this text originated in the third redaction.

The metaphoric saying about the narrow door is introduced in Q^3 13:24. This conveys many instructions regarding the kingdom of God. First, the image of the door informs readers of the matter of entering. In other words, the kingdom of God is a place where a person can get in through a door. If the second redactor described the kingdom of God with a background of the garden of Eden with the five petitions of the Lord's Prayer (Q^2 11:2–4), it could be strengthened by the image of a door mentioned in the third redaction since the garden of Eden had been surrounded by a fence, supposedly with a door (Gen 3:24). The intertestamental writings further developed the description that the garden of Eden had a door (*TLevi* 18:10; cf. *Apoc. Mos.* 19:1). Second, the narrow door informs readers of difficulty of getting through it. In other words, it is very difficult to enter the kingdom of God. While the first and second redactors promised the kingdom of God to the poor, the hungry, and the mourner (Q^1 6:20b; Q^2 6:21), the third redactor limited the number of those who would enter it with the metaphor of a narrow door (Q^3 13:24). Third, the third redactor used the contrast between "many" and "few" regarding the entrants of the kingdom of God. Although many people seek to enter, only a few people will enter through it. While the second redactor used the phrase "search [ζητεῖτε] and you will find" (Q^2 11:9), the third redactor said that many seek [ζητήσοθσιν] but few will enter. The further the redaction of Q progressed, the slimmer the chance of getting in and obtaining what a person seeks in connection with the kingdom of God.

The metaphor of the door provides two sets of dialogue. The first set of dialogue is described in Q^3 13:25. After the door had been shut, the visitors asked the householder to open it. However, the householder replied that he did not know who they were. It is noteworthy that the visitor called the householder "Lord." The parable of the manager also used the title "Lord" for the household (12:42–46). This reminds readers of various texts of the third redaction in which Jesus is designated as the Lord (6:46; 7:6; 12:42, etc.). This description is accordant with the emphasis on one's relationship with Jesus (6:22–23b; 10:16, 21–22; 12:8–9, etc.). According to one's relationship with Jesus, his or her fate will be determined by entering the kingdom of God or not. Only those who were selected by Jesus the Son of Man would enter the house that represents the kingdom of God. Although the kingdom of God is still growing in order to accommodate as many people as possible (13:18–21), the narrow door is not big enough to allow all of them entrance. However, the householder denied the request of those who wanted the door to be opened again. This reminds readers of the denial by the Son of Man in front of the messengers of God (12:8–9). In other words, those who denied Jesus the Son of Man in front of people will be prevented from entering the door that leads them to the kingdom of God. In this respect, the third redactor reveals the eschatological judgment through the first dialogue between the householder and the visitors.

The second set of dialogue is described in Q^3 13:26–27.[13] The visitors insisted that they were eating and drinking in front of the householder and they taught as he had instructed. The second redactor already used the theme of eating and drinking in the application of the third petition of the Lord's Prayer (Q^2 12:29). It was related with daily life in that context. On the other hand, the third redactor already used the theme of eating and drinking as a critique against "this generation" (Q^3 7:31–34). The matter of eating

---

13. The Lucan and Matthean versions reveal a significant difference in detail (Luke 13:26-27; Matt 7:22-23). However, I would like to believe that the Lucan version reflects the original wording of Q because it does not divide the text into three as the Matthean one did. Matthew seems to modify the content according to his theological intention to fit them in the context.

and drinking with the householder represents the intimacy of the disciples with Jesus in this context. Although the visitors insisted on their relationship with the householder, they were told that he did not know them. This means that Jesus did not regard them as disciples, namely the entrants of the kingdom of God. Intimate relationship with Jesus is not the only precondition to enter the kingdom of God. Rather, they were identified as those who did unrighteousness.[14] While the first redactor described John coming to the world for the righteousness of God (Q^1 7:29–30), the third redactor described the unrighteous who called Jesus "Lord!" but did not observe his words (Q^3 6:46–47). Thus, the third redactor introduced those who did not live righteously. They called Jesus "Lord" but were excluded from the kingdom of God. Thus, the householder told them to get away from him. This is somewhat different from the previous sayings when the second redactor urged the followers of Jesus to gather people for the kingdom of God (Q^2 10:9). The third redactor revealed the authority to drive the unworthy disciples out of the kingdom of God. This indicates that there were some who did not fit in the entrance of the kingdom of God.

As dealt with above, the parable of the narrow door consists of two sets of dialogues between the householder and the visitor. While a set of dialogue was found in the second redaction (Q^2 9:57–58; 11:14–15, 17–20), the third redactor developed the pericope by increasing the number of dialogues. Two sets of dialogues were already used in the story about the centurion (Q^3 7:1–10). Then, the third redactor added another pericope with two sets of dialogues in the metaphor of the door to describe the characteristic of the kingdom of God. This shows that as the redaction of Q progressed, the form of narrative developed further. Then, it can be surmised that the third redactor was one of the well-trained scribes who were fond of using dialogue as instruction.

Later Addition

Then, some added texts are found in Q 13:28–17:2. They were added in order to strengthen the meaning of the kingdom of God described by the third redactor. It is, however, remembered that the added texts reflect the theology of the fourth redactor.

---

14. The Matthean version uses the term "lawlessness" rather than "unrighteousness." To my judgment, the Matthean version does not reflect the original wording of Q in that the law itself is not mentioned in the third redaction of Q, although allusion to the law appears in Q^3 11:39–42. According to the Jewish tradition, living by the law is the righteous way of life.

Instruction about eschatological reversal is introduced in Q 13:28–30 (Luke 13:28–30; Matt 8:11–12; 20:16). This text follows Q^3 13:24–27 by the theme of being thrown out of the kingdom of God. It is, however, noteworthy that this text "is inappropriate in this context because it is addressed more widely to Israel in general . . . It appears to be a later addition."[15] This text shows a different aspect of the kingdom of God in that it reveals the transcendental aspect. Then, the names "Abraham, Isaac, and Jacob" call our attention to the phrase "Abraham and his descendants" in Q^4 3:8bc. Especially, the eschatological reversal between the Jews and the Gentiles is totally new in Q. It seems that this text shows a more developed aspect than that in the third redaction regarding the matter of the Gentiles (Q^3 7:1–10; 11:31–32). This indicates that Q 13:28–30 belongs to the fourth redaction with 3:8bc.

A similar tendency is found in the lamentation about Jerusalem in Q 13:34–35 (Luke 13:34–35; Matt 23:37–39).[16] This text reveals many differences from its surrounding texts. First, Jerusalem is mentioned for the first time in Q. Second, the martyrdom of prophets reminds readers of Abel and Zechariah in Q^4 11:51. This can be connected with the texts which deal with the theme of death (4:9–12; 9:59–60a; 10:3; 11:47–51; 12:4–5).[17] Third, the house which refers to the temple also reminds readers of the house mentioned in 11:51.[18] Then, the Jerusalem temple is described as the place of martyrdom (4:9–12).[19] In this respect, 13:34–35 seems to belong to the fourth redaction with 4:1–11; 11:51; and 12:4–5.

The controversy about Sabbath is written in Q 14:5 (Luke 14:5; Matt 12:11–12).[20] Q 14:5 does not fit into its present context; in other words, it does not go along with its surrounding texts (13:34–35; 14:11). This tells people about the possibility that this text was added to Q^3 6:39 by the linking phrase "fall into a pit" [βόθυνος].[21] On the other hand, the fact that 14:5

---

15. Jacobson, *First Gospel*, 208.

16. The original location of Q 13:34–35 has been debated among scholars. Cf. Jacobson, *First Gospel*, 209–10.

17. For the opposite opinion, see Seeley, "Blessing," 131.

18. Tuckett says that Q 13:34–35 in general coheres with 11:51 (Q, 175).

19. Mack points out the possibility that Q 13:34–35 belongs to the redaction in which 4:1–13 is included (*Lost Gospel*, 173).

20. Q 14:5 seems to belong to Q. Cf. Neirynck, "Luke 14:1–6," 183–204. On the other hand, Robinson does not think that this text belongs to Q (*Critical Edition*, 424–29).

21. For this, the Matthean version is preferred to the Lucan (Matt 12:11; Luke 14:5). It seems that the Matthean term βόθυνος represents the original word of Q 14:5 rather than the Lucan one φρέαρ.

conveys the controversy regarding the law informs readers of its origin in the fourth redaction with 4:1–13. It seems that Q⁴ 14:5 was attached to 6:39 by the fourth redactor.

The instruction about the reversal appears in Q 14:11 (Luke 14:11; Matt 23:12). The theme of reversal reminds readers of Q⁴ 13:28–30 in which the eschatological reversal appears between the Jews and the Gentiles. When 14:5 is removed on account of its relocation to the original place in the fourth redaction, 14:11 follows 13:34–35 by the theme of reversal; in other words, Jerusalem abandoned her religious place by refusing the prophets of God and this can be compared to the one who exalted himself or herself but was forcefully lowered down. This implies that 14:11 also originated in the fourth redaction with 13:28–30, 34–35.

In addition, the parable of the banquet is written in Q 14:16–24 (Luke 14:16–24; Matt 22:1–10).[22] This parable deals with the eschatological reversal between those who were invited and those who were not invited. This seems to be used as an example of the reversal mentioned in Q⁴ 13:28–30 and 14:11.[23] In this respect, the parable of the banquet belongs to the fourth redaction with 13:28–30 and 14:11.

Instruction about discipleship is introduced in Q 14:26–27 (Luke 14:24–27; Matt 10:37–38).[24] The disciples were asked to run the risk of death on the cross. In this respect, this text deals with the matter of death and life. This reminds readers of the second temptation of Jesus in Q⁴ 4:9–12; in addition, the same theme appears in 9:59–60a; 11:47–51 and 12:4–5. In this respect, the text of 14:26–27 seems to belong to the fourth redaction with 4:1–13; 9:59–60a; 11:47–51; and 12:4–5. It is, however, noteworthy that the text 14:26–27 does not fit well in its context because the themes of hating one's family members and carrying the cross do not go along with the parables of banquet and its following text. Although it is difficult to relocate 14:26–27 in its original place, it will be discussed later when 17:33 is treated.

The parable of the salt is located in Q 14:34–35 (Luke 14:34–35; Matt 5:13). This parable mentions salt being thrown out when it loses its taste. This text follows Q⁴ 14:16–24 by the theme of being thrown out. In a sense, this also conveys the theme of reversal. Then, this supports the possibility that 14:26–27 is out of context. On the other hand, the parable of the salt could be a supplement to the saying in 13:28–30 in that the phrase βάλλω is

22. Although the Lucan and Matthean versions reveal great differences in details, they convey many common elements. In this respect, the parable of the banquet seems to be a part of Q. Cf. Jacobson, *First Gospel*, 216.

23. Kloppenborg, *Formation*, 229.

24. Jacobson, *First Gospel*, 223. In addition to discipleship, he also argues for the theme of exclusion.

used in both places. These two texts also deal with eschatological judgment. In this respect, 14:34-35 also seems to belong to the fourth redaction along with 13:28-30 and 14:16-24.

The parable of the lost sheep is found in Q 15:4-7 (Luke 15:4-7; Matt 18:12-14). This parable conveys the theme that the lost are found.[25] This also deals with the reversal of one's fate; in this respect, Q 15:4-7 continues 14:16-24 in terms of common theme. The term "sheep" makes readers see that it was already mentioned in Q^4 10:3 and probably 14:5 (Matt 12:11). In this respect, the parable of the lost sheep is also to be included in the fourth redaction.

Instruction about material possessions is found in Q 16:13 (Luke 16:13; Matt 6:24). This text is out of context in its present order; in other words, it does not have any common element with its previous text Q^4 15:4-7. Rather, it seems to follow Q^3 12:33-34 as reflected in the Matthean order by the theme of material possessions (Matt 6:19-21, 24). The disciples of Jesus should serve God not Mammon; Mammon represents the lord of material possessions. The choice between them points to the temptation story in which the devil seduced Jesus with all the kingdoms of the world and their splendor (Q^4 4:5). The devil demanded Jesus to choose between God and Mammon. This shows that 16:13 originated in the fourth redaction.

The division of salvation history is described in Q 16:16 (Luke 16:16; Matt 11:12-13). It seems that this text originally followed Q^4 7:28 as they are reflected in the Matthean order.[26] John is described as the one who seemed to be excluded from the kingdom of God because he belonged to the period of the law and the prophet. This is the worst description of his status so far in Q and collides with his positive role as the one better than the prophets and as the messenger sent ahead of Jesus by God in the third redaction (Q^3 7:24-27). In this respect, 16:16 as well as 7:28 were probably added by a later redactor. Then, it can be said that 16:16 belonged to the fourth redaction along with 7:28.

The virtue of the law is described in Q 16:17 (Luke 16:17; Matt 5:18). This text follows Q^4 16:16 by the connecting word "law." It is difficult to recover the original place of 16:17 since the Matthean version uses it in a different context from the Lucan one; however, it seems to be best to conclude that it followed 16:16 in the fourth redaction.

The commandment about adultery is introduced in Q 16:18 (Luke 16:18; Matt 5:32). This text follows Q^4 16:17 by the fact that it also deals

---

25. Jacobson, *First Gospel*, 226.

26. Jacobson, *First Gospel*, 116, 229; Kloppenborg, *Formation*, 112-13; and Allison, *Jesus Tradition*, 18.

with the matter of law. However, its original location is ambiguous because Luke and Matthew used it in different contexts. While Luke placed it after 16:16–17 (Q^4 6:16–17), Matthew located it after 5:18, 25–26 (Q^4 6:17; 12:58–59). It is, however, noteworthy that the term "law" is a connecting word between the two. In this respect, Q 16:18 seems to follow 16:16–17 and belong to the fourth redaction.

Finally, a woe is written in Q 17:1–2 (Luke 17:1–2; Matt 18:6–7). This text seems to follow Q^4 15:4–7 by the theme of not losing even one of many. This is a warning against those who do harm to others. This is, however, somewhat different from those of the third redaction because this is not against the opponents (Q^3 10:13–15; 11:39–46, 52). In addition, the fact that the woe deals with the theme of death reminds readers of many texts such as Q^4 4:9–12; 10:3; 11:47–51; 12:11–12; 13:34–35, etc. In this respect, 17:1–2 also seems to belong to the fourth redaction.

A saying about faith and obedience is written in Q 17:6 (Luke 17:6; Matt 17:20). This is connected to Q^4 17:1–2 by the connecting word "sea."[27] In this respect, 17:1–2 and 17:6 drew a contrast regarding faith: a person of faith and one of little faith. In reality, it is impossible for the mulberry tree [or mountain] to be planted in the sea. This reminds readers of the saying in Q^4 3:8bc, in that making the descendants of Abraham out of stones is also impossible in reality. It seems that 17:6 belonged to the fourth redaction along with 3:8bc and 17:1–2.

C. THE COMING OF THE SON OF MAN

The phenomena at the time of the coming of the Son of Man are described in Q 17:23—22:30. This part conveys the theme of eschatological reward for the disciples of Jesus. Of course, this is composed in two redactions. Thus, it is necessary to distinguish the third redaction. From a literary point of view, this part constitutes a corresponding pair of 12:39–40, 42–46 in the main texts of the third redaction which shows an *inclusio*.

The Coming of the Son of Man (Q 17:23–24)

The coming of the Son of Man is depicted from an apocalyptic perspective in Q 17:23–24 (Luke 17:23–24; Matt 24:26–27). The coming of the Son of Man was already mentioned in Q^3 12:39–40 and supplemented by the

---

27. Luke uses the term "sea" (Luke 17:6), whereas Matthew adopts the term "there" (Matt 17:20). It seems that Luke represents the original wording of Q because the term could be the connection word.

parable of the manager in 12:42–46. While his sudden and unexpected coming was compared to that of a thief there, it is described in connection with lightening here. In this respect, 17:23–24 constitutes a corresponding pair with 12:39–40 because they surround the texts about the kingdom of God. Along with a description about the coming of Jesus after John in 3:16–17 and 7:18–23, the third redactor identified the Son of Man with Jesus in 6:22; 7:34; 12:8–9 and 12:40. In this respect, Jesus is defined as the eschatological figure who will come at the end of time. In consequence 17:23–24 seems to originate in the third redaction with the texts listed above.

The third redactor gave a warning against wrong expectation about the Son of Man.[28] According to the text, Jesus taught his disciples to neglect the saying that the Son of Man was here or there. This implies that some of the disciples of Jesus believed that the Son of Man has already come. However, the third redactor denied the mysterious and private coming of the Son of Man. On the contrary, he will come in public, as lightening seen by everybody. While comparison with a thief was made in reference to the sudden and unexpected coming of the Son of Man (Q^3 12:39–40), the comparison with lightening was made in reference to the universally known phenomenon. In spite of a belief in his coming like lightening, specifics are not explained. For this, the third redactor adopted only the apocalyptic slogan.[29] It is noteworthy that the Son of Man is described as a transcendental figure for the first time. However, the third redactor was hesitant to describe the apocalyptic timetable.[30] Although the third redactor was interested in the apocalyptic point of view, he was still silent on the precise description about the coming of the Son of Man.

The third redactor attributed an eschatological role to the Son of Man. As explained before, the title "Son of Man" does not appear in the first redaction. Then, the second redactor used it in substitute for the first person (Q^2 9:58; 11:30).[31] In this case, the Son of Man refers to an earthly figure. Moreover, the third redactor used the title in three different ways. First, when the title "Son of Man" was interpolated into the main texts of the first redaction, it referred to the earthly figure (Q^3 6:22; 7:34). Second, when the title was added into the main texts of the second redaction, his features were ambivalent (12:8–9); in other words, his role is interpreted differently depending on the identity of ἄγγελοι of God. If the term ἄγγελοι refers to

28. Kloppenborg, *Formation*, 159.
29. Ibid., 160.
30. Jacobson, *First Gospel*, 233.
31. Vermes, *Dead Sea Scrolls*, 162–68. There is also an opinion that the title "Son of Man" did not refer to a person in general sense at the time of Jesus (Owen and Shepherd, "Speaking Up," 81–122).

"the angels," the Son of Man would also be a transcendental figure. On the other hand, if it refers to "the messengers," he would be an earthly figure. To my judgment, the third redactor used it as a transitional role in this context for the next step. Third, in the main texts of the third redaction, the Son of Man appears as an eschatological figure (12:39–40) and then finally a transcendental figure in the apocalyptic context (17:24).[32] As the redaction of Q progressed, the concept of the Son of Man also theologically developed. In this respect, the status and role of Jesus was getting heightened as the servant of God from a theological perspective at the stage of the third redaction.

It seems that the Son of Man was described in light of the Bible. As mentioned in the explanation of Q² 9:58, the earthly aspect of the Son of Man seems to be described against the backdrop of the title "son of man" [בן אדם] in the Bible (Job 16:21; Ps 8:4 58:1; 80:17; Prov 8:4, 31; Jer 49:33; 50:40; 51:43; Ezek 2:1; 3:1; 4:1, etc.). On the other hand, when the third redactor imposed a transcendental aspect to the Son of Man in Q³ 17:24, it seems that the Aramaic phrase "one like a son of man" [כבר אנש] was its theological background (Dan 7:13–14). In other words, "the one like a son of man" turned into the "Son of Man" at the stage of the third redactor. In this respect, the third redactor used the title "Son of Man" with literary and theological intention.[33] The more the redaction of Q progressed, the more theological meaning was imposed to the Son of Man as the eschatological agent of God.

The Indifference of People (Q 17:26–27, 30)

The indifference of people about the Son of Man is mentioned in Q 17:26–27, 30 (Luke 17:26–27, 30; Matt 24:37–39). This text follows Q³ 17:23–24 by linking words such as "for as," "on the day(s)," and the title "Son of Man."[34] In addition, the common theme appears in both texts that the Son of Man will come to the world. It seems that 17:26–27, 30 plays the role of supplement to 17:23–24 regarding the phenomenon that will happen at the time of the coming of the Son of Man. In this way, the third redactor continues

32. "Building on Philipp Vielhauer's view that the apocalyptic Son of man sayings do not go back to Jesus himself," Koester argues for their late appearance in Q (Robinson et al., *Critical Edition*, lx; quoted from Koester and Robinson, *Entwicklungslinien*, 129n66).

33. The title "Son of Man" is also found in 1 En 46:1–6; 48:2–6 which was supposed to be written in the middle of the 40s CE probably a little later than Q.

34. While the Matthean version uses ὥσπερ, the Lucan uses καθὼς in Q 17:26. On the other hand, both versions use ὥσπερ in Q 17:24.

to describe the coming of the Son of Man. In consequence, Q 17:26–27, 30 seems to belong to the third redaction.

In order to describe the phenomenon at the time of the coming of the Son of Man, the third redactor employed the literary pattern of *inclusio* in Q^3 17:26–27, 30. For this, the terms οὕτως [so it will be], ἡμέρα [the day], and ὁ υἱὸς τοῦ ἀνθρώπου [the Son of Man] are used in 17:26 and 17:30. With this literary pattern, the third redactor emphasized the phenomena written in the middle of them: eating and drinking, marrying and being given in marriage (17:27). Although each redactor used a different term for "eating," the theme of eating and drinking is mentioned in Q^2 12:29; Q^3 7:33–34 and 17:27, and a more negative perspective is reflected in the texts according to this order. In addition, the image of marriage appears for the first time in the third redaction (17:27). It is, however, noteworthy that the wedding ceremony was described as a place no other than the joyful feast. The third redactor described what the people will do on the day of the coming of the Son of Man from a negative perspective as simply enjoying their daily life. This is the reason that the Son of Man will come to pass judgment upon the world.

The third redactor adopted the social situation at the time of Noah as the background for the description about the day of the coming of the Son of Man. Noah is used for the contrast between salvation and destruction: while entering the ark represents the salvation of God, the flood is used as the means of destruction of those who enjoyed daily life as if it were a wedding feast. It is noteworthy that Noah is used for the description about eschatological judgment for the first time. While Jonah and Solomon appeared in the second redaction (Q^2 11:30; 12:27), Noah as well as the Queen of the South, Solomon, the Ninevites, and Jonah were used for the description about the eschatological judgment in the third redaction (Q^3 11:31–32; 17:27). The further the redaction of Q progressed, the less known figures were used for the description about eschatological judgment. The third redactor attempted to identify the disciples of Jesus with the less known servants of God. It seems to show that the disciples of Jesus segregated themselves from the major Jewish tradition at the time of the writing of the third redaction. In this respect, Jesus the Son of Man is described as the eschatological judge rather than the savior.[35]

---

35. Jacobson, *First Gospel*, 237.

The Reversed Fate (Q 17:33)

The instruction about the reversal of one's fate is mentioned in Q 17:33 (Luke 17:33; Matt 10:39). However, this text does not show a natural flow with its surrounding texts. Rather, this text follows Q^4 14:26–27 as reflected in the Matthean version (Matt 10:37–39). In other words, Matt 10:26–27, 28–33, 18–19, 37–39 represent Q 12:2–3, 4–7, 11–12; 14:26–27; 17:33. The fact that 14:26–27 and 17:33 deal with the matter of death implies that they originated in the fourth redaction. In addition, they follow Q^4 16:13 by the linking word "hate" in the fourth redaction. Then, it seems that Q^4 14:26–27 and 17:33 were placed after Q^2 17:3–4 by the fourth redactor, so that they might play the role of conclusion to the mission of the disciples of Jesus described in the main texts of the second redaction.

Two Different Groups (Q 17:34–35)

The contrast between the taken and the left is drawn in Q 17:34–35 (Luke 17:34–35; Matt 24:40–41). This text follows Q^3 17:26–27, 30 by the theme of eschatological phenomena. This text shows what will happen at the end of the world. The sharp contrast between two groups carries the typical characteristic of the third redaction. Then, a male and female pair calls our attention to previous ones (11:31–32; 13:18–21). In addition, the authority to select reminds readers of 10:22. In this respect, 17:34–35 seems to originate from the third redaction.

The third redactor emphasized eschatological distinction. Two men will be in a field; while one will be taken, the other will be left. In addition, it is said that two women will be grinding grain; while one will be chosen, the other will be abandoned. A sharp contrast is drawn between those taken and left. While the former represents those who will be saved by the Son of Man, the latter are those who will not be saved. This kind of contrast has been continually used in the third redaction (Q^3 6:43–44, 48–49; 7:31–34; 12:42–46, etc.). In addition, the authority to choose or abandon recalls the announcement of Jesus the Son of God that he had the right to reveal God to whom he wanted (10:22). The similarities listed above inform readers of the fact that 17:34–35 belonged to the third redaction with the texts listed above.

The third redactor introduced a male-female pair in connection with the eschatological judgment. The male-female pair was already used in Q^3 11:31–32 and 13:18–21. It seems that the third redactor "has a striking habit of pairing male and female examples."[36] This shows that the third redactor was concerned with the equality of male and female from a sociological perspective. It seems to reflect that female disciples will share the same benefit from God as male disciples. Without doubt, this shows the social aspect of the disciples of Jesus at the time of the writing of the third redaction in that the number of female disciples increased.

The third redactor seems to describe the role of the Son of Man taking the chosen and leaving the abandoned against the backdrop of Dan 7:13–14 and Gen 5:24. It is supported by the fact that the apocalyptic title "Son of Man" came from the "one like a son of man" (Dan 7:13) and that the idea of taking the chosen seems to be from the description that Enoch was taken by God after walking with him (Gen 5:24). However, it has not been known where he was taken to. In this manner, the third redactor did not mention the eschatological destination of the disciples of Jesus who will be taken by the Son of Man. Nevertheless, the kingdom of God is supposed to be the destination, since it was described as the eschatological place in the previous texts.

Later Addition

Q then introduces some texts added to the third redactor in Q 17:37; 19:12–26; 22:30. It seems that they were irrelevant to each other. However, they are also connected to their previous texts by the themes described in the fourth redaction.

A metaphoric saying is found in Q 17:37b (Luke 17:37b; Matt 24:28). The image of eagle appears for the first time in connection with corpse. The theme of death has been frequently used in the text of the fourth redaction. For instance, there are Q^4 4:9–12; 9:59–60a; 10:3; 11:47–51 and 12:4–5. These texts show that the fourth redactor introduced the theme of death and developed it further. In this respect, 17:37b seems to originate from the fourth redaction with the texts listed earlier.

The parable of the accounting is described in Q 19:12–26 (Luke 19:12–26; Matt 25:14–29). This parable is placed here because this also shows the theme of eschatological judgment. However, this is a well-developed pericope composed of three sets of dialogue between the master and his servants. This reminds readers of the story about the temptation of Jesus because it is also composed of three sets of dialogue between Jesus and the devil (Q^4 4:1–13). In addition, the authority to reign over others appears in both texts (4:5–8; 19:17, 19). Moreover, the parable of the banquet also

36. Batten, "More Queries," 47.

revealed the well-developed pericope in 14:16–24. In this respect, the parable of the accounting seems to belong to the fourth redaction with the story about the temptation and the parable of the banquet.

Finally, the promise of eschatological reward is mentioned in Q 22:30 (Luke 22:30; Matt 19:28).[37] The disciples of Jesus are promised to be seated on the twelve thrones in order to reign over the twelve tribes. The theme of twelve tribes started in Q^4 3:8bc where the descendants of Abraham were mentioned for the first time. Then, the temptation story described Jesus as the representative of the Israelites composed of twelve tribes (4:1–13). In addition, Q lists the names of the twelve apostles who represent the new Israel (6:12–16). In this way, the fourth redactor developed the theme of the new twelve tribes of Israel. In consequence, 22:30 seems to originate in the fourth redaction with the texts listed above.

---

37. Cf. Bammel, "Ende," 39–50.

4

Conclusion

The third section of Q was also expanded by the third redactor. He interpolated many texts into the main texts of the first and second redactions; and then attached the main texts at the end of the second redaction. By doing so, Jesus was described as the Son of God and the Son of Man. In this way, the third redaction theologically depicts Jesus as the eschatological servant of God.

The third section of Q consists of two redactions. The third redaction includes Q^3 12:39–40, 42–46; 13:18–21, 24–27; 17:23–24, 26–27, 30, 34–35. On the other hand, the fourth redaction carries Q^4 12:49, 51–56, 58–59; 13:28–30, 34–35; 14:11, 16–24, 34–35; 15:4–7; 17:1–2, 37b; 19:12–26; 22:30. The texts of the third redaction in the third section of Q show a well-arranged structure—*inclusio*—regarding the preparation of the Son of Man, the kingdom of God, and the coming of the Son of Man. In this respect, the main texts of the third redaction were collected and arranged according to the theological purpose of the third redactor.

After the third redaction was completed, the texts that belong to the third redaction are as follows: (1) The texts interpolated into the first redaction are Q^3 3:16–17, 21–22; 6:22–23b, 28, 39–49; 7:1–10, 18–27, 31–34; (2) the texts interpolated into the second redaction are 10:2, 13–16, 21–24; 11:21–23, 31–32, 33–35, 39–46, 52; 12:2–3, 8–9, 33–34; (3) the main texts of the third redaction are 12:39–40, 42–46; 13:18–21, 24–27; 17:23–24, 26–27, 30, 34–35. As the list above shows, an abundant amount of texts were added to the main texts of the first and the second redactions by the third redactor. For a theological description of Jesus, the third redactor needed an abundance of sources; in fact, he used them for the instruction that he had wanted to deliver.

It is then necessary to see how Q went through a process of redaction up to the third redaction. When the third redaction was completed, Q was likely as follows:

I. John the Baptist and Jesus

  A. John

      Q^1 3:2–4 (Luke 3:2–4 / Matt 3:1–3, 5–6)

      Q^1 3:7–8a (Luke 3:7–8a / Matt 3:7–9a)

      Q^1 3:9 (Luke 3:9 / Matt 3:10)

      Q^3 3:16–17 (Luke 3:16–17 / Matt 3:11–12)

      Q^3 3:21–22 (Luke 3:21–22 / Matt 3:16–17)

  B. Jesus

    1. The Sermon

        Q^1 6:20b (Luke 6:20b / Matt 5:2b–3)

        Q^2 6:21 (Luke 6:21 / Matt 5:4, 6)

        Q^3 6:22–23b (Luke 6:22–23b / Matt 5:11–12b)

        Q^1 6:27 (Luke 6:27 / Matt 5:44a)

        Q^3 6:28 (Luke 6:28 / Matt 5:44b)

        Q^1 6:29–38 (Luke 6:29–38 / Matt 5:39–40, 42, 45–48; 7:1–2, 12)

        Q^3 6:39–42 (Luke 6:39–42 / Matt 15:14; 10:24–25; 7:3–5)

        Q^3 6:43–45 (Luke 6:43–45 / Matt 7:16, 18; 12:33–35)

        Q^3 6:46–49 (Luke 6:46–49 / Matt 7:21, 24–27)

    2. The Activity

        Q^3 7:1–10 (Luke 7:1–10 / Matt 8:5–10, 13)

  C. Jesus and John

      Q^3 7:18–27 (Luke 7:18–27 / Matt 11:2–10)

      Q^1 7:29–30 (Luke 7:29–30 / Matt 21:31–32)

      Q^3 7:31–34 (Luke 7:31–34 / Matt 11:16–19a)

II. Jesus' Commission of His Disciples and Their Missions

  A. The Followers of Jesus

      Q^2 9:57–58 (Luke 9:57–58 / Matt 8:19–20)

B. The Manual for Ministry

    Q^3 10:2 (Luke 10:2 / Matt 9:37–38)

    Q^2 10:4–12 (Luke 10:4–12 / Matt 10:7–15 (11:24))

    Q^3 10:13–16 (Luke 10:13–16 / Matt 11:21–23; 10:40)

    Q^3 10:21–24 (Luke 10:21–24 / Matt 11:25–27; 13:16–17)

C. The Lord's Prayer and Its Application

  1. The Lord's Prayer

    Q^2 11:2–4 (Luke 11:2–4 / Matt 6:9–13)

  2. Confidence in Prayer

    Q^2 11:9–10 (Luke 11:9–10 / Matt 7:7–8)

  3. Confidence in the Father: The Vocative of God

    Q^2 11:11–13 (Luke 11:11–13 / Matt 7:9–11)

  4. The Kingdom of God: The Second Petition

    Q^2 11:14–15, 17–20 (Luke 11:14–15, 17–20 / Matt 12:22–28)

    Q^3 11:21–23 (Luke 11:21–23 / Matt 12:29–30)

  5. The Temptation: The Fifth Petition

    Q^2 11:16, 29–30 (Luke 11:16, 29–30 / Matt 12:38–40)

    Q^3 11:31–32 (Luke 11:31–32 / Matt 12:41–42)

    Q^3 11:33–35 (Luke 11:33–35 / Matt 5:15; 6:22–23)

    Q^3 11:39–46 (Luke 11:39–46 / Matt 23:4, 6–7, 23, 25–28)

    Q^3 11:52 (Luke 11:52 / Matt 23:13)

    Q^3 12:2–3 (Luke 12:2–3 / Matt 10:26–27)

  6. The Fear of God: The First Petition

    Q^2 12:6–7 (Luke 12:6–7 / Matt 10:29–31)

    Q^3 12:8–9 (Luke 12:8–9 / Matt 10:32–33)

  7. Daily Bread: The Third Petition

    Q^2 12:22–31 (Luke 12:22–31 / Matt 6:25–33)

    Q^3 12:33–34 (Luke 12:33–34 / Matt 6:19–21)

  8. Forgiveness: The Forth Petition

    Q^2 17:3–4 (Luke 17:3–4 / Matt 18:15, 21–22)

III. The Coming of the Son of Man and the Kingdom of God

CONCLUSION

A. Preparation for the Son of Man

Q^3 12:39–40 (Luke 12:39–40 / Matt 24:43–44)

Q^3 12:42–46 (Luke 12:42–46 / Matt 24:45–51)

B. The Kingdom of God

Q^3 13:18–21 (Luke 13:18–21 / Matt 13:31–33)

Q^3 13:24–27 (Luke 13:24–27 / Matt 7:13–14, 22–23; 25:10–12)

C. The Coming of the Son of Man

Q^3 17:23–24 (Luke 17:23–24 / Matt 24:26–27)

Q^3 17:26–27, 30 (Luke 17:26–27, 30 / Matt 24:37–39)

Q^3 17:34–35 (Luke 17:34–35 / Matt 24:40–41)

The texts listed above show the formation of Q when the third redaction was completed. It shows that Q has been developed well according to the theological themes and the literary patterns in each redaction.

The third redactor added an abundance of sources to the main texts of the first and second redactions. However, the redactor did not change the previous texts according to the Jewish tradition of redaction. By doing so, the redactors make readers recognize the differences among the three layers of redaction and trace how the third redaction developed. The third redactor made a tremendous effort to describe the status and role of Jesus as the Son of God and the Son of Man. In other words, the third redactor imposed a lot of theological aspects to Jesus. As a result, Jesus was believed to be the eschatological and transcendental being at last and respected as the leader of his disciples. In this respect, the third redaction does not seem to contain the words and actions of the historical Jesus and John. Rather, they were theologically interpreted by the third redactor in order to meet and overcome the contemporary circumstances.

The third redactor projected the socio-religious situation to the sayings and activities of Jesus and John. It seems that the disciples of Jesus faced serious opposition from the people of Galilee. Thus, the third redactor planted a lot of instruction to overcome their insult and hatred. In response, the third redactor pronounced woe to the opponents. The disciples of Jesus advanced to urban areas such as Capernaum, Chorazin, and Bethsaida. It seems that the third redaction was written by a Pharisaic scribe in the region of Galilee.[1]

---

1. Cf. Arnal, *Jesus*, 159–64.

PART 4

The Fourth Redaction

Q underwent a fourth redaction. Its texts were already distinguished from those of the previous three redactions. The fourth redactor should have been credited with a significant achievement in the description of Jesus' biography. Taking after the Israelites who wandered in the wilderness for forty years, the fourth redactor completed the typological description about the life of Jesus for the first time. Although it does not have the passion narrative, it is sufficient enough to deliver the redactor's own theology defining Jesus as the one who represented the people of God. In this respect, the fourth redactor tried to say that the disciples of Jesus are the true descendants of Abraham. Focusing on observation of the law, Q reveals its Jewish characteristic. From a socio-historical perspective, the fourth redaction reflects resistance against the Roman emperor Gaius Caligula who attempted to erect his statue in the Jerusalem temple. As a result, the disciples were encouraged to run the risk of death in spite of persecution and martyrdom. It seems that the disciples of Jesus advanced to the center of Israel—that is, Jerusalem—at the time of the writing of the fourth redaction. The texts of the fourth redaction will be divided into three parts for examination: the texts interpolated into the main texts of the first redaction, those added to the main texts of the second redaction, and those found in the main texts of the third redaction.

1

The Texts Added to the First Redaction

The first section of Q was expanded by the fourth redaction once again. The fourth redactor interpolated his sources into the main texts of the first redaction to which the second and third redactors already added some texts for their own theological purposes. By interpolating the texts, the fourth redactor laid a stepping stone to the typological description of Jesus in comparison to the Israelites.

A. THE DESCENDANTS OF ABRAHAM (Q 3:8BC)

The fourth redactor interpolated Q^4 3:8bc in between Q^1 3:7–8a and 3:9. This text deals with the descendants of Abraham in the middle of John's preaching about bearing the fruit worthy of repentance. In this way, the fourth redactor made a significant shift with this text from the matter of repentance to that of identity.

The fourth redactor dealt with the identity of the disciples of Jesus as the descendants of Abraham. According to the fourth redactor, Jesus told people that they should not regard Abraham as their forefather from a perspective of blood relationship. In other words, they should not consider themselves as his descendants. According to the Jewish tradition, "descendants of Abraham" is a technical term for the people of God—namely, the Israelites. Then, this means that the fourth redactor raised a question about the identity of the people of God with this saying. This implies that the disciples of Jesus were in serious controversy with their opponents about identity: who are the real people of God? It is noteworthy that the term

"Israelites" was already used for the description of the faithless Jews in contrast with the Gentile centurion in the third redaction (Q^3 7:9). It is clear that the disciples of Jesus faced a certain situation that caused them to deal with the matter of identity at the time of the writing of the fourth redaction.

The fourth redactor used the phrase λέγω γὰρ ὑμῖν [for I tell you] as an introductory formula. This reminds readers of the phrase λέγω ὑμῖν [I tell you] used in Q^1 6:27; Q^2 10:12; 11:9; 12:22; and Q^3 7:9, 26. It is, however, noteworthy that this formula was applied to Jesus in the texts listed above, whereas it is adopted for the sayings of John for the first time in Q^4 3:8bc. As shown before, this phrase usually refers to the sayings of God through the prophets in the Bible—namely, יאמר יהוה [for YHWH says] (Isa 1:11, 18; 3:16; Jer 1:11; 2:5; 44:11; Ezek 3:16; 7:1; etc.). If this interpretation is right, the fourth redactor kept assigning the prophetic feature to John. As we have seen, the third redactor already described John as the one more than a prophet (Q^3 7:26); in addition, Jesus was identified as the one more than Jonah the prophet (11:32). Thus, the fourth redactor was able to apply the prophetic feature to John with the introductory formula mentioned above.

The fourth redactor described that Jesus had mentioned an extraordinary way of being descendants of Abraham. In other words, God could make the descendants of Abraham out of stones. The term λίθος [stone] was once used for the description of paternal affection in the second redaction when it was said that even an evil father would not give a stone to a son who had asked for bread (Q^2 11:12; cf. Matt 7:9). It is impossible for a stone to turn into bread if not by a miracle of God. Having inherited the previous description about the stone, the fourth redactor heightened the divine power that could make impossible things possible and used it for the description about the relationship between the forefathers and the descendants. It was written in order to show the eschatological reversal that could happen regarding the identity of the people of God.[1] At this point, it is to be noted that the interest in the Gentiles has also reduced when the fourth redactor treated the matter of making the descendants of Abraham out of stones rather than making the Gentiles the people of God. In other words, this reflects that the occasion for writing was that the identity of the disciples of Jesus became the top priority at the stage of the fourth redaction.

The matter of identity was an important issue for the disciples of Jesus. It was out of dispute at the stage of the second redaction because they began their ministry to the neighbors in the region of the Jordan. On the other hand, the third redaction reflects the opposition of the neighboring people

---

1. The eschatological reversal of one's fate was mentioned in Q^2 6:21. However, it is important to observe that the eschatological reversal of two different parties appear in Q^4 3:8bc.

because they followed the teaching of Jesus the Son of Man (Q³ 6:22b–23; 7:33–34, etc.). Opposition probably led them to think about the identity of the people of God in the region of Galilee. Finally, the fourth redactor concluded that the blood relationship did not guarantee the status of the people of God. It seems that the fourth redactor began to articulate that the disciples of Jesus were the only people of God, not by blood relationship but by the bearing of fruit worthy of repentance based on the observation of the instruction of Jesus. It seems that the fourth redactor provided the disciples of Jesus with their own theological basis regarding their identity.

The fourth redactor reduced the interest in miracles. It is said that God can make the descendants of Abraham out of stones. While the second redactor had described the expulsion of the demon from the mute by the finger of God (Q² 11:19–20), the third redactor mentioned the healing miracle two times (Q³ 7:1–10, 22). On the other hand, the fourth redactor mentioned the possibility that the stones could turn into the descendants of Abraham. However, everybody knows that it is impossible. As the redaction of Q progressed, it seems that the difficulty of performing miracles was getting increased. This means that the disciples of Jesus diminished their interest in the divine miracle because it did not occur as many times as they wished. Or it is possible that the surrounding situation made it difficult to expect divine miracles.

B. THE TEMPTATION OF JESUS (Q 4:1–13)

The temptation of Jesus is described in Q⁴ 4:1–13 (Luke 4:1–13; Matt 4:1–11). This text follows Q⁴ 3:8bc in the fourth redaction by the theme of "people of God." In addition, the temptation story is placed after his baptism by the linking word "Spirit" and the title "Son of God" (Q³ 3:21–22). As a result, the matter of identity, John's introduction of Jesus, the baptism by the Spirit, and the temptation of Jesus by the devil constitute the beginning part of his biography (Q⁴ 3:8bc; Q³ 3:16–17, 21–22; Q⁴ 4:1–13). Generally, critical scholars insist that the story of temptation was written at the final stage of redaction.[2]

The fourth redactor described Jesus being led to the wilderness by the Spirit (Q⁴ 4:1). The term "Spirit" is used here because it already appeared in the third redaction (Q³ 3:16–17, 21–22). There is, however, a difference

---

2. Kloppenborg, *Formation*, 247–48; and Jacobson, *First Gospel*, 90–91, 94. He introduces the opinion of Petr Pokorný who regarded the temptation story as "a summary created by its learned collector" and then lists the possible allusions. Cf. Pokorný, "Temptation," 126.

in that the fourth redactor personified the Spirit, while the third redactor did not. Although the third redactor introduced the concept of the Spirit at the beginning part, he did not develop it further in the rest of the third redaction. On the other hand, the fourth redactor significantly developed the concept of the Spirit by personifying it. Then, it can be said that the Spirit was defined as the one superior to Jesus at the stage of the fourth redaction because the Spirit led Jesus to the wilderness. The wilderness is described as the place where the Spirit led Jesus. It is important to observe how the term "wilderness" has been used in Q. The first redactor described it as the place where John was working (Q^1 3:2, 4). As shown before, the wilderness was used in allusion to the second exodus—that is, the liberation from the Babylonian exile (Isa 40:3). Then, the third redactor once again recognized it as his working place (Q^3 7:24). The fact that John was described as the one more than a prophet there indicates that the third redactor received the previous perspective on John and used it again. Finally, the fourth redactor depicted the wilderness as the place where Jesus had been led by the Spirit. This is the first text that connects Jesus with the wilderness in Q. It is noteworthy that Jesus took over the place where John had been active for his ministry. However, it has not been known yet where the wilderness was. It seems that the wilderness was adopted not simply for its barrenness. Rather, it is to be noted that the wilderness was already adopted for a theological purpose by the first and third redactors.

The fourth redactor described that Jesus had been led to the devil in order to be tempted (Q^4 4:2).[3] The theme of temptation came to the fore at the stage of the fourth redaction. It is, however, noteworthy that the second redactor already mentioned it in the fifth petition of the Lord's Prayer: "lead us not into temptation" (Q^2 11:4). Then, it was written that some people asked Jesus for a sign in order to tempt him (11:16). Jesus who taught his disciples not to be led into temptation was tempted by the crowds in the second redaction. On the other hand, no text about the temptation is found in the third redaction. Later, having succeeded the previous tradition, the fourth redactor described that Jesus had been led to the devil by the Spirit in order to be tempted. A significant change is found regarding the tempted person; in other words, Jesus who taught his disciples not to be led into temptation in the second redaction becomes the one being tempted by the devil in the fourth redaction. Having put the temptation story in Q^4 4:1–13, the fourth redactor tried to explain how one can be led into temptation

---

3. The Lucan and Matthean versions take different forms of the word "tempt." While the Lucan (Luke 4:2)version takes the form of the participle, indicating the duration of temptation, the (Matt 4:1) Matthean version takes the form of the infinitive, indicating the purpose.

more in detail. On the other hand, when Q was completed, the temptation story of Jesus became the model for the disciples regarding how to overcome temptation because he had already overcome it in the wilderness (Q^4 4:1–13; Q^2 11:4).

It is important to observe that the temptation of Jesus by the devil was initiated by the Spirit. It seems that there was a reason for writing about the more intimate relationship with the Spirit in connection with the temptation. To my judgment, from a redaction critical perspective, it is to be remembered that although Jesus was tempted by the crowds to show a sign, he only referred to the sign of Jonah in the second redaction (Q^2 11:16, 29–30). It is, however, to be noted that he did not respond to it except mentioning the sign of Jonah whose meaning was not clear in that context. It was probably the proclamation of Jonah to Nineveh. On the other hand, as shown before, the third redactor wished to say of the Spirit descending from heaven upon Jesus as the sign ahead of Q^2 11:16, 29-30 because its descent at the time of baptism was a supernatural event and the dove refers to Jonah [יונה] in Hebrew (Q^3 3:21–22). Having inherited these texts, the fourth redactor created the story of temptation in response to the demand of the crowds for a sign in connection with the Spirit. When the fourth redaction was completed, the victory over the temptation of the devil could be the answer of Jesus to the crowds who tempted him to show a sign, because Q^2 11:16, 29–30 comes later than Q^2 4:1–13 according to the final form of Q.

The devil is mentioned for the first time in the fourth redaction. It is to be observed how each redactor revealed interest in the evil being. While no evil being appears in the first redaction, the second redactor introduced the demon, Beelzebul, and Satan (Q^2 11:14–15, 17–20). Then, the demon is simply mentioned again in the third redaction (Q^3 7:33). Later, the fourth redactor described the active role of the devil in the temptation story (Q^4 4:2). This shows that as Q went through a process of redaction, interest in evil became greater by each redactor. The devil was the opponents that Jesus faced directly according to the fourth redactor. Although Jesus was acquainted with the evil being, the fourth redactor did not explain the identity of the devil at all. Nevertheless, it is definite that the devil represented the most powerful being among the evil ones.

The fourth redactor wrote about the duration of temptation. It is said that Jesus was tempted for forty days. The number "forty" appears for the first time in Q. However, it reminds readers of the forty years the Israelites were tempted by God. If the typological approach to the Israelites is possible on the basis of the number "forty" in connection with the term "wilderness," it can be said that the fourth redactor tried to describe Jesus with a background of the Israelites who wandered for forty years in the wilderness of Sinai (Exod 16:35; Num 14:33–34; 32:13; Deut 2:7; 8:2, 4; 29:5; Josh 5:6, etc.). The wilderness is to be approached from a typological perspective in that the fourth redactor attempted to connect Jesus with the Israelites in the wilderness. In other words, Jesus is introduced as the one who represents the Israelites—namely, the people of God. It seems that the number "forty" in connection with the term "wilderness" is the stepping stone to understanding Jesus as the one who represented the descendants of Abraham (Q^4 3:8bc).

The fourth redactor described Jesus being hungry for forty days in the wilderness. The term ἐπείνασεν [became hungry] reminds readers of πεινῶντες [the hungry] used in Q^2 6:21a. This makes readers expect that Jesus would be blessed on account of his hunger. His hunger recalls the instruction that the disciples should not worry about what to eat (12:22–31). This makes readers think about whether Jesus would not worry about his satisfaction with food provided by God. In addition, from a typological perspective, Jesus' hunger for forty days in the wilderness recalls the historical description that the Israelites were provided with manna for forty years in the Sinai wilderness when they were hungry. This makes readers think about the divine provision of food for the hungry Jesus in the wilderness. The information listed above points to the possibility that Jesus would be provided with food by God.

The first temptation of Jesus is depicted in Q^4 4:3–4. According to the fourth redactor, the devil called Jesus "a son of God, which acknowledged Jesus' filial relationship with God."[4] The devil was supposed to hear the heavenly voice addressed to Jesus saying "my [God's] Son" at his baptism because he was a transcendental being (Q^3 3:21–22). As shown before, the third redactor kept attributing the filial relationship to Jesus as reflected in his thanksgiving to God (10:21–22). It is, however, noteworthy that Jesus was defined as the Son of God from a weak typological perspective in the third redaction. The title simply referred to his filial relationship with God the Father in the third redaction only with slight reference to the Israelites. Having inherited this tradition, the fourth redactor applied the title "Son of God" to Jesus, so that he might represent the Israelites. This reflects that the occasion for writing was that the disciples of Jesus were in a serious dispute with their opponents who were strong enough to be compared to the devil regarding the matter of their identity as the descendants of Abraham—that is, the people of God.

---

4. The conditional clause refers to a real situation in Matt 4:3, 6. This is equivalent to "since," rather than the hypothetical "if." Cf. Kelly, "Exposition," 58. From the fact that Matt 4:3, 6 reflects the wording of Q, the same interpretation can be applied here.

The fourth redactor described the first temptation (Q^4 4:3). The devil asked Jesus to turn the stones into loaves of bread. The term "stones" plays the role of connecting the temptation story with 3:8bc in the fourth redaction. This supports the possibility that these two texts should be interrelated for their interpretation. As shown before, the stone and the bread were used for the paternal affection in the second redaction (Q^2 11:2–3, 11; cf. Matt 7:9). Having succeeded these texts, the fourth redactor applied them to the temptation of the devil, whether God the Father provides him with the loaves of bread made from stones. In this way, the filial relationship of Jesus with God the Father was tested by the devil. This temptation seems to reflect the need to write about the identity of the disciples of Jesus as the people of God at the time of the writing of the fourth redaction.

The first answer of Jesus to the devil is reported in Q^4 4:4. According to the fourth redactor, Jesus refused the request of the devil by quoting Deut 8:3. As the stones cannot be turned into the descendants of Abraham, they cannot actually become loaves of bread. While the second redactor described the expulsion of the demon from the mute in the Beelzebul story (Q^2 11:14–15, 17–20), the third redactor mentioned the healing of the servant of the centurion (Q^3 7:1–10) and listed the sort of miracles that Jesus performed (7:22). On the contrary, the fourth redactor described that Jesus had refused to perform miracles (Q^4 4:3–4) although making the stones into loaves of bread is much easier than creating descendants of Abraham out of the stones (3:8bc). His refusal of the devil's request to perform a divine miracle reveals the intention to keep a distance from miracles at the time of the writing of the fourth redaction.[5] It seems that the disciples of Jesus were reluctant to show miracles because they would not happen as they had expected.

It is noteworthy that the fourth redactor used the introductory formula γέγραπται [as it is written] for the quotation. As shown before, this was already used in order to cite a verse from the Bible and define the role of John in the third redaction (Q^3 7:27). Having inherited the tradition, the fourth redactor applied it to the answer of Jesus. It is, however, to be noted that there is a difference between Q^3 7:27 and Q^4 4:4 regarding the role of scriptural texts quoted with the introductory formula. While the third redactor used it for the description of John, the fourth redactor used it for the answer of Jesus. The ability to interpret the role of John and Jesus under the light of the Bible shows the Pharisaic aspect of the third and fourth redactors. At any rate, according to the fourth redactor, Jesus answered to live according to the words of God, not by the loaves of bread. This recalls the

---

5. Jacobson, *First Gospel*, 89–90.

event of manna written in Exod 16:1-12 and Deut 8:3. In this way, Jesus is contrasted with the Israelites who were not satisfied with manna provided by God every day.

The fourth redactor seems to emphasize observing the words of God. According to him or her, Jesus responded to the devil's request by emphasizing the observance of the words of God rather than making loaves of bread out of stones although he was starving to death. Then, the fourth redactor did not seem to believe that the hungry would be satisfied with the food as written in the second beatitude (Q^2 6:21). This means that the emphasis changed from the divine provision of food to the observance of the words of God. In this way, the observance of the divine words comes to the fore in the fourth redaction. As shown before, while the theme of "observance of the words" appears in connection with the Lord Jesus in the third redaction (Q^3 6:46-47; 7:6), the fourth redactor applied it to God through the answer of Jesus. This means that while the third redactor was eager to produce the words of Jesus the Lord, the fourth redactor emphasized the observance of the words of God by describing that Jesus observed them. This seems to reflect the changed circumstances that the disciples of Jesus faced during their ministry. They tried to establish their own theology based on the words of Jesus during the conflict with the opponents at the time of the writing of the third redaction. However, later, they faced a certain situation that caused them to focus on the words of God in order to show their faith in him at the stage of the fourth redaction.

Then, the second temptation is depicted in Q^4 4:9-12. It is, however, noteworthy that the temptation occurred at the pinnacle of the temple. The temple is mentioned for the first time. First of all, it is provocative to describe that the temple was used as a place for the temptation of Jesus by the devil. This means that something happened that caused them not to consider the temple as the holiest place anymore. This reflects that the occasion for writing was that the temple was seriously threatened by a powerful one. The second temptation provides glimpses of the disciples of Jesus who advanced to Jerusalem from the region of Galilee at the time of the writing of the fourth redaction. While the third redactor revealed that they were active in the Galilean cities such as Capernaum, Chorazin, and Bethsaida (Q^3 7:1; 10:13-15), the fourth redactor seems to show that they advanced to Jerusalem where the temple was (Q^4 4:9-12). It is natural that the more active and successful their ministry was in the region of Galilee, the more zealous they were to advance to Jerusalem, which was the center of Jewish society.[6] This informs readers that Jerusalem was the place of the writing of the fourth redaction.

The content of the second temptation is described in Q^4 4:9–11. The devil demanded Jesus to throw himself from the pinnacle of the temple, so that God might send angels to lift him up before his feet reached the ground. First, this text follows 4:3–4 by the linking word "stone," the title "Son of God," and the quotation from the Bible. The devil quoted a verse from the Bible in response to the first answer of Jesus which emphasized living according to the words of God. In this respect, the second temptation was a way of tightening the screws on the beleaguered Jesus. It is, however, noteworthy that the devil cited a verse from the Bible for his own intention. Second, it was a temptation which asked him for total dependence upon God. It reminds readers of the confidence in God written as the application of the third petition of the Lord's Prayer in the second redaction (Q^2 11:3; 12:22–31).[7] The disciples of Jesus were taught to rely upon God's care. Having inherited the tradition, the fourth redactor tried to instruct them to rely completely upon God even to death. Third, the second temptation is related to the matter of salvation from death. While the second redactor mentioned the fate of birds in the sky (Q^2 12:6) and the third redactor used the term dirge in a metaphor (Q^3 7:32), the fourth redactor referred to the theme of the death of human beings for the first time (Q^4 4:9–12). Whereas the second redactor depicted the challenge of the crowds (Q^2 11:14–15, 17–20) and the third redactor showed their opposition (Q^3 6:22; 7:33–34; 17:26–27), the fourth redactor revealed the circumstance of martyrdom (Q^4 4:9–12). This implies that the disciples of Jesus were facing the situation of running the risk of death in the Jerusalem temple. Fourth, it is noteworthy that the devil mentioned the angels. They seem to be the transcendental beings sent by God. As shown before, the messenger(s) or angel(s) of God is mentioned in the third redaction (Q^3 7:27; 12:8–9). While they were probably human messenger(s) of God in the third redaction, they appeared as the transcendental angels in the fourth redaction. In this manner, the fourth redactor added one more transcendental being to the devil in the temptation story.

---

6. It seems that the disciples of Jesus advanced to Jerusalem before 35 CE. It can be known from the description that Paul had persecuted them in the region of Judea before he received the revelation from God about his son around 35 CE, which was fourteen years prior to the apostolic meeting held at Jerusalem around 49–50 CE (Gal 1:13—2:10; 1 Thess 2:14). Ra, *Origin*, 18–19.

7. Cf. Jacobson, *First Gospel*, 159. After looking at the terminological and thematic relationship, he concludes that "the Q temptation account thus counters tendencies which I have contended are to be found in Q 11:9–13." Rather, I would argue that the temptation story reflects the elements in Q 11:9–13.

This means that the further the redaction of Q progressed, the more the redactor paid attention to the transcendental being.

The second answer of Jesus is mentioned in Q^4 4:12. For this, he quoted Deut 6:16, which says that no one must put the Lord God to temptation. In this way, the request of the devil was refused by Jesus. First, the second answer recalls the event that happened at Massah (Exod 17:1–7). Once again, the fourth redactor interpreted the temptation of Jesus against the backdrop of the Israelites who were tested in the wilderness on their way to the land of Canaan. This implies that the disciples of Jesus faced a serious situation regarding the temptation of God at the temple. Second, the second answer reflects the wisdom tradition in that the tempted Jesus is similar to the suffering of the righteous servant of God written in Wis 2:17–20.[8] This is shown in the description that the righteous son of God was tempted regarding whether his words were true and whether God would deliver him from the hands of his adversaries. In addition, he was tempted to a shameful death. The righteous one will receive the wisdom as well as the holy and disciplined spirit (Wis 1:4–6). In the description that Jesus was tempted as a Son of God by the devil, there is a similarity between the righteous servant and Jesus. In this respect, the wisdom tradition is the mirror for the second temptation of God. While the second redactor introduced the name "Solomon" (Q^2 12:27), the third redactor used the phrase "wisdom [σοφία] of Solomon" (Q^3 11:31) and the term "wise" [σοφός] (10:21). On the other hand, the fourth redactor described the temptation of Jesus against the background of the wisdom tradition (Q^4 4:12).

The fourth redactor described the environment of the third temptation in Q^4 4:5. The term "mountain" appears for the first time. The reason that this term was adopted here is because it recalls Moses who climbed up the mountain Nebo at the end of his life in the wilderness (Deut 34:1). In this way, the third temptation can be also connected with the event of the Israelites in the wilderness. The description that the devil showed him all the kingdoms of earth and promised to give them to him is reminiscent of Deut 34:1–4.[9] In this way, the fourth redactor strengthened the connection between the temptation of Jesus and the event of the Israelites from a typological perspective. The third temptation heightens the typological description about the comparison between Jesus and the Israelites.

The fourth redactor mentioned the kingdom of the world with its splendor. It is to be acknowledged that Jesus mentioned "every kingdom" in

---

8. Jacobson, *First Gospel*, 93–94. Wisdom of Solomon was probably written around 100 BCE.

9. Allison, *Intertextual Jesus*, 28.

the second redaction (Q^2 11:17). Then, the second redactor introduced the kingdom of Satan in contrast to the kingdom of God (11:18, 20). Later, the third redactor mentioned the kingdom of God a couple of times without any clue about the kingdom of Satan. Having succeeded this tradition, the fourth redactor could describe the kingdoms of the world which the devil had reigned over. The further the redaction of Q progressed, the bigger the kingdom of the evil being was getting as the redactor described. This seems to reflect that the occasion for writing was a serious challenge regarding the kingdom of God at the time of the writing of the fourth redaction.

The content of the third temptation is written in Q^4 4:6–7. According to the fourth redactor, the devil asked Jesus to prostrate him and then promised to give him all the kingdoms of the world and their splendor. However, prostration to the devil is nothing but idolatry from which the disciples of Jesus were prohibited. This is blasphemy against God according to the Jewish tradition. The temptation of prostration recalls the worship of the golden calf on Mount Sinai by the Israelites (Exod 32:1–14). It is definite that the fourth redactor wrote the third temptation of prostration from a typological perspective. It is, however, noteworthy that the theme of prostration appears for the first time. It seems that the disciples were exposed to an environment of temptation regarding blasphemy at the time of the writing of the fourth redaction.

The third answer of Jesus is described in Q^4 4:8. Quoting Deut 6:13, he told the devil to bow down to the Lord God and serve him only. First, the fourth redactor was able to describe Jesus' refusal of the devil's request because the third redactor already depicted that Jesus was given everything from God (Q^3 10:21–22). Therefore, Jesus was not deceived by the devil in the temptation story of the fourth redaction. Second, the fourth redactor once again showed the typological perspective on the temptation of Jesus. It was described against the background of the Israelites who were asked not to follow other gods of other races in the wilderness (Deut 6:15). Third, the fourth redactor revealed the theocentric perspective three times by mentioning prostration to God only. As shown before, Jesus focused on God in every answer to the devil: living by the word of God, not testing God, and prostrating before God only. Fourth, prostration to God could be related to the fear of God. The second redactor already mentioned it in the first petition of the Lord's Prayer and its application (Q^2 11:2; 12:6–7). Then, the third redactor attached the testimony of the Son of Man in front of God's messengers in order to strengthen the theme of the "fear of God" (Q^3 10:8–9). Having inherited this tradition, the fourth redactor described that Jesus was tempted regarding prostration before God. According to the fourth redactor, Jesus consistently emphasized the fear of God in the third answer to the devil. Fifth, the theme of prostration reflects that the occasion for writing was a challenge against divine authority. This means that as the redaction of Q progressed, the redactor consistently conveyed instruction about reliance upon God.

The fourth redactor depicted the departure of the devil from Jesus (Q^4 4:13). The devil left Jesus after he had failed in tempting him. This is a little different from the description of Jesus casting out the demon from the mute in the second redaction (Q^2 11:14). While the second redactor described the compulsory expulsion of the demon from the mute by Jesus, the fourth redactor mentioned the voluntary departure of the devil from Jesus. It is, however, to be noted that the devil was not completely defeated, rather only repulsed.[10] In this respect, the fourth redactor opened the way to the further activity of spiritual beings in the following texts at the final stage of redaction.

The story of the temptation shows a well-developed form of pericope. It is noteworthy that the temptation story is composed of three sets of dialogues between Jesus and the devil with a setting. As the redaction of Q progressed, the number of dialogue sets increased one by one. While the second redactor showed a set of dialogues (Q^2 9:57–58; 11:14–15, 17–20; 11:16, 29–30), the third redactor described two sets of dialogues (Q^3 7:1–10; 13:24–27). On the other hand, having inherited the literary tradition, the fourth redactor created a story of temptation that consisted of three sets of dialogues between Jesus and the devil (Q^4 4:1–13). As the redaction of Q progressed further, the literary form of pericope developed more by the redactor. This implies that the fourth redactor was probably a well-trained scribe from a literary point of view.[11]

The fourth redactor applied the theology of Deuteronomy to the temptation story. This is seen in the three verses quoted from Deuteronomy by Jesus for his answers to the devil. Without doubt, Jesus is depicted as the faithful son of God "in contrast to the faithless generation addressed by Moses in Deuteronomy 6–8."[12] While the faithful observance of the law had been explained for the first time in the third redaction (Q^3 11:39–42), it was represented by the quotations from Deuteronomy in the fourth redaction (Q^4 4:4, 8, 12).[13] This implies that the fourth redactor adopted the theology of Deuteronomy rather than that of Leviticus, which appeared in the third redaction. In addition, it can be said that apocalyptic instruction

---

10. Jacobson, *First Gospel*, 87.
11. Cf. Horsley, "Questions," 202–3.
12. Jacobson, *First Gospel*, 88.
13. Kloppenborg, *Formation*, 258.

was diminished in the fourth redaction.[14] The fourth redactor seemed to be a well-trained scribe with regard to the law because he cited verses from Deuteronomy that focuses on the description of the law.[15] It seems that at the stage of the fourth redaction the disciples of Jesus were active in the Jerusalem area, whereas the people of the Galilean region did not observe the law well.[16]

The fourth redactor imposed the Israelites typology to the temptation story of Jesus in combination with the baptism. Considering that the temptation of Jesus was attached to his baptism (Q^3 3:21–22), these two stories allude to the Israelites who crossed the Red Sea and then faced temptation in the wilderness. "Jesus is here repeating Israel's history in the desert . . . Q 4:1–3 appears to present Jesus as one like Moses."[17] In this manner, the fourth redactor applied the Israelites typology to the baptism and temptation of Jesus. Then, Jesus is described as the representative of the Israelites by the fourth redactor. While the third redactor was supposed to be one of the Pharisees (Q^3 7:22; 11:31–32, 39), the fourth redactor was also a well-trained scribe in that he applied a typological interpretation to Jesus. Then, this typological attempt heightens the status of Jesus in comparison to the Israelites—namely, the descendants of Abraham (Q^3 3:8bc)—in the fourth redaction. In this respect, the fourth redactor adhered to the Jewish tradition with regard to the identity of the people of God.[18] This implies that the further the redaction of Q progressed, the more theologically Q developed.

The story of the temptation of Jesus reflects the historical event that occurred in 40–41 CE. According to Gerd Theissen, the Roman emperor Gaius Caligula attempted to erect his statue in the Jerusalem temple and forced the Jews to prostrate in front of it.[19] This was idolatry to the Jews. Thus, they could not help but resist his attempt. Therefore, Theissen insists that this historical event is especially reflected in the third temptation because the devil represents Gaius Caligula who could give kingdoms to whomever he wanted.[20] On the other hand, Jesus represented the Jews including his

14. Jacobson, *First Gospel*, 88–89, 95.

15. Kloppenborg, *Formation*, 197; and Jacobson, *First Gospel*, 88, 90.

16. Horsley, "Questions," 197.

17. Allison, *Intertextual Jesus*, 26–27. He lists the parallels between Jesus and the Israelites in the temptation more in detail.

18. Jacobson, *First Gospel*, 95.

19. Theissen, *Gospels*, 206–21. As for opposition to this interpretation, see Allison, *Jesus Tradition*, 51. Allison insists on the interpretation of the temptation story against the backdrop of the event in Exodus. However, Theissen believes that the writer of Q reflected his or her historical perspective in the description of Jesus (*Gospels*, 204).

20. According to Pagels, Satan represents the adversary in the Hebrew Bible (Zech

disciples who opposed idolatry according to the instruction of Deut 6:13. Theissen convinces us to accept his argument that there are many points of contact between the two incidents. To my judgment, the third temptation undoubtedly reflects the historical crisis that Gaius Caligula attempted to erect his statue at the temple in Jerusalem.

In addition, I would argue that the first and second temptations also reflect the historical event caused by Gaius Caligula. First of all, the forty days could be related to the historical event of the Jews resisting the attempt to erect the statue for forty days in Jerusalem (*Jewish Antiquities*, 18:272).[21] This is accordant with the description that Jesus was tempted after forty days had passed (Q^4 4:2). As a result, the Jews missed the appropriate time to sow the seeds. This could be reflected in the first temptation which was about the loaves of bread—that is, the food (4:3). Second, the Jews asserted that they would not violate the law during their resistance (*Ant.*, 18:266). This recalls the descriptions that Jesus answered with a quotation from Deut 8:3, which mentions the importance of living according to the words of God—that is, the law (Q^4 4:4, 9, 12). Third, the Jews ran the risk of death to protect the temple from being defiled by the statue of Gaius Caligula (*Ant.*, 18:264). This is reflected in the description that Jesus was seduced to throw himself from the pinnacle of the Jerusalem temple (Q^4 4:9). Fourth, in order to scatter the crowd, the Roman envoy Petronius quoted the plagiarized letter of Gaius Caligula (*Ant.*, 18:280-283). This reminds readers of the devil's quotation from Ps 91:11-12 for his own purpose in the second temptation (Q^4 4:10-11). It is possible that the fourth redactor described the intriguing quotation of the devil in allusion to Petronius' plagiarized letter of Gaius Caligula. From the comparisons listed above, it can be concluded that the first and second temptations of Jesus also reflect the confrontation between Petronius and the Jews when Gaius Caligula attempted to erect his statue in the Jerusalem temple in 40-41 CE. If this interpretation can be acceptable, this makes it possible to decide the date of the composition of the fourth redaction—that is, 41 CE.

3:1-5) ("Social History," 105-28). This kind of description was inherited by the intertestamental documents. Of course, the writer of Q also received this kind of tradition and applied the devil to the Roman emperor Gaius Caligula in the temptation story.

21. On the other hand, Josephus described that it was for fifty days in *Jewish War*, 2:200. Of course, the number forty or fifty was not written based on an accurate counting; rather they reflect the perspective of Josephus at the time of writing.

C. THE TWELVE APOSTLES (Q 6:12-16)

The fourth redactor provided a list of the twelve apostles in Q^4 6:12-16 (Luke 6:12-16; Matt 5:1a; 10:2-4). This text follows Q^4 4:1-13 by the linking word "mountain" and the theme of the descendants of Abraham. In other words, the twelve apostles represented the twelve tribes of the Israelites as the descendants of Abraham. In this respect, the fourth redaction maintains the flow of the story regarding the people of God.

The term "mountain" is described in Q^4 6:12a.[22] There are, however, many things to be discussed regarding the mountain. It is to be noted that the term "mountain" appeared as the place of the third temptation (4:5-8). Then, it is natural that the mountain could be the place where Jesus selected the twelve apostles in the fourth redaction. This reminds readers of the mountain Sinai where the twelve tribes of the Israelites were rearranged (Exod 19:1-3; Num 1:1—3:4). In this respect, the fourth redactor kept applying the typological interpretation to Jesus regarding the people of God on the mountain. This reflects that the disciples of Jesus faced a serious challenge regarding identity at the time of the writing of the fourth redaction. Then, it can be said that the mountain where Jesus selected his apostles could correspond to Mount Zion, on which the Jerusalem temple stood. In this respect, the fourth redactor tried to impose authority to the twelve apostles as the people of God.

The phrase "twelve apostles" is mentioned in Q^4 6:13a.[23] It is, however, noteworthy that the appearance of twelve apostles in this text is natural; after the descendants of Abraham were mentioned in Q^4 3:8bc and Jesus was described as the representative of the new Israelites in 4:1-13, then the twelve apostles are introduced as those who replaced the twelve tribes of the Israelites—namely, the descendants of Abraham. It is legitimate to conclude that the list of the twelve apostles strengthens the typological description of Q regarding the people of God. Especially, the fourth redactor used the title ἀπόστολος [apostle] for the first time which came from the verb "send" [ἀποστέλλω]. The "apostle" seems to be created on the basis of previous descriptions that Jesus was the one "sent" [ἀποστείλαντά] by God (Q^3 10:16). In other words, the fourth redactor succeeded this concept, applied it to the twelve disciples of Jesus, and created the title "apostle," which refers to those chosen in order to represent the new people of God. This accords well with

---

22. A majority of scholars would not accept the mentioning of "mountain" in this text. Cf. Jacobson, *First Gospel*, 87.

23. A majority of scholars do not think that their list was not in Q. For instance, Robinson, Hoffmann, and Kloppenborg do not list the names of the twelve apostles in their book *The Critical Edition of Q*.

the prophets in that they were also sent by God.[24] The disciples were already given the prophetic feature in that they had heard what the prophets had wanted to hear but had not heard (Q^3 10:24). Based on this concept, the fourth redactor was able to apply the prophetic aspect to the apostles.

The fourth redactor listed the names of the twelve apostles in Q^4 6:13b–16. No specific description appears regarding how Jesus selected them.[25] It is, however, noteworthy that the second redactor already described the voluntary follower of Jesus (Q^2 9:57–58). This implies that some followed Jesus at the stage of the second redaction. Although the third redactor did not mention the disciples of Jesus directly, it was supposed that there were some disciples of Jesus, in that they were insulted and hated on account of him (Q^3 6:22–23b). In addition, the third redactor began to use the term "disciple" (6:40). In consequence, the fourth redactor introduced the twelve apostles who were chosen among the disciples of Jesus.[26] They seemed to be the leaders among the disciples at the time of the writing of the fourth redaction. However, the list of twelve apostles needs to be examined carefully because the Lucan and the Matthean versions are different from each other.[27] While Matthew includes Thadaeus rather than Judas son of James, Luke reverses these.[28] It seems that both were originally in the list of the twelve apostles in Q. On the contrary, Judas Iscariot was invented by Mark later.[29] This means that Mark substituted Judas Iscariot for Judas son of

---

24. Meier argues that the title "apostle" is to be understood against the background of the Hebrew term שלח [send] which was used for the prophets sent by God ("Circle," 639).

25. A certain number of scholars deny the fact that Jesus had twelve disciples. For example, Crossan believes that Jesus was a wandering Cynic and that they provided only symbolic meaning (*Historical Jesus*, 72–90). On the other hand, most scholars agree the existence of the twelve disciples. Cf. Sanders, *Jesus*, 61–119; Eddy, "Jesus," 449; and Meier, "Circle," 635–72.

26. It seems that Mark created the story about the summoning of Peter, Andrew, James, and John at the shore of the Lake Galilee (Mark 1:16–20), and then Levi at the custom office (2:13–14). Mark tried to explain their selection more in detail on the contrary to the description of Q which suddenly introduces the twelve apostles at once.

27. I learned this interpretation from Dr. Dennis R. MacDonald when I studied at the joint PhD program of the University of Denver and Iliff School of Theology in 1992. Matthew lists the same names with Mark (Matt 10:2–4; Mark 3:16–19). It seems that Matthew followed Mark regarding the twelve disciples of Jesus.

28. Meier insists that the difference between the Lucan and Matthean versions regarding the names of twelve disciples is insignificant ("Circle," 645–47, 652).

29. While Matthew and Luke list the first four disciples in the order of Peter, Andrew, James, and John, Mark lists them differently in that he changed the order between John and James. Thus, Mark provides the foundation, so that Jesus could take Peter, Andrew, and John to the mountain of transfiguration and the front of Gethsemane (Mark 9:2; 14:33).

James.[30] This is supported by the fact that John mentions Judas son of James as one of the disciples of Jesus (John 14:22). Moreover, Paul mentioned "the twelve" to whom Christ had appeared after the resurrection (1 Cor 15:5). If Judas Iscariot had been one of the twelve, Paul could not have mentioned the twelve. This means that Judas Iscariot was not one of the twelve apostles. The twelve apostles were listed as those who represented the twelve tribes of the Israelites, the descendants of Abraham.

The fourth redactor completed the beginning part of Jesus' biography with the list of the twelve apostles. Having taken after the journey of the Israelites from Egypt to the land of Canaan, the fourth redactor located the list of twelve apostles after the baptism and temptation story of Jesus. In this respect, Jesus and his twelve apostles were depicted as the new people of God—namely, the descendants of Abraham. Then, Jesus can be compared with Moses the leader of the Israelites in the wilderness. It is clear that the fourth redactor had the Moses/Exodus typology in his or her mind when he or she introduced the selection of the twelve apostles of Jesus.

D. PERSECUTION (Q 6:23C)

Instruction about the persecution of the prophets by the forefathers is written about in Q^4 6:23c (Luke 6:23c; Matt 5:12b). In this respect, the theme of persecution appears for the first time in the fourth redaction. It seems that the socio-historical situation was getting worse at the time of the writing of the fourth redaction.

The fourth redactor mentioned the persecution of the prophets by the forefathers in Q^4 6:23c.[31] By adding this to Q^3 6:22–23b, the insulted and

---

30. Mark created the motive that Judas Iscariot betrayed Jesus. It seems that the writer described Judas Iscariot as the traitor in order to emphasize that Jesus Christ was killed unlawfully (Luke 6:16; John 14:22). Matthew succeeded the description of Mark since the motive of Judas Iscariot's betrayal was an important theme; thus, Matthew described that Jesus Christ appeared to the eleven disciples on the mountain in Galilee, excluding Judas Iscariot (Matt 28:16). Luke also succeeded the betrayal of Judas Iscariot from Mark and described it as it is. He also mentioned Judas' suicide while writing Acts (cf. Acts 1:18–19). However, there are differences between the descriptions of Matthew and Acts relating to the suicide of Judas Iscariot (Matt 27:3–10). Mark seemed to create Judas Iscariot to describe that Jesus Christ was bought at a price for the redemption of people. It is historical that Jesus was killed by the Jews as Paul simply reported in his first letter (1 Thess 2:15). It seems that Jesus was not handed over to death on account of the betrayal of Judas Iscariot. The reason of his death has not been known.

31. Luke uses the term "their forefathers" (Luke 6:23c), while Matthew simply adopts the pronoun in the form of the third person plural (Matt 5:12b). To my judgment, the Lucan version represents the original of Q in the fact that the term "forefathers" reflects the theme of the descendants of Abraham (Q 3:8bc). Cf. Robinson et al.,

hated disciples were juxtaposed against the prophets persecuted by the forefathers at the stage of the fourth redaction. This was possible because the third redactor had already defined the disciples of Jesus as the prophets (Q^3 10:23–24). Having inherited this tradition, the fourth redactor could put the disciples of Jesus in parallel with the prophets persecuted by the forefathers. This means that the twelve apostles were particularly regarded as the persecuted prophets of God at the stage of the fourth redaction. This indicates that the intensity of opposition was getting stronger as Q went through the process of redaction. The disciples of Jesus had to make up their mind to endure the persecution at the time of the writing of the fourth redaction.

The fourth redactor applied the Deuteronomistic historical tradition to the disciples of Jesus. As shown in the temptation story, verses were quoted from Deuteronomy three times. However, the quotation itself does not mean that the Deuteronomistic historical tradition was applied to Jesus. Rather, it is reflected in the persecution of prophets (Q^4 6:23c).[32] This means that the fourth redactor understood the persecution of the disciples of Jesus from a perspective of the Deuteronomistic tradition.[33] The persecution of the prophets was already implied in the story of temptation in that Jesus was seduced to death by the devil at the pinnacle of the temple of Jerusalem. Although Jesus did not surrender to the demand of the devil, it is clear that he was threatened to death leading to the description of persecution of the prophetic disciples in 6:23c.

E. CONTROVERSY ABOUT THE LAW (Q 14:5)

Controversy about the law is written of in Q^4 14:5 (Luke 14:5; Matt 12:11–12). This text follows Q^3 6:39 by the theme of "falling into a pit." On the other hand, this text starts dealing with the role of the law specifically in the fourth redaction.

The fourth redactor raised a question about the law regarding the observance of the Sabbath in Q^4 14:5. It says, "If any of you have a sheep and it falls into a pit on the Sabbath, will you not take hold of it and lift it out?" (Matt 12:11).[34] The fourth redactor dealt with the matter of how to observe

Critical Edition, 52–53.

32. Cf. Steck, *Israel*, 257–60; Jacobson, "Literary Unity," 383; Jacobson, *First Gospel*, 100; and Kloppenborg, *Formation*, 173, 190.

33. Cf. Seeley, "Blessings," 131–45.

34. Luke uses the terms "son" and "ox" (Luke 14:5), while Matthew adopts "sheep" (Matt 12:11). It is difficult to choose one of them for the original wording of Q. I would like to use the Matthean version because the fourth redactor used "sheep" in Q 10:3 and 15:4–7.

the commandment about the Sabbath for the first time. This implies that the fourth redactor was involved in the controversy about its interpretation with the Jews in Jerusalem. This reveals the fact that the fourth redactor interpreted the law in a different way from the Jewish tradition by arguing to rescue the one falling into a pit on the Sabbath. As shown before, the interpretation of the law started in the third redaction regarding cleansing and tithing (Q^3 11:39–42). Having succeeded this interpretation, the fourth redactor showed his interest in the law by citing three verses from Deuteronomy in the temptation story (Q^4 4:4, 8, 12) and then began to discuss the interpretation of the law regarding the observance of the Sabbath (14:5). While the third redactor emphasized how to observe the original virtue of the law, the fourth redactor attempted a different interpretation from the customary one. In this respect, a new perspective on the law was suggested by the fourth redactor. This implies that the disciples of Jesus were getting more interested in the observance of the law on the basis of the interpretation of Jesus resulting in the separation from the ordinary Jews at the stage of the fourth redaction.

F. THE STATUS OF JOHN (Q 7:28; 16:16)

The status of John is described in Q^4 7:28 and 16:16. He seems to be excluded from the kingdom of God. This shows the most negative perspective on John in the fourth redaction.

The fourth redactor described the downgraded John in Q^4 7:28 (Luke 7:28; Matt 11:11). Although there is no one greater than John among those born of a woman, he is less than the least in the kingdom of God. In order to define his identity, the comparative and superlative are adopted here. The comparative was already used in the second redaction (Q^2 10:12; 11:13; 12:7, 23–24) and the third redaction (Q^3 3:16; 7:26; 10:14; 11:22, 31–32). The comparative was used in connection with John in 7:26. In this vein, the fourth redactor was able to use the comparative for the description of John. On the other hand, the superlative appears for the first time in that the term "the least" is found in the description of John's status. It is ambiguous whether John belongs to the kingdom of God or not because he is less than the least in the kingdom.[35] Therefore, his status was radically downgraded from an eschatological perspective. While John was described as the one who came to the world on the way of God's righteousness in the first redaction (Q^1 7:29–30), he was identified as the one more than a prophet in the

---

35. On the contrary, some scholars believe that John belongs to the kingdom of God according to Q (Catchpole, "Beginning," 212).

third redaction (Q^3 7:18–27). Then, he was regarded as the one who was not included in the kingdom of God in the fourth redaction (Q^4 7:28). This means that his status was downgraded as the redaction of Q progressed.[36] This reveals the social environment of the disciples of John at the time of the writing of the fourth redaction, because his status was extremely weakened among the disciples of Jesus. Even if he was criticized as the one less than the least in the kingdom of God, there was no one who protected him from such critique and reproach. The text of Q^4 7:28 "seeks to subordinate John to Jesus."[37]

The fourth redactor described the kingdom of God as a place of residence. This aspect has not been found in the previous three redactions. It is noteworthy that a hierarchical system is introduced in connection with the residents of the kingdom. This is found in phrases such as "less" and "least" in the kingdom of God. The ranking system was supposed to be among the disciples of Jesus following the Jewish tradition. It seems to reflect that the occasion for writing was the evaluation of the disciples at the stage of the fourth redaction. This is supported by the selection of twelve apostles among them who were supposed to be their leaders (Q^4 6:12–16). On the other hand, this reflects that there were enough people to classify them according to their level of faith in God and Jesus at the time of the writing of the fourth redaction.

The fourth redactor alluded to the first prophecy about the messianic figure. Although the phrase "born of woman" could be applied to everyone because he or she was born of woman, the fourth redactor did not use it for that meaning. Rather, it seems that it conveys a theological meaning with an allusion to the prophecy written in Gen 3:15. Of course, "the offspring born of woman" refers to the messianic figure. Then, the description that John was greater than any of those "born of woman" means that he was the greatest messianic figure. The fourth redactor was able to use this description because the second redactor already alluded to the garden of Eden with the second beatitude (Q^2 6:21a) and the Lord's Prayer (11:2–4). Also, the third redactor used a reference to the primordial creation with the phrase "the Lord of heaven and earth" (Q^3 10:21) and to the garden of Eden with the agricultural aspect of the kingdom of God (13:18–19). Having inherited the tradition regarding the primordial event, the fourth redactor could use the phrase "born of woman" for the status of John with allusion to Gen 3:15 when he was identified in connection with the kingdom of God. As the

---

36. Tuckett, Q, 119.
37. Jacobson, "Literary Unity," 381n45.

redaction of Q progressed, more attention was paid to the primordial times for the description of eschatological aspect.

The fourth redactor continued dealing with the status of John in Q^4 16:16 (Luke 16:16; Matt 11:12–13). His status is defined in connection with the kingdom of God. The fourth redactor drew a contrast between the period of the law and prophets and that of the kingdom of God. According to Q, John belongs to the period of the law and the prophets rather than the period of the kingdom of God.[38] This is accordant with the preceding text that described John as the one who belonged to the group of prophets even though he was more than a prophet in the third redaction (Q^3 7:26). In addition, the fourth redactor also applied the prophetic aspect to John with the phrase "for I tell you" in the middle of his announcement (Q^4 3:8bc). In this vein, the idea was developed that John did not belong to the kingdom of God (7:28) rather to the period of prophet (16:16). Finally, John was described as the one much inferior even to the disciples of Jesus—the entrants of the kingdom of God—in the fourth redaction.

The fourth redactor defined the characteristic of the kingdom of God. It is noteworthy that the kingdom of God is coming forcefully and the violent enter it.[39] It seems the fourth redactor developed the previous tradition about the kingdom. When the first redactor designated the poor as those who entered the kingdom of God, they were required of no other particular precondition except poverty (Q^1 6:20b). Then, the second redactor announced its imminent coming (Q^2 10:9; 11:2; 12:31). The kingdom of God was a realm to experience when a certain precondition—that is, the expulsion of the demon by the finger of God—is met (Q^2 11:19–20). In this respect, the kingdom of God was a realm that has to come but is not completely fulfilled yet in the second redaction. On the other hand, the third redactor avoided direct description of the kingdom; rather, it was described figuratively through the parables (Q^3 13:18–21). The kingdom of God is a place that has been expanded to accommodate as many people as possible. It is a place to enter through something compared with the narrow door

---

38. The Lucan and Matthean versions differ from each other. While Luke excludes John from the kingdom of God, Matthew includes him in it. It seems, however, that the Lucan version represents the original wording of Q because the fourth redactor excluded him from the kingdom in Q 7:28. The Matthean version reflects his own theology in the fact that John was the first person who proclaimed the coming of the kingdom of God which does not appear in Luke's Gospel (Matt 3:2). Cf. Robinson et al., *Critical Edition*, 464–66.

39. Robinson et al. believe that the Greek term βιάζεται represents the original wording of Q (*Critical Edition*, 466). However, they interpret it as a verb of passive voice. On the other hand, Verseput argues for the middle voice (*Rejection*, 94–96). Then, this indicates the kingdom coming forcefully.

(13:24-27). Having inherited these texts, the fourth redactor was able to describe the residents in the kingdom of God (Q^4 7:28). However, its forceful coming to the world was argued for; thus, those who try violently to grasp the kingdom can enter it (16:16). Thus, the disciples of Jesus must desire the kingdom of God and make a strong decision to observe the instruction of Jesus to enter it.

G. THE PERFECT LAW (Q 16:17-18)

The law is dealt with again in Q^4 16:17-18 (Luke 16:17-18; Matt 5:18, 32). Although this follows 16:16 by the connecting word "law," why they are connected is not clear. It is, however, definite that the fourth redactor significantly concentrated on the matter of the law on account of the surrounding environment.

The characteristic of the law is described in Q^4 16:17. The fourth redactor focused on the perfect nature of the law. The positive view on the law started with the third redactor emphasizing how to observe the nature of the law rightly (Q^3 11:39-42). Then, the fourth redactor continued to take a positive view on the law with three quotations from Deuteronomy in the temptation story (Q^4 4:4, 8, 12) and then the new interpretation of observance of the Sabbath (14:5). In this vein, the law was used as a criterion to divide the period of divine salvation (16:16). In this respect, the fourth redactor kept developing the idea regarding the law by mentioning its perfectness (16:17). As Q went through a process of redaction, the virtue of the law was getting strengthened. This informs readers that theologically the disciples of Jesus were within the range of the Jewish tradition at the stage of the fourth redaction.

The fourth redactor emphasized the virtue of the law. It is seen in the description that even if heaven and earth pass away, not one iota or one serif of the law will fall. There is nothing in the world more important and valuable than the law. It is noteworthy that the phrase "heaven and earth" was already used in reference to God the Father in the third redaction (Q^3 10:21). However, the fourth redactor used it in contrast to the law. If the phrase was used against the background of the creation of the world (Gen 1:1; 2:4), it seems that the fourth redactor considered the law to be more valuable than the creation itself. This shows that the disciples of Jesus had faith in the law interpreted in the name of Jesus.

The commandment about adultery is written in Q^4 16:18. It is said that the one who divorces his wife and marries another woman commits adultery. The terms "divorce" and "adultery" appear for the first time. This is to be understood in the context of a man and woman who got married (Gen 2:24–25). Thus, according to the fourth redactor, it is against the will of God that a man divorce his wife and marry another woman. As shown before, interest in the creation story began in the second redaction (Q^2 6:21; 11:2–4) and then developed in the third redaction (Q^3 10:21; 13:18–19). It seems that as Q went through a process of redaction, the redactor seemed to plant more clues about the relationship with primordial creation. It seems that the primordial events became the mirror for the interpretation of the marital relationship in connection to the law. In other words, the law was the most valuable virtue to the disciples of Jesus at the time of the writing of the fourth redaction.

H. JESUS AS WISDOM (Q 7:35)

The fourth redactor treated "wisdom" in connection to Jesus in Q^4 7:35 (Luke 7:35; Matt 11:19b). It seems that this text was added as the conclusion to Q^3 7:31–34. It is noteworthy that wisdom was personified in the fourth redaction.

Wisdom is personified for the first time in Q^4 7:35. This calls our attention to the personification of the Spirit in the fourth redaction (4:1–2). Although the phrase "wisdom of Solomon" was mentioned in the third redaction (Q^3 11:31), it was not personified there. Having inherited the tradition regarding wisdom, the fourth redactor developed it further in connection with Jesus. As described before, the wisdom tradition was detected in the second temptation of Jesus alluding to Wis 2:17–20 (Q^4 4:9–12). Then, the fourth redactor introduced the personified Wisdom, which seems to refer to Jesus. Therefore, Wisdom reminds readers of Prov 8:22–31 where she was depicted as a personification of God. It is noteworthy that Wisdom was not a transcendental being yet in the fourth redaction.[40] In this respect, it can be said that the theological interpretation was made regarding the role of Jesus with reference to Wisdom in the fourth redaction.

The children of Wisdom seem to refer to the disciples of Jesus. It is noteworthy that the term τέκνον [children/descendants] was already used in Q^4 3:8bc. Although some scholars argue that the children of Wisdom refer to John and Jesus,[41] it is to be noted that John was downgraded in

---

40. It is to be noted that wisdom is a transcendental being who dwells in heaven according to the author of the Book of Parables which was believed to be written in 40s CE (1 En 42:1–2). In this respect, the Book of Parables is supposed to be written a little later than Q.

41. Cf. Kloppenborg, *Formation*, 111–12; and Carlson, "Wisdom," 102.

the fourth redaction (7:28; 16:16). It is, therefore, unacceptable that John is included in the children of Wisdom. Rather, they probably refer to the disciples of Jesus at the stage of the fourth redaction.[42] This is in accord with the fact that they were in contrast with "this generation" in the third redaction (Q^3 7:31–34).[43] Their filial relationship with Wisdom is a substitute for their "teacher and disciples" relationship found in the third redaction (Q^3 6:40). Therefore, they were identified as the new descendants of Abraham (Q^4 3:8bc) and the twelve apostles (6:12–16) in the fourth redaction. In this respect, the fourth redactor imposed the theological meaning to Jesus and his disciples.

The fourth redactor treated the theme of the vindication of Wisdom by her children. Vindication is another expression for "being proved as righteous." This seems to reflect the wisdom tradition in that the righteous will receive wisdom as well as the holy and disciplined spirit which had filled the world (Wis 1:4–7). It is not quite clear whether wisdom, that is the spirit, was personified or not by the author of Wisdom of Solomon. On the other hand, the fourth redactor of Q seemed to apply the wisdom tradition to Jesus, in that he would be proven to be righteous by his disciples.

---

42. A certain number of scholars believe that the children of wisdom refer to those who responded to the teaching of John and Jesus (Tuckett, Q, 176–80; and Piper, Wisdom, 168).

43. Tuckett, Q, 178–79. He considers John and Jesus the messengers of wisdom. However, I would not agree with him; I will discuss this more in detail when I discuss Q 13:34–35 later.

2

The Texts Added to the Second Redaction

The second section of Q was expanded further by the fourth redactor. The last redactor interpolated his or her sources into the main texts of the second redaction, into which the third redactor already interpolated many texts. By doing so, the fourth redactor developed the theology of Jesus and his disciples. In addition to the theme of sending the disciples and the Lord's Prayer, the fourth redactor emphasized the instruction that they should take part in ministry in spite of persecution and martyrdom. In this respect, the fourth redactor was a theologically trained scribe.

A. THE INVITED FOLLOWER (Q 9:59-60A)

The fourth redactor described a person who was invited to follow Jesus in Q^4 9:59-60a (Luke 9:59-60a; Matt 8:21-22). When this text was added to Q^2 9:57-58, they made a pair of examples regarding the disciples of Jesus. In consequence, their status changed from voluntarily followers to invited ones at the stage of the fourth redaction.

The fourth redactor seemed to emphasize the authority of Jesus by asking someone to follow him (Q^4 9:59). It seems that the person, who was asked to join Jesus, failed to follow him due to his dead father's funeral. In this respect, the fourth redactor instructed that one had to follow Jesus when being called by him. This reminds readers of 6:12-16 which describes the selection of twelve apostles by Jesus. In this vein, the request of Jesus to follow him indicates his authority to choose the people of God. This implies that the disciples of Jesus faced a critical situation in that they had to respond to the calling of Jesus in spite of death.

The fourth redactor mentioned the matter of family. The disciples of Jesus should abandon their family in order to follow Jesus. He did not allow the person to hold even the funeral of his dead father. The son is responsible for the funeral of his dead father. It is shameful of him if he does not hold the funeral[1] because this would be to deny filial piety.[2] Nevertheless, according to the fourth redactor, Jesus hindered the person from holding the funeral of his dead father. No precondition was allowed in order to be the disciples of Jesus. At this point, it should be reminded that the fourth redactor mentioned the matter of being descendants of Abraham (Q^4 3:8bc). Although the phrase "descendants of Abraham" carries a broader concept than the family, it possibly refers to the new family of God gathering around Jesus. Then, the fourth redactor introduced the twelve apostles as those who represented the new family of God, the descendants of Abraham (16:12–16). In this respect, the fourth redactor specified the new family of the disciples of Jesus. This seems to reflect that the disciples had reason to leave their genealogical families for Jesus. However, this does not mean that all the disciples of Jesus left their families in order to join and live together. There is no clue whether they constituted a separate community or not.

The fourth redactor clearly mentioned the theme of death for the first time. Even though it was not the death of disciples, its appearance is significant in this context. The theme of death can be detected from the fate of those who were compared to the tree which would be chopped down and thrown into the fire in the first redaction (Q^1 3:9), and the illustration of the bird and grass in the second redaction (Q^2 12:6, 28). The third redactor also dealt with a topic related to death (Q^3 7:22, 32; 11:44). On the other hand, the fourth redactor dealt with the death that could happen to Jesus (Q^4 4:9–12). Then, finally, it was related with the matter of disciples (9:59–60a). As the redaction of Q progressed, the theme of death was more closely connected with the disciples of Jesus. It seems to reflect a critical situation that could lead them to death—that is, martyrdom.

---

1. Vaage, "Q1," 171.

2. Jacobson, *First Gospel*, 134. According to Batten, "A son or daughter's repudiation of his or her parents would be impious and in some cases deserving even to death (Josephus, *Ant.*, 4.8)" ("More Queries," 49).

B. THE POSSIBILITY OF MARTYRDOM (Q 10:3)

The martyrdom of disciples is implied in Q^4 10:3 (Luke 10:3; Matt 10:16a). This text was added to Q^3 10:2 in order to allude to the fate of eschatological workers of God. On the other hand, in the fourth redaction, Q^4 10:3 followed 9:59–60a by the theme of death. In this respect, the matter of death developed steadily.

The warning is given in the form of a simile (Q^4 10:3). It is said that the disciples sent out to ministry were like sheep in the middle of wolves.[3] It is noteworthy that Isaiah also used the image of sheep and wolf in the context of a peaceful situation fulfilled at the end of the world (Isa 65:25). However, the fourth redactor used them for a hostile climate at the time of its writing. While the second redactor had used animals such as foxes, birds, sparrows, and ravens for the description of daily life (Q^2 9:58; 12:6–7, 24), the third redactor adopted animals such as a dove and birds for the spiritual aspect (Q^3 3:22; 13:19). On the other hand, the fourth redactor used sheep first (Q^4 14:5; cf. Matt 12:11–12) and then added wolves for the adversarial relationship between the disciples of Jesus and their opponents (Q^4 10:3). Without doubt, the sheep will be taken and killed by the wolves. Thus, this image refers to the death of disciples during their ministry. In this respect, this text is to be connected to Q^4 9:59–60a regarding the theme of death. The disciples who had to abandon the funeral of the dead father could not help but face their own death during their ministry (10:3) as Jesus had been seduced to death (4:9–12). As the fourth redaction advanced, the theme of death was being clearly emphasized.

The fourth redaction reflects the critical situation at the time of its writing. The disciples had to worry about their life. While the second redactor said that life [soul] is more than food and the body than clothing (Q^2 12:22–31), the fourth redactor dealt with worry about the fate of the disciples (Q^4 10:3). Economic crisis turned into a matter of life and death as Q went through a process of redaction. This indicates that the surrounding circumstances were getting worse. When Q^4 10:3 is understood in connection with the second temptation of Jesus (4:9–12), its meaning becomes clear, that the disciples faced crisis caused by Gaius Caligula. In other words, they had to run the risk of death—that is, martyrdom—when they followed Jesus by keeping the words of God.

---

3. As for the image of wolves, refer to Gen 49:27; Prov 28:15; Jer 22:27; Ezek 22:27; Zeph 3:3; TGad 1:3; TBen 11:1–2; John 10:12; Acts 20:29. Cf. Catchpole, "Mission Charge," 167.

C. THE PARABLE OF THE UNCLEAN SPIRIT
(Q 11:24–26)

The parable of the unclean spirit is written in Q^4 11:24–26 (Luke 11:24–26; Matt 12:43–45). This text was added to the parable of the strong man (Q^3 11:21–23), so that it might convey the instruction that if a person is not with Jesus, the situation will be worsened by the stronger evil spirit. Furthermore, in the fourth redaction, this text follows Q^4 10:3, so that it might deliver instruction on how to save one's life from unclean and evil spirits that can be compared to wolves.

The parable introduces the unclean spirit for the first time (Q^4 11:24). It is noteworthy that the fourth redactor paid more attention to the spiritual being. As shown before, the third redactor introduced the Spirit for the first time (Q^3 3:16, 21). Having received this tradition, the fourth redactor mentioned the Spirit in the temptation story (Q^4 4:1) and then the unclean spirit and seven other evil spirits in this parable (11:24–26). In this respect, the unclean and evil spirits are in sharp contrast with the Spirit. As Q went through a process of redaction, the spirit was getting personified. In addition, two groups of spirits are sharply contrasted in the fourth redaction. This indicates that the disciples of Jesus understood the phenomena occurring around them from a spiritual perspective. In this way, they seemed to take the shape of religion.

The fourth redactor described that the unclean spirit came out of a person. It is noteworthy that the unclean spirit is described as a spiritual being which can dwell in a human being. While the second redactor had described Jesus as an exorcist, casting a demon out of the mute (Q^2 11:14), third redactor mentioned John being slandered by the people saying he had a demon (Q^3 7:33). Furthermore, the fourth redactor described that the devil left Jesus voluntarily when he failed seducing him (Q^4 4:13). In the same manner, the unclean spirit also left the person voluntarily (11:24). It seems that the fourth redactor was confident in the authority of the disciples of Jesus, being spiritually strong enough to make the evil spirit get away voluntarily.

The fourth redactor mentioned the unclean spirit wandering through waterless land seeking rest without a result. The image of a waterless place and rest calls attention to Hagar who wandered in the waterless region without rest, being afraid of Sarah, but finally bore Abraham a son named Ishmael (Gen 16:1–16). It is noteworthy that Ishmael was a descendant of Abraham, but he was not the legitimate son. In this respect, the parable of the unclean spirit is related with the matter of being a descendent of Abraham (Q^4 3:8bc). The fourth redactor seemed to teach the disciples of Jesus that they should not be possessed by the unclean spirit who makes them the illegitimate people of God. In this respect, the fourth redactor used the parable of the unclean spirit as an example of those who went astray from the instruction of Jesus in the middle of religious crisis such as the attempt to erect the statue of Gaius Caligula in the Jerusalem temple. It seems that the fourth redactor urged the disciples of Jesus to stay in his instruction.

The fourth redactor compared the house to a person (Q^4 11:24). It is said that the unclean spirit returned to the house from which he had come. The return of a spiritual being to a house appears for the first time in the fourth redaction. This means that even if the unclean spirit was expelled from a person, it could return to the person. Once the house referred to the shelter which the disciples had to find for rest during their ministry in the second redaction (Q^2 10:5), and then it was figuratively compared to obedience to the Lord's words in the third redaction (Q^3 6:46–48; cf. 11:21). On the other hand, the fourth redactor compared it to a person in which the spirit can dwell. This was possible because the second redactor already mentioned the dwelling of demon in a mute (Q^2 11:14). The spiritual being can dwell in human being. Having inherited this tradition, the fourth redactor was able to mention the dwelling of the evil spirit in a person. In a sense, the evil spirit was also personified in the fourth redaction. The reason that the fourth redactor described it in this way was because some of the disciples of Jesus were going astray by abandoning the law, that is the word of God, during the crisis caused by Gaius Caligula.

The fourth redactor described the situation of the person in Q^4 11:25. It is figuratively said that when the unclean spirit returned to the house, he found [εὑρίσκει] it "swept clean and put in order." This refers to the situation of a person without any unclean or evil spirit. The Greek term εὑρίσκω was once used in the second redaction (Q^2 11:9–10). While it was used in the context of prayer there, it appears in the context of one's spiritual condition in the fourth redaction. In addition, the image of cleaning was once used for the eschatological judgment with the term διακαθαίρω in the third redaction (Q^3 3:17). In this vein, the fourth redactor used the image of cleaning for one's spirituality although he used different terms σαρόω and κοσμέω (Q^4 11:25). This reminds readers of the situation of the absence of the devil after he departed Jesus. In this respect, the person was described in the neutral perspective.

The unclean spirit accompanied the seven other spirits (Q^4 11:26). It is said that the seven spirits were more evil than the unclean spirit, and they came to the person whose inside was swept clean and put in order. This implies that when a person is not filled with the Spirit of God, the more evil spirits take over him or her. In other words, although Jesus had defeated the devil, the disciples should not feel relieved at the absence of the evil spirit. When they slacken their effort to protect themselves from the unclean spirit, they could be possessed by it again and be in a worse situation than they previously were. This is a warning to be alert against the evil spirit.[4] In other words, the disciples of Jesus should stay alert to watch for the spiritual attack of opponents, namely the contemporary religious group of people. It is, however, noteworthy that the number "seven" appears regarding the spiritual being. It was already used with regard to the complete forgiveness of sins in the second redaction (Q^2 17:3-4). Then, the fourth redactor used the number "seven" for the description of more evil spirits. By doing so, the fourth redactor seemed to express the worst condition of those who did not receive the Spirit of God.[5] This implies that the disciples of Jesus were in the middle of conflict with their opponents in an extreme situation at the time of the writing of the fourth redaction.

The fourth redactor used the comparative twice in the parable of the unclean spirit (Q^4 11:26). Whereas the seven other spirits were defined as those more evil than the unclean spirit, the circumstances of the person became worse. The comparative was already used in the second redaction (Q^2 10:12; 12:7, 23-24) and in the third redaction (Q^3 3:16; 7:26, 28; 10:14). On the other hand, the combination of comparative and superlative was used in the fourth redaction (Q^4 7:28). It is, however, noteworthy that the comparative is used twice in order to explain a certain case (11:26). The double use of the comparative indicates emphasis on the worsened situation of a person because of the unclean and evil spirits. It seems that the fourth redactor warned the disciples of Jesus against the evil power represented by Gaius Caligula who attempted to erect his statue in the Jerusalem temple.

D. WOE (Q 11:47-51)

Another woe is introduced in Q^4 11:47-51 (Luke 11:47-51; Matt 23:29-31, 34-36). This text was interpolated into the six woes of the third redaction (Q^3 11:39-46, 52). Then, in the fourth redaction, this woe makes it possible to continue the number "seven" which also appears in the preceding text—namely, the parable of the unclean spirit (Q^4 11:24-26). Thus, it can be said that the woe against the Jerusalem temple was intentionally placed here in order to show the extremely evil situation that the disciples of Jesus faced.

---

4. Kloppenborg, *Formation*, 126-27. On the contrary, Jacobson would not accept this kind of general interpretation. This seems to result from his effort to change the original location of Q 11:24-26 (*First Gospel*, 170).

5. Cf. Jacobson, *First Gospel*, 171. See also 171n66.

The fourth redactor mentioned the tombs of the prophets (Q^4 11:47). The term "tombs" is used as a linking word to connect this woe to the fourth woe in which the indistinct tomb was already mentioned in the third redaction (Q^3 11:44).[6] The word "tombs" carries the image of death which started to be mentioned in the second temptation (Q^4 4:9-12). Then, the persecution of the prophets reminds readers of 6:23c in that the forefathers were already defined as the persecutors of the prophets. The fourth redactor also mentioned the theme of death in the description of the invited follower (9:59-60a). Moreover, describing the disciples as sheep in the middle of wolves, the fourth redactor intensified the instruction that they were destined for the martyrdom (10:3). Furthermore, having inherited the description that the disciples of Jesus were the prophets in Q^3 10:24, the fourth redactor mentioned the martyrdom of prophets, namely the disciples of Jesus, by their fellow Jews in Q^4 11:47. As Q went through a process of redaction, the fourth redactor finally mentioned the martyrdom of prophets with a literary device "woe" here. This reflects that the occasion for writing was a critical situation regarding their relationship with the Jews at the stage of the fourth redaction.

The role of forefathers is mentioned in Q^4 11:47-48. Their role reaches the acme in the description that they killed the prophets. As the fourth redaction advanced, they were described from a more negative perspective. Without doubt, this reflects the Deuteronomistic tradition.[7] According to the fourth redactor, the fellow Jews were accused for witnessing the killing of the prophets. In other words, they participated in killing the prophets as their forefathers did. Their relationship recalls that of the Jews and their children regarding the exorcism in the second redaction (Q^2 11:19). Having succeeded this tradition, the fourth redactor probably applied it to the fellow Jews and their forefathers regarding the killing of the prophets. At this moment, it is necessary to see who the prophets were in the fourth redaction. As shown before, the third redactor already defined the disciples as the prophets (Q^3 10:23-24). Having inherited this tradition, the fourth redactor could define them as the persecuted and martyred prophets (Q^4 11:47-48). In this respect, the fourth redactor cannot help but announce extreme woe against the Jews.

The personification of Wisdom is mentioned once again (Q^4 11:49). It is said that Wisdom had sent out the prophets, but the Jews killed them.[8]

---

6. It is possible that Q^4 11:47-51 followed Q^3 11:44 as reflected in the Matthean version (Matt 23:27-36). No matter which version stands for the original order of Q, I will not treat it anymore because it is not the primary issue in this book.

7. Jacobson, "Literary Unity," 383-84. Cf. Steck, *Israel*, 26-58, 222-39.

8. The Lucan and Matthean versions show the difference. While Luke uses "the

As already mentioned, the second temptation reflects the wisdom tradition (4:9–12) and then it is said that Wisdom would be vindicated by her children in the fourth redaction (7:35). It is clear that Wisdom was personified as the agent of the prophets in 11:49. The fourth redactor described Jesus as the personified Wisdom of God.[9] In this sense, Jesus the personified Wisdom is described as the one who has sent out the sages and the prophets who were destined for martyrdom.[10] This reminds the reader of the sequence between 10:2 and 10:3. While the third redactor depicted Jesus as the one asking the Lord of the harvest to send workers (Q^3 10:2), the fourth redactor attached to it the metaphor of sheep among wolves that describes the disciples as those destined for martyrdom (Q^4 10:3). In consequence, the role of the Lord as the eschatological worker is substituted with Wisdom, who was the sender of sages and prophets, identified as her children in the fourth redaction. In this respect, the fourth redactor developed the wisdom tradition in the description of Jesus and his disciples. While Wisdom was usually depicted as an attribute of God, she sometimes refers to a special agent of God,

> calling people to obedience but meeting refusal and rejection (cf. Prov 1:20ff). In Sir 24, Wisdom is portrayed as seeking to find a home in Israel (and indeed finding a home: the identification is made between Wisdom and Torah); in *I En* 42, Wisdom also seeks a home but finds none, and so withdraws.[11]

Relying upon the Jewish tradition, the fourth redactor was probably able to describe that Wisdom had sent the prophets to Israel. This is how the fourth redactor theologically interpreted the role of Wisdom.

The fourth redactor mentioned the result of killing the sages and the prophets sent by Wisdom (Q^4 11:50–51). It is said that "this generation" was responsible for all the blood of the prophets shed since the beginning of the world. First, the blood shed by the martyred prophets would be asked from this generation. It is noteworthy that the term "blood" is used for the first time with the meaning of unlawful death. Second, it is also to be noted that the term ζητέω [ask] is used in various ways in Q. While the term was used in the context of prayer in the second redaction (Q^2 11:9) and in the context of the kingdom of God in the third redaction (Q^3 13:24), the fourth redactor used it in the context of retaliation for the martyred prophets (Q^4 11:50).

---

wisdom of God," Matthew adopts "I" for Jesus. It seems that the Lucan term represents the original of Q. Cf. Jacobson, *First Gospel*, 176–77.

9. Kloppenborg argues that Q 7:35 and 11:47–51 belong to the same redaction (*Formation*, 112).

10. Cf. Miller, "Rejection," 230.

11. Tuckett, *Q*, 170.

The fourth redactor showed a determined attitude toward martyrdom. Third, "this generation" was designated as the object of God's retaliation. The fourth redactor was able to use "this generation" since it had already been used in the previous redactions. While the second redactor had used the term "evil generation" in the context of challenge (Q^2 11:29), the third redactor adopted the phrase "this generation" in the context of opposition (Q^3 7:31; 11:31–32). On the other hand, the fourth redactor used it in the context of persecution and martyrdom (Q^4 11:50–51). The situation of animosity is reflected in the three redactions, and a stronger animosity is reflected in the texts according to this order. This indicates that as time passed, the animosity of their fellow Jews had grown more against the disciples of Jesus. In consequence, the fourth redactor could not help but announce divine retaliation against the contemporary Jews. Fourth, using the term ἵνα [in order to], the fourth redactor revealed that the judgment upon this generation was the final purpose.[12] In this way, the fourth redaction reflects the serious confrontation between the disciples of Jesus and their opponents.

The fourth redactor listed the names of the martyred prophets. Abel is the first who was killed since the founding of the world. It is, however, dubious whether he was a martyred prophet. Then, Zechariah is introduced as the one killed by the contemporary Jews between the sacrificial altar and the temple (Q^4 11:51). Although it is not easy to identify Zechariah, it is definite that he was known to the disciples as one of the martyred prophets at the time of the writing of the fourth redaction. By mentioning him, the fourth redactor delivered the message that some prophets were killed at the Jerusalem temple. The temple was not considered the place of offering anymore; rather, it was a place of murder since it was already implied in the second temptation (4:9–12). Then, Zechariah could be one of those who were killed during the resistance to the attempt of erecting Gaius Caligula's statue in the temple. At any rate, the animosity toward the temple reached its peak in the description of the martyred Zechariah.

The fourth redactor concluded the woe by saying, λέγω ὑμῖν [I tell you] (Q^4 11:51). This phrase was already used in Q^1 6:27; Q^2 10:12; 11:9; 12:22; Q^3 7:9, 26; Q^4 3:8c; and 7:28. As shown before, this was usually used for the prophetic introduction to the words of YHYH in the Bible. This means that the fourth redactor also attributed the prophetic aspect to Jesus when he had announced the judgment to this generation. In other words, the fourth redactor had a self-understanding of prophets of God when he used the prophetic announcement made by Jesus.

---

12. Miller, "Rejection," 232.

The woe reveals the social environment that the disciples of Jesus faced. They seem to have advanced to Jerusalem where the temple was at the time of the writing of the fourth redaction.[13] This is supported by the mentioning of the temple in Jerusalem (Q^4 4:9; 11:51). However, the disciples faced serious persecution such as martyrdom in the temple.[14] It was so serious that the fourth redactor claimed the retaliation of God upon the opponents through the announcement by Jesus. The insult and hatred mentioned in the third redaction changed into persecution and martyrdom in the fourth redaction (Q^3 6:22–23b; Q^4 11:50–51). Therefore, the disciples of Jesus had double fronts against whom they had to fight: on the one hand, the Roman emperor Gaius Caligula, and on the other hand, the fellow Jews who would not accept the instruction addressed in the name of Jesus.

E. WORRY ABOUT THE WORLD AFTER DEATH (Q 12:4–5)

Instruction about the world after death is mentioned in Q^4 12:4–5 (Luke 12:4–5; Matt 10:28). As mentioned before, this text follows Q^3 12:2–3 without any linking words. Rather, this text follows Q^4 11:47–51 by the theme of death in the fourth redaction. On the other hand, the fourth redactor placed this text in front of Q^2 12:6–7 by the connecting phrase "do not fear" in order to make a transition from Q^3 12:2–3 to Q^2 12:6–7. In consequence, the text Q^4 12:4–5 provides a supplementary explanation for the fifth petition of the Lord's Prayer regarding the theme of "temptation" by being added to the main texts of the second redaction (Q^2 11:16, 29-30).

According to the fourth redactor, Jesus taught the disciples not to be afraid of those who can kill the body but not the soul (Q^4 12:4). Rather, they had to fear the one who can kill both the body and the soul; of course, "the one" is no other than God. The theme of death recalls the texts that belong to the fourth redaction such as Q^4 4:9–12; 9:59–60a; 10:3; and 11:47–51. With these texts, the fourth redactor encouraged the disciples of Jesus to

---

13. This is supported by the description that Paul met Cephas, namely Peter, and James the Lord's brother in Jerusalem after he had received the revelation of God (Gal 1:16–19). This means that the disciples of Jesus were in Jerusalem at the time of Paul's visit. It was probably around 38 CE.

14. Many scholars were suspicious of killing people in the temple at that time because no record is found about it in the historical documents. Thus, Mack argues that the martyrdom could have occurred during the Jewish war in 66–70 CE. In this respect, he designates the final date of Q to that period (*Lost Gospel*, 172–76). See also Seeley, "Blessings," 144; and Han, *Jerusalem*, 175–80. Cf. Steck, *Israel*, 237–39; and Jülicher und Fascher, *Einleitung*, 337–38.

run the risk of persecution and martyrdom. The text of 12:4 shows that human beings are composed of body and soul. Although the term "body" was already used in the second redaction (Q² 12:22–23) and in the third redaction (Q³ 11:34–35), it means the flesh of human beings. However, if the Matthean version stands for the original wording of Q⁴ 12:4, the word ψυχή [soul] appears a second time in addition to Q² 12:23. It seems that this text reflects the Jewish concept that human beings are composed of body and soul.

The fourth redactor introduced gehenna [γέεννα] (Q⁴ 12:5). This is the place where the soul goes after the death of the body. This is a transcendental place that appears in contrast to the kingdom of God in the fourth redaction (7:28; 16:16). Although "hades" appeared in contrast with "heaven" in the third redaction (Q³ 10:15), it is not clear whether gehenna is to be identified as hades or not. It seems that they are different places from each other. While the third redactor introduced hades as the symbol of humiliation, the fourth redactor regarded gehenna as the place where one's soul goes after the death of the body. Then, this means that the fourth redactor developed the description of the third redactor regarding the matter of transcendental realm.

F. THE STATUS OF THE SPIRIT (Q 12:10–12)

The status and role of the Spirit is described in Q⁴ 12:10–12 (Luke 12:10–12; Matt 12:32; 10:18–19). This text follows Q³ 12:8–9 by a common title "Son of Man." In addition, this text follows Q⁴ 12:4–5 by the theme of fearing the divine being in the fourth redaction. On the other hand, this plays the role of supplement to the first petition of the Lord's Prayer which deals with the theme of "fear of God" written in the main texts of the second redaction (Q² 11:2; 12:6–7) when the fourth redaction was completed.

The matter of speaking against the Son of Man and the Spirit is described in Q⁴ 12:10. It is said that whoever speaks a word against the Son of Man will be forgiven, but whoever speaks against the Spirit will not be forgiven. This implies that the Spirit is superior to the Son of Man with regard to the status. While the third redactor did not compare between the Spirit and the Son of Man regarding the status, the fourth redactor made a comparison between them. Whereas the third redactor defined the Spirit as the power of God (Q³ 3:16–17, 21–22) and used the title "Son of Man" for Jesus (6:22–23b; 7:34; 12:8–9; 17:24), the fourth redactor described the Spirit leading Jesus to the devil in the wilderness (Q⁴ 4:1–2). In this vein, the fourth redactor continued saying that one who speaks against the Spirit cannot be forgiven but the one who speaks against the Son of Man could be forgiven (12:10). It seems that the fourth redactor tried to argue that the Spirit was superior to Jesus the Son of Man. In this respect, the theological focus was moved from the Son of Man in the third redaction to the Spirit in the fourth redaction.

The Spirit was personified in Q^4 12:10. The status of the Spirit was enhanced in that while the third redactor did not describe the Spirit as a personified being at all, the fourth redactor personified the Spirit as the one who led Jesus to the devil (Q^4 4:1). Wisdom was also personified in the fourth redaction (7:35; 11:49). In this respect, the fourth redactor personified the divine agent. The personified Spirit appears in connection with the matter of speaking against it in 12:10. The reason that the fourth redactor personified the Spirit has not been known. It is, however, to be remembered that the Spirit was once described as the eschatological agent in the third redaction (Q^3 3:17). Having received this tradition, the fourth redactor seemed to apply the eschatological status to the Spirit. In this respect, there is no time to be forgiven when a person speaks against the Spirit.

The theme of forgiveness is written about a second time. As mentioned before, the Lord's Prayer dealt with the instruction about forgiveness and its application appeared in the second redaction (Q^2 11:4; 17:3–4). The principle of reciprocity between God and human beings was adopted there. In the fourth redaction, a similar principle was applied to the relationship between the Spirit and human beings in that the one who speaks against the Son of Man could be forgiven, but the one who speaks against the Spirit cannot be forgiven. Although this saying has been disputed among scholars, there is no scholarly consensus of its meaning.[15] To my judgment, the matter of speaking against Jesus the Son of Man is reminiscent of the devil who issued three demands to Jesus during the temptation (Q^4 4:3–12). It is, however, noteworthy that when the devil failed in seducing Jesus, he was not punished but he simply left him. On the other hand, the devil did not say even a word to the Spirit. The reason that the devil spoke to Jesus but not to the Spirit could be understood in light of 12:10. As Jesus obeyed the Spirit, the disciples should also be obedient to the Spirit. This shows that the fourth redactor concluded the figurative story of temptation with the saying in 12:10.

The role of the Spirit is described in Q^4 12:11–12. The fourth redactor taught the disciples of Jesus not to worry about what to say when they were dragged to the authorities. It is noteworthy that the authority of the world is mentioned for the first time. However, the fourth redactor did not reveal

---

15. Cf. Kloppenborg, *Formation*, 211–13.

who the authority was. At any rate, this reflects the occasion that the disciples were dragged to a certain authority. It could be the Roman governor in Jerusalem, or the high priest of the Sanhedrin, or the provincial officer, etc. The authority calls our attention to the devil who alleged his authority over the kingdom of world (Q^4 4:5–8). The fourth redactor consistently implied that the disciples of Jesus faced a serious situation of having to cope with worldly authority.

The fourth redactor instructed that the Spirit will provide the disciples with the words to say in front of the authority (Q^4 12:12). The authority reminds readers of those who can kill the body (12:4–5). On the other hand, those who do not speak against the Spirit will receive the words when they have to vindicate themselves before the persecutors (12:10–12). The disciples are promised they will get through the interrogation and win the spiritual battle. This is how Wisdom is vindicated by her children (7:35) and how the disciples imitate Jesus who answered to the devil with the words from Deuteronomy and overcome temptation (4:1–13). While the third redaction defined the disciples as those who had the words of the Lord and observed them (Q^3 6:46–49), the fourth redactor described that they had to speak to the worldly authority what the Spirit had given them. In this respect, the disciples of Jesus had to do what was assigned to them. This is how the disciples are led by the Spirit in order to overcome the critical situation they face.

The fourth redactor revealed the historical situation which the disciples of Jesus faced. They were exposed to the circumstance of being dragged to the authoritative administrations. This could be understood if the crisis caused by Gaius Caligula is the historical background of the fourth redaction to which Q^4 12:10–12 belonged. The disciples seemed to be afraid of the thought that they could be dragged to the Roman authority, imprisoned, and sentenced to death. In this situation, the fourth redactor needed to make them assured of divine guidance and protection. Thus, he delivered the instruction that the Spirit would give them what to say in front of the authority.

G. TWO MASTERS (Q 16:13)

A sharp contrast between God and Mammon is drawn in Q^4 16:13 (Luke 16:13; Matt 6:24). This text is put just after Q^3 12:33–34 by the theme of material possession. As a result, this text becomes the supplementary explanation for the application of the third petition of the Lord's Prayer (Q^2 11:3; 12:22–31). On the other hand, in the fourth redaction, this text follows

12:10–12 by a theme of depending upon the divine being—that is, the Spirit and God.

According to the fourth redactor, Jesus taught the disciples to choose between God and Mammon. No one can serve both masters at the same time. This instruction reminds readers of the third temptation which depicts the seduction of the devil to make Jesus choose the kingdoms of the world rather than God (Q^4 4:5–8). However, as Jesus relied completely upon God, the disciples also have to be dependent upon God rather than Mammon. While the third redactor described how two different managers served the master in the parable of the manager (Q^3 12:42–46), the fourth redactor listed two sorts of masters and made the disciples choose one between them. This informs readers of the changed circumstance among the disciples of Jesus in that they faced serious temptation regarding material possessions. The difference between God and Mammon is too big to serve at the same time. On this, three sets of contrast are suggested as three sets of dialogue between Jesus and the devil appear in Q^4 4:1–13. A person will either hate or love the other, will either be devoted to or despise the other, and will either serve God or Mammon (16:13). If the fourth redaction reflects the crisis caused by Gaius Caligula, then this text also reveals the situation that the disciples of Jesus had to choose between God and the Roman emperor. They faced a crisis of having to serve God by observing the law or to serve the Roman emperor to preserve their material possessions.

H. DISCIPLESHIP (Q 14:26–27; 17:33)

Instruction about discipleship is written in Q^4 14:26–27; 17:33 (Luke 14:26–27; 17:33; Matt 10:37–39). As reflected in the Matthean version, Q^4 14:26–27 and 17:33 were connected to each other in order to impose the instruction about discipleship. They follow Q^4 16:13 by the linking word "hate" in the fourth redaction. The fourth redactor taught the disciples to abandon not only material possessions but also their families. On the other hand, being located in the present place, 14:26–27 and 17:33 play the role of conclusion to the instruction about the ministry of the disciples described in the main texts of the second redaction.

The fourth redactor wrote that a person should hate his or her family to be the disciples of Jesus (Q^4 14:26). This makes the readers think of 9:59–60a in which Jesus did not allow a person to hold the funeral of his dead father.[16] While only the term "father" was mentioned in 9:59–60a, the extended members of family are mentioned in 14:26. This implies that the

---

16. Cf. Jacobson, *First Gospel*, 224.

fourth redactor extended the boundary of family to hate in order to be the disciples of Jesus. While the former text dealt with the matter of the funeral of the dead father, the latter treats the matter of the living members of family. This shows that as the story of the fourth redaction advances, animosity against the family is described more strongly. Although many disciples probably remained with their families, some of them would have left their family in order to campaign for the primacy of discipleship over domestic affairs at the stage of the fourth redaction.[17] It is, however, unclear whether they lived together in a separate place.

The fourth redactor mentioned instruction about taking up the cross (Q^4 14:27). From a literary perspective, the parallelism between hating one's family and taking up the cross indicates that those who love their family cannot bear the cross.[18] The disciples are those who take up the cross and follow him.[19] This carries the theme of martyrdom with the reference to the cross. Carrying the cross is far more difficult than the wandering life (Q^2 9:57–58), the insult and hatred (Q^3 6:22–23b), and abandoning the funeral of a dead father (Q^4 9:59–60a). This implies that they faced a situation at the stage of the fourth redaction that was critically serious. When it is considered that the cross was the Roman method of executing traitors, the disciples of Jesus had to run the risk of persecution and even martyrdom (Q^4 10:3).[20] This reflects the historical situation that they had to determine to lose their life on the cross (11:47–51; 12:4–5). When the members of the Q community faced the crisis caused by Gaius Caligula in order to erect his statue in the Jerusalem temple (4:1–13), the fourth redactor taught them not to avoid the possibility of being sentenced to death on the cross, being accused as traitors against the Roman Empire (14:27).

The instruction about the reversal of one's fate is described in Q^4 17:33 (Luke 17:33; Matt 10:39). This is a proverbial saying about life and death. Those who would like to seek their life will lose it; on the other hand, those who would like to lose it will seek it. The reversal of one's fate appears for the first time. While the second redactor encouraged the disciples not to worry about food and clothes for their life (Q^2 12:22–31), the third redactor talked about life after the general resurrection of the Gentiles (Q^3 11:31–32). On

17. Kloppenborg, *Formation*, 231.

18. There is an opinion that Q 14:26–27 is an early tradition reflecting the remembrance of the cross of Jesus (cf. Seeley, "Blessings," 138). This is the only text that includes the term "cross" in Q. This could reflect the historical crucifixion of Jesus (cf. Jacobson, *First Gospel*, 222). It is, however, to be noted that the redactor did not give any clue to the cross of Jesus.

19. Seeley, "Death," 226.

20. This could remind readers of the crucifixion of Jesus (cf. Kloppenborg, *Q*, 75).

the contrary, the fourth redactor urged them to lose their life so as to seek life (Q^4 17:33). It seems that the fourth redactor thought of life after death in connection with the earthly life. This is reminiscent of the instruction of 12:4–5 in that life after death attracts the eyes of people in the fourth redaction. Then, the life that the disciples will gain when they lose it could refer to the life that the soul will enjoy after the death of body. This tells people about the possibility that the third and fourth redactors were from the Pharisees who believed in the general resurrection at the end of the world. This implies that the disciples of Jesus faced a critical situation of running the risk of death when they followed Jesus.[21]

---

21. Cf. Kloppenborg, *Formation*, 232.

3

The Texts Interpolated into the Third Redaction

The third section of Q was expanded further by the fourth redaction. The fourth redactor interpolated some texts into the main texts of the third redaction. By doing so, the fourth redaction shows its theology conveyed not only by the previous addition to the main texts of the first and second redactions but also by the interpolation into the main texts of the third redaction. For instance, the reason that Jesus came to the world is explained, reconciliation before the final judgment is asked, eschatological reversal at the end of the world is emphasized, eschatological judgment at the end of the world is described in various ways, and the authority that will be given to the twelve apostles is mentioned. With these descriptions, the fourth redactor tried to make the disciples ready for what would happen, identified them as the people of God, and described the eschatological judgment. By doing so, the texts about the coming of the Son of Man and the kingdom of God were reoriented by the fourth redaction.

A. THE PURPOSE OF THE COMING OF JESUS (Q 12:49, 51–53)

The purpose of Jesus coming into the world is described in Q^4 12:49, 51–53 (Luke 12:49, 51–53; Matt 10:34–36). This text follows Q^4 14:26–27; 17:33 by the theme of family in the fourth redaction. This text was added to Q^3 12:39–46 which deals with preparation for the Son of Man in the third redaction. While the third redactor talked about preparation for his sudden coming, the fourth redactor described one's preparation for what would happen on account of Jesus.

The fourth redactor described the reason why Jesus had come to the world in Q^4 12:49, 51. He came to the world not to give peace but to give fire and/or a sword. Peace was once mentioned in the second redaction (Q^2 10:5-6); however, the fourth redactor wrote that Jesus had come to give fire and sword rather than peace. On one hand, the proclamation of peace was once accepted in the region of Galilee; as a result, many people gathered in the name of Jesus at the stage of the third redaction though the opposition increased. On the other hand, it was not easy to manage in the region of Jerusalem at the stage of the fourth redaction. This reflects that circumstances were not peaceful; rather, the disciples were under persecution and martyrdom.[1] The term "sword" appears for the first time. It seems that the fourth redactor used the wordplay between μακάιρος [blessed] and μάχαιρα [sword]. This is supported by the fact that while the first three redactors wrote the beatitudes starting with the term "blessed" [μακάιροι] in Q 6:20b-22; 7:23; 10:23, the fourth redactor did not use it. This implies that the situation was not good enough to announce blessing to the disciples of Jesus. The sword is a weapon either to attack or to defend oneself from opponents. If the fourth redaction was done in the middle of the crisis caused by Gaius Caligula, it is understandable that the fourth redactor taught the disciples to hold the sword against the enemy. They had nothing to do but resist and fight against the opponents.[2]

The fourth redactor mentioned the division among the family members in Q^4 12:52-53. This reminds readers of 9:59-60a and 14:26-27 regarding the family. As a person was asked to leave family to follow Jesus in spite of a funeral of a dead father (9:59-60a), he or she was demanded to love Jesus more than his or her parents and children (14:26-27). Then, the fourth redactor dealt with division among family members: between father and son, mother and daughter, and mother-in-law and daughter-in-law. As the story of the fourth redaction advances, the intensity of division and conflict among family members was getting stronger. This reflects the social situation of the disciples in relationship with their family members. Probably, this division was resulted from the crisis caused by Gaius Caligula who attempted to erect his statue in the Jerusalem temple. Some of the family members wanted to deal with the Roman soldiers in order to keep God holy, but the others would not in order to protect their material possessions.

---

1. Kloppenborg, *Formation*, 152.
2. Tuckett argues there was a real situation to hold the sword (*Q*, 239).

In this respect, the division among the family members was inevitable at the stage of the fourth redaction.

The allusion to the Bible is detected in Q^4 12:53. Division among family members is interpreted against the background of Mic 7:6. The fourth redactor already revealed interest in the Bible in that he quoted Deuteronomy three times and Psalms once in the temptation story (4:4, 8, 10–11, 12); in addition, he mentioned Abel and Zechariah (11:49–51). Moreover, the parable of the unclean spirit alludes to the story of Hagar (11:24–26). In this sequence, the fourth redactor made another allusion to Mic 7:6. In other words, division among family members was the mirror for the understanding of the contemporary situation as the corrupted one. In this respect, the fourth redactor was a well-trained scribe in his interpretation of the teaching of Jesus in light of the Bible.

B. THE SIGN ABOUT THE TIMES (Q 12:54-56)

The fourth redactor mentioned the sign about the times in Q^4 12:54–56 (Luke 12:54–56; Matt 16:2–3). This text follows Q^4 12:49, 51–53 with terms derived from the same root πῦρ [fire] as that used in the fourth redaction.[3] In this respect, division among family members on account of Jesus is a sign of the end of the world. Having attached this text to the main texts of the third redaction, the fourth redactor intended to deliver instruction to see the crisis raised by Gaius Caligula as the sign of the coming of Jesus the Son of Man at the end of the world.

The fourth redactor mentioned the changing appearance of the sky in Q^4 12:54–55. It is said that a tiny change of meteorological phenomena makes people forecast the weather that will happen later. The instruction regarding the sign learned from nature appears a second time in Q. For example, the second redactor argued that people should learn divine care from the ravens in the sky and the lilies in the field (Q^2 12:24, 27). It is, however, too weak to be interpreted as a sign from the nature. On the other hand, the third redactor mentioned rain and floods as signs of eschatological judgment, wind in comparison to prophet, and lightening for the coming of the Son of Man (Q^3 6:48–49; 7:24; 17:23–24). However, these meteorological phenomena are not adequate to be used as the sign of the

---

3. While πῦρ [fire] is used in Luke 12:49, πυρράζω [flame red] is adopted in Matt 16:2. Cf. Robinson et al., *Critical Edition*, 376, 388. It is not easy to decide which version represents the original wording of Q. It seems that the Lucan version represents the weather of Ephesus which is supposed to be the place of its writing. Then, it could be said that the Matthean version represents the original of Q.

times. On the contrary, having inherited this tradition, the fourth redactor put an emphasis on learning meteorological signs from nature. It seems that learning from nature was emphasized in order to make the disciples of Jesus look for the divine sign for the designated time in the middle of crisis caused by the Roman emperor Gaius Caligula. They were required to look at every kind of sign that could occur in their normal life.

The fourth redactor emphasized interpreting the sign of the times (Q^4 12:56). It is said that since the disciples of Jesus knew to interpret the appearance of the sky, they had to know the sign of the times. This is a way of argument called *a minori ad maius* which means an inference from smaller to bigger.[4] As implied above, this argument was already used in the second redaction (Q^2 12:6-7, 22-31). Although the argument of *a minori ad maius* is not directly used in the third redaction, its logic seems to be applied to texts such as Q^3 10:14 and 12:2-3. Having inherited this tradition, the fourth redactor urged the disciples of Jesus to recognize the sign of the times from their surroundings. This means that they were in a critical and unstable situation and they had to be cautious of what would happen.

C. RECONCILIATION (Q 12:58-59)

Instruction about reconciliation is given in Q^4 12:58-59 (Luke 12:58-59; Matt 5:25-26). This text follows Q^4 12:54-56 by the theme of solving the problem that was already anticipated. On the other hand, this text was added to Q^3 13:18-21, 24-27 of the third redaction in order to be ready for the eschatological judgment.

The fourth redactor dealt with instruction about the effort to reconcile oneself with one's adversary (Q^4 12:58). According to it, Jesus asked the disciples to be reconciled with the adversary to whom they had done something wrong before they would be handed over to the judge and finally put into prison. The legal term ἀντιδίκος [adversary] appears for the first time in the fourth redaction. This implies that there were lawsuits between the disciples and their opponents. While Jesus taught his disciples to do something good first to others in the first redaction (Q^1 6:31-38), the fourth redactor applied it to the disciples who did something wrong first. Although they were persecuted or martyred, they made an effort to make themselves reconciled with their fellow Jews. Appearance in front of a judge reminds readers of Q^4 12:11-12 in that the disciples could be dragged before the authority of the world. This implies that they faced the situation of having to appear in front of judges at the stage of the fourth redaction.

4. Cf. Doewe, *Jewish Hermeneutics*, 106-10.

The fourth redactor instructed that the disciples should pay to the last penny (Q^4 12:59). This is seen in the description that the term ἔσχατος [last] is used to be exempted from their debt. This is the only way to be freed from prison. This refers to the accounting at the end of the world. The fourth redactor encouraged the disciples to avoid the eschatological judgment with regard to punishment. The theme of eschatological judgment at the end of time has been developed since the third redaction. Having received this tendency, the fourth redactor described eschatological judgment in the future with the image of accounting. In this respect, Q focuses on one's consistent preparation for the end of the world especially facing the crisis raised by Gaius Caligula with regard to the matter of idolatry.

D. ESCHATOLOGICAL REVERSAL (Q 13:28-30)

The theme of eschatological reversal is introduced in Q^4 13:28-30 (Luke 13:28-30; Matt 8:11-12; 20:16). This text follows Q^4 12:58-59 in the fourth redaction by the linking word "last" that shows interest in the end of world. In addition, this text was added to Q^3 13:18-21, 24-27 of the third redaction in order to define those who enter the kingdom of God. The fourth redactor depicted it as a transcendental realm in a more specific way.

The fourth redactor described the transcendental aspect of the kingdom of God in regard to the entrants (Q^4 13:28-29). It is said that many people will come from east and west and sit with Abraham, Isaac, and Jacob in the kingdom of God, while others will be cast out of it into the darkness where there will be wailing and grinding of teeth. The mentioning of Abraham, Isaac, and Jacob recalls the terms "forefather" and "descendants of Abraham" (3:8bc). Then, the descendants of Abraham refer to the entrants of the kingdom of God in the fourth redaction. In this respect, the kingdom is described as the transcendental realm which people will enter after their death. This calls attention to the kingdom of God which is contrasted with the kingdom of the world (4:5-8). In addition, the kingdom of God is the place opposite to gehenna where the soul goes after death according to the fourth redactor (12:4-5). In this respect, the fourth redactor was much interested in transcendental places.

It is necessary to see how the concept of kingdom changed as the redaction of Q progressed. As mentioned before, the first three redactors treated the kingdom of God from their own perspectives (Q^1 6:20b; Q^2 10:9; 11:2, 20; 12:31; Q^3 13:18-21). Especially, the garden of Eden was the mirror for the kingdom of God when the second redactor introduced the five petitions of the Lord's Prayer (Q^2 11:2-4). Then, the third redactor figuratively described the kingdom as a place to enter (Q³ 11:52; 13:18-19, 24-27). In addition, the fourth redactor depicted the kingdom as a place that the disciples had to be eager to enter (Q⁴ 16:16) and as the realm in which many people already entered according to their hierarchical system (7:28). Finally, it is depicted as the place where many people has entered and dwell, including Abraham, Isaac, and Jacob (13:28-29). The description above shows how the kingdom of God changed to a transcendental place to enter and dwell as the redaction of Q progressed.

The fourth redactor introduced a proverbial saying in Q⁴ 13:30. It is about the eschatological reversal that the last will be first and the first will be last. The eschatological reversal was already implied in 13:28-29, because those who had been supposed to enter were announced to be thrown out of the kingdom. Then, it presupposes division among the two parties although it is not clear whether the division occurred "within the Q community or within the Jesus movement."[5] The fourth redactor seemed to open the door of the kingdom of God to the Gentiles. While the Gentiles were treated with favor in the third redaction (Q³ 7:1-10),[6] the fourth redactor showed the possibility that the Gentiles were involved among the residents of the kingdom when he mentioned those from east and west[7] The fourth redactor developed the theme of eschatological reversal and applied it to the status of the Jews and the Gentiles regarding entrance into the kingdom of God. This kind of reversal was shocking to the Jews who had regarded themselves as the people of God. In this respect, it seems that the disciples of Jesus turned their eyes to the Gentiles at the stage of the fourth redaction.

E. LAMENTATION OVER JERUSALEM (Q 13:34-35)

Lamentation over Jerusalem is written about in Q⁴ 13:34-35 (Luke 13:34-35; Matt 27:37-39).[8] This text follows Q⁴ 13:28-30 by the theme of reversal in that the Jews excluded themselves from the people of God. This text was attached to Q³ 13:18-21, 24-27 in order to explain the reason that the Jews were kicked out of the kingdom of God.

---

5. Jacobson, *First Gospel*, 208.

6. The third redactor mentioned the Queen of the South and the Ninevites in Q³ 11:31-32. It is, however, to be noted that they were mentioned to heighten the unfaithfulness of the Jews.

7. Kloppenborg, *Formation*, 236.

8. Miller believes that Q 13:34-35 is the saying of prophets in the name of resurrected Jesus ("Rejection," 238, 235-40).

The fourth redactor mentioned the name "Jerusalem" for the first time (Q^4 13:34). While the temple is mentioned in 4:9–12 and 11:47–51, Jerusalem itself appears only in 13:34. After the temple was described from a negative point of view in those texts, Jerusalem and temple were used in connection with increased animosity toward the Jews. This implies that the disciples of Jesus were active in Jerusalem at the stage of the fourth redaction. The fourth redactor identified Jerusalem as the place of martyrdom. This is seen in the description that the prophets were stoned to death there. This reminds readers of the second temptation of the devil who seduced Jesus to death (Q^4 4:9–12) and the martyrdom of Abel and Zechariah in the temple (11:47–51). The place of sacrificial offering to God changed to that of killing the prophets—that is, the disciples of Jesus. In other words, they experienced a serious confrontation with the authorities of Jerusalem. This implies that those who were in charge of Jerusalem were in cooperation with the Roman emperor and killed some disciples of Jesus in the temple during the crisis caused by Gaius Caligula.

The fourth redactor identified the disciples of Jesus as the prophets. As mentioned before, the third redactor started describing them as the prophets, since they were those who saw and heard what the prophets had wanted to see and hear but had not (Q^3 10:23–24). In a sense, they were more than the prophets. Having succeeded the tradition, the fourth redactor defined them as the prophets sent to Jerusalem. Once it was written that the disciples of Jesus were the children of Wisdom (Q^4 7:35) and that Wisdom sent the prophets (11:47–51). "Q 13:34–35 has the characteristic of a discourse of the personified Wisdom."[9] In other words, they were the prophets sent by Jesus from the perspective of the Deuteronomistic tradition (6:23c; 10:3).[10] In this respect, Jesus was defined as Wisdom who sent the prophets to Jerusalem.

The fourth redactor attributed the reason of eschatological reversal to the Jews. This is described with the metaphor that a hen tried to gather her nestlings under her wings but they were not willing. The lamentation reveals the wisdom tradition. According to Tuckett,

> The image of the hen gathering its brood has a parallel in a saying about Wisdom in Sir 1:15 (Gk). Furthermore, the motif of the withdrawal of the speaker (v. 35a) has a parallel in the idea of

---

9. Sato, "Shape," 174. Cf. Sato, *Q*, 43; Jacobson, *First Gospel*, 212.

10. Miller, "Rejection" 238–39; Kloppenborg, *Q*, 76–77; and Jacobson, *First Gospel*, 212. There is an alternative interpretation that this saying talks about the time of salvation according to the repentance of the Israelites. Cf. Allison, "Matt 23:39," 77–81.

Wisdom withdrawing (to heaven) when she cannot find a dwelling place on earth (*I En* 42).[11]

It is clear that the fourth redactor kept using the wisdom tradition in this text. Then, it can be said that Jesus was speaking as Wisdom. In this manner, Jesus is identified as Wisdom which has sent out the prophets martyred even at the temple (11:49–51). The metaphor of hen seems to be developed from Q³ 3:21–22 in which appears the image of the dove descending from heaven upon Jesus the Son of God. Applying this image to the hen, the fourth redactor conveyed the instruction that Jerusalem rejected their identity as the children of God. In addition, Q⁴ 13:34–35 is reminiscent of 4:9–13 in that three elements appear in common: the theme of death, the temple, the term "wing" [πτέρυξ] or "pinnacle" [πτερύγιον]. In other words, the Jewish authority of the temple was in parallel with the devil who seduced Jesus to death. This indicates "the escalation in the harshness of the judgment."[12] They reflect the occasion for writing 13:34–35 against the backdrop of the second temptation of Jesus in order to heighten the reason that the Jews were kicked out of the people of God. In this respect, the Jewish authority of the temple was responsible for the eschatological reversal.

The fourth redactor depicted Jerusalem as the place of dissolution (Q⁴ 13:35). This is seen in the saying of Jesus, "You will not see me again until you say, 'Blessed is he who comes in the name of the Lord.'" For this, the fourth redactor used the phrase λέγω ὑμῖν depicting Jesus as the prophet of God (Q¹ 6:27; Q² 10:12; 11:9; 12:22; Q³ 7:9, 26; Q⁴ 3:8C; 7:28; 11:51). As Q went through a process of redaction, the prophetic aspect of Jesus was strengthened. It seems that the fourth redactor adopted the quotation from Ps 117:26a (LXX).[13] Then, Jesus is identified with the one who will come in the name of the Lord.[14] While God was defined as the Lord in Q¹ 3:4; Q³ 10:2 and then Jesus was identified as the Lord in Q³ 6:46; 7:6, the fourth redactor used the title "Lord" again in an ambivalent way in Q⁴ 13:35. It can refer to God or Jesus. On the basis of the theme of coming developed in the third redaction (Q³ 3:16–17; 7:24–27; 12:39–40; 17:23–24), it seems that the fourth redactor applied the theme of coming to the one who will come in the name of the Lord. In this respect, the eschatological appearance of Jesus continued in the fourth redaction.

---

11. Tuckett, *Q*, 175.
12. Sato, *Q*, 42; and Sato, "Shape," 174.
13. Jacobson, *First Gospel*, 211.
14. Cf. Sato, *Q*, 43; and Sato, "Shape," 174.

F. REVERSAL OF POSITION (Q 14:11)

Instruction about the reversal of one's position is found in Q^4 14:11 (Luke 14:11; Matt 23:12). This text follows Q^4 13:34–35 by the theme of reversal in the fourth redaction. Furthermore, this text was added to Q^3 13:18–21, 24–27 of the third redaction in order to ascribe the aspect of reversal to those who will enter the kingdom of God.

The fourth redactor introduced a proverbial saying regarding the reversal of one's position (Q^4 14:11). It is said, "For everyone who exalts himself will be humbled, and he who humbles himself will be exalted." The theme of reversal already appeared with regard to life and death in 17:33. It seems that this kind of eschatological reversal started when the self-boasting of Capernaum was criticized in the third redaction (Q^3 10:15). In addition, the third redactor criticized those who liked the best seat at a banquet and received greetings at the marketplace (Q^3 11:43). Having inherited these texts, the fourth redactor could write about the eschatological reversal of one's position in Q^4 14:11. It is, however, to be noted that although this text carries the theme of eschatological reversal, it does not fit well with its context. The surrounding texts deal with the reversed fate of the Jews and the Gentiles in Q^4 13:28–30 and 14:16–24.

The fourth redactor introduced eschatological reversal from an ethical perspective. It has not been known why it was written in the middle of texts that treat eschatological reversal between the Jews and the Gentiles (Q^4 13:28–30; 14:16–24). It seems that the instruction was given to the disciples of Jesus as a warning not to boast about their reversed status. They were instructed to be humble although they were promised entrance into the kingdom of God.

G. THE PARABLE OF THE BANQUET (Q 14:16–24)

The parable of the banquet is described in Q^4 14:16–24 (Luke 14:16–24; Matt 22:1–10). This text follows Q^4 14:11 by the theme of reversal in the fourth redaction. Furthermore, this text was added to the texts of Q^3 13:18–21, 24–27 in order to show reversal in the kingdom of God.

The fourth redactor introduced a well-developed pericope in Q^4 14:16–24. This consists of three sets of dialogues between the master and the servants. The dialogue has been developed as the redaction of Q progressed. For instance, no dialogue is found in the first redaction because only unilateral address is used for the preaching of John and Jesus (Q^1 3:7–8a, 9; 6:20b, 27, 29–38). A set of dialogues is found in the second redaction (Q^2 9:57–58;

11:14–15, 17–20), while two sets of dialogues are found in the third redaction (Q³ 7:1–10; 13:24–27). On the other hand, the fourth redactor already created a pericope equipped with three sets of dialogues in Q⁴ 4:1–13. In this vein, three sets of dialogues between the master and the servants were adopted in the parable of the banquet (Q⁴ 14:16–24). The further the redaction of Q progressed, the longer the pericope was getting. This implies that the fourth redactor was a well-trained scribe from a literary perspective.

The parable of the banquet reveals the pattern of invitation and rejection. It is described in that the master invited guests through his servants but the invitees rejected his invitation three times with an excuse in this parable.[15] This type of pattern was already used in the temptation story when the devil invited Jesus to seductions but he rejected them three times (Q³ 4:1–13). In addition, the invitation of guest reminds readers of Jesus' invitation of a follower who refused on account of the funeral of his dead father (9:59a–60). This shows that the fourth redactor was consistent in the use of the literary pattern of invitation and rejection that is a typical characteristic of the Deuteronomistic historical point of view. This seems to reflect the social situation that the disciples of Jesus frequently asked their fellow Jews to accept the instruction of Jesus but they refused to accept it. It seems that ministry in Jerusalem was not successful because the Jews refused to accept the instruction of Jesus often.

The parable of the banquet teaches the disciples of Jesus about eschatological reversal. The invitees refused to participate in the banquet, while the uninvited will enter in their place. It is to be observed that the invitees voluntarily refused to go to the banquet. If the banquet represents the feast at the kingdom of God (Q⁴ 13:34–35), the eschatological reversal between the invitee and the randomly chosen becomes clear. This probably means that while the Jews voluntarily refrained from the kingdom of God, the uninvited Gentiles fortunately took part in it. It seems that the further the disciples of Jesus faced the opposition and persecution of the fellow Jews, the more the redactor emphasized the eschatological reversal in order to encourage the disciples to hold their faith in God and follow the instruction of Jesus. Eschatological reversal is the most important theme in the parable of the banquet.[16]

The parable of the banquet provides glimpses of the economic environment at the time of the writing of the fourth redaction. It seems that some of the disciples were in a stable situation from an economic perspective in that they were rich enough to provide a banquet, have a number of servants,

---

15. Jacobson, *First Gospel*, 217.
16. Jacobson, *First Gospel*, 219.

and have fellowship with various groups of people. While the third redactor depicted the household who entrusted his property to the manager in order to sustain the servants (Q³ 12:42-46), the fourth redactor mentioned the kingdoms of the world and their splendor (Q⁴ 4:1-12) and described a person who provided a banquet for the guests outside of his house (14:16-24). This means that as the redaction of Q progressed, the disciples advanced to Jerusalem and became affluent enough to describe a banquet.

H. THE PARABLE OF THE SALT (Q 14:34-35)

The parable of the salt is described in Q⁴ 14:34-35 (Luke 14:34-35; Matt 5:13). This text is located in the present place as the conclusion to the parable of the banquet, in that as the insipid salt can do nothing but be thrown out, those who lose the nature of disciple will be thrown out of the kingdom. This is accordant with the instruction that Q⁴ 13:28-30 delivers. The parable of the salt was attached to the texts of Q³ 13:18-21, 24-27 in order to show that the entrants of the kingdom should not lose the nature of the disciples of Jesus.

Salt appears for the first time in Q⁴ 14:34. It is said that salt is good. This means that salt is useful. The term καλός was used for the fruit in the first redaction (Q¹ 3:9). Then, the third redactor applied it to the tree (Q³ 6:43). Then, it was adopted for the characterization of salt in the fourth redaction (Q⁴ 14:34). The texts listed above evince the fact that the term καλός is applied to a plant in the second and third redactions and to a mineral in the fourth redaction. When salt has lost its flavor, it will be thrown out. However, neither the earth nor the dunghill accommodates it. This reminds readers of wailing and grinding of teeth in the darkness (Q⁴ 13:29). In this way, the fourth redactor emphasized the eschatological reversal of one's status.

I. THE PARABLE OF THE LOST SHEEP (Q 15:4-7)

The parable of the lost sheep is found in Q⁴ 15:4-7 (Luke 15:4-7; Matt 18:12-13). This text follows Q⁴ 14:34-35 by the theme of "going astray" either voluntarily or compulsorily, and it can be connected to 14:16-24 by the linking word "find" [εὑρίσκω]. The parable of the lost sheep was written in order to find the people of God. The parable was placed after the texts Q³ 13:18-21, 24-27 of the third redaction in order to heighten the importance of entering and remaining in the kingdom of God.

The fourth redactor introduced the parable of the lost sheep to emphasize taking care of others. This is seen in the description that one out of a hundred was lost but finally found. The delight of finding the one is greater than that of the ninety-nine left in the safe place. In this way, the parable urges the disciples to take care of others until they have found every last one. Then, this makes readers think of his summoning of people on the road in order to fill the empty seat (Q^4 14:16–24). As a result, the parable of the lost sheep plays the role of conclusion to the parable of the banquet which mentions the eschatological reversal of the marginal people who were called to the kingdom of God, probably including the Gentiles.

The parable of the lost sheep conveys the instruction that the lost one should be found. It seems to reflect the effort to find the one who left the group of the disciples of Jesus. Probably some members walked away from the instruction of Jesus on account of continuous persecution and even martyrdom. Nevertheless, the fourth redactor delivered the parable of the salt in order to teach them not to lose the nature of disciples of Jesus and then conveyed the parable of the lost sheep in order to teach them to get the lost back. In this way, the fourth redactor showed the effort to find even the last one. While the parable of the banquet described the effort to fill the empty seats, the parable of the lost sheep depicts the effort to find the last one. In this way, the fourth redactor conveyed the instruction to do the best to find the lost.

J. WOE AGAINST SCANDAL (Q 17:1–2)

Woe against scandal is mentioned in Q^4 17:1–2 (Luke 17:1–2; Matt 18:6–7). This text follows Q^4 15:4–7 by the theme of taking care of the little ones. Both texts carry a common element in that the sheep was one out of hundred (15:4–5) and no one should entice one of these little ones (17:1–2). This text was planted in the present place in order to support the texts of Q^3 13:18–21, 24–27 in that the disciples should take care of even the least one in their community.

The fourth redactor described that Jesus had announced a woe against those who had enticed others. The term σκανδαλίζω [entice] appears a second time. While it was used for the case of the disciples being enticed on account of Jesus in the third redaction (Q^3 7:23), it appears here for the case of disciples enticing other disciples (Q^4 17:1). This indicates that the fourth redactor tried to strengthen the solidarity among the disciples in confrontation with their opponents. In addition, the literary device "woe" was frequently used in the third redaction: two woes in Q^3 10:13–15 and six woes in 11:39–46, 52. Having inherited this literary device, the fourth redactor used it once in Q^4 11:47–51 and wrote another one in 17:1–2. It is, however, noteworthy that both are related with the theme of death in the fourth redaction. While the "woe" was addressed to those who insulted and hated the disciples in the third redaction, it was said to the disciple who had enticed other people of little faith in the fourth redaction. With the literary device of "woe," the fourth redactor would like to make the disciples of Jesus keep solidarity.

The fourth redactor prescribed death to those who enticed other disciples. In case of scandal, they had to put a millstone around their neck and throw themselves into the sea. This is a sentence of death for the person. It is, however, noteworthy that this is in contrast with the cases described in Q^4 4:9–12; 11:47–51; and 13:34–35. While these texts dealt with the death of the persecuted disciples of Jesus, 17:1–2 deals with the case of those who enticed other disciples. It seems that the fourth redactor warned those who divided the disciples. Then, this reminds readers of 12:49, 51–53 which deals with division among family members on account of Jesus.

The fourth redactor referred to the little ones (Q^4 17:2). They are supposed to be the ones who did not have strong faith in Jesus. It is noteworthy that the fourth redactor paid attention to stratification among the disciples. The fact that the term "little ones" [μικροί] is mentioned indicates the existence of those bigger and stronger than them among the disciples. This recalls the stratification that John was defined as the one less than the least in the kingdom of God (7:28). These texts mentioned above are sufficient enough to show stratification among the disciples at the stage of the fourth redaction. This reflects that the occasion for writing was new members who had joined the disciples of Jesus in Jerusalem. In this way, the fourth redactor urged the disciples of Jesus to raise them up with careful nursing.

K. FAITH (Q 17:6)

Instruction about the result of faith is written about in Q^4 17:6 (Luke 17:6; Matt 17:20). This text follows Q^4 17:1–2 with the connecting word "sea." On the other hand, this text was put in front of Q^3 17:23–24, 26–27, 30, 34–35 in order to make the disciples have faith in the eschatological judgment.

The fourth redactor introduced a proverbial saying regarding the miracle resulting from faith. It is said, "If you have faith as small as a mustard seed, you can say to this mulberry tree [or mountain], 'Be uprooted and planted in the sea,' and it will obey you."[17] The combination of faith and obe-

17. The Matthean version of Q 17:6 uses the term "mountain" instead of the Lucan

dience was already used in the story of the centurion (Q³ 7:1–10) and the term "mustard seed" is found in the parable of the mustard seed in the third redaction (13:18–19). There is, however, a difference in that while the third redactor believed in the miracle (7:1–10, 22), the fourth redactor did not expect it to actually occur (Q⁴ 3:8b; 4:1–13). In this vein, the fourth redactor knew that the mountain cannot be actually uprooted and planted in the sea by faith. Nevertheless, this saying conveys an important teaching that the disciples of Jesus have to have faith in God in their difficult circumstance.

L. THE EAGLE AND THE CORPSE (Q 17:37B)

Instruction about death is written in Q⁴ 17:37b (Luke 17:37b; Matt 24:28). This text follows Q⁴ 17:6 in the fourth redaction. It is, however, noteworthy that there is no linking word or theme between them. On the other hand, the metaphor was added to the texts of the third redaction in order to describe the result at the end (Q³ 17:23–24, 26–27, 30, 34–35).

The metaphoric saying about the eagle appears for the first time. It is said, "Where there is a dead body, there the vultures will gather." The eagle seems to stand for the Roman Empire because it was her emblem.[18] Then, this saying could mean death by the Roman soldiers. Furthermore, this saying seems to be closely related to the crisis caused by Gaius Caligula who attempted to erect his statue in the temple of Jerusalem. Those who resisted his attempt would be sentenced to death. Rather, the fourth redactor delivered the instruction that those who had faith as small as a mustard seed in God and followed the instruction of Jesus could be killed by the Roman soldiers (Q⁴ 13:34–35). Being taken by the Son of Man was the only way to avoid being killed by them, not to compromise with them (Q³ 17:34–35). In this way, the fourth redactor insisted on the hope of divine salvation.

M. THE PARABLE OF THE ACCOUNTING (Q 19:12–26)

The parable of the accounting is introduced in Q⁴ 19:12–26 (Luke 19:12–26; Matt 25:14–29).[19] This text follows Q⁴ 17:37b in the fourth redaction by the

---

term "mulberry tree" (Luke 17:6; Matt 17:20b; cf. 21:21). It is not easy to know which version represents the original text of Q. However, some critical scholars prefer the Lucan version to the Matthean. Cf. Robinson et al., *Critical Edition*, 492–93. In my judgment, "mountain" should be preferred on account of its use in Q⁴ 4:5 and 6:12a. My argument can be supported by Paul who indirectly cited this saying in 1 Cor 13:2.

18. Jacobson, *First Gospel*, 235–36.

19. It is difficult to decide which version represents the original wording of Q,

theme of punishment. Although their sequence is not natural, the fourth redactor seemed to focus on it. In addition, Q^4 19:12–26 was added to the texts of Q^3 17:23–24, 26–27, 30, 34–35 in order to explain the eschatological judgment at the time of the coming of the Son of Man.

The fourth redactor developed the literary device "pericope" by composing the parable with three sets of dialogue. They are found between the master and his three servants. Three sets of dialogue were already found in the temptation story (Q^4 4:1–13); in addition, three attempts to send the servants and invite the quests appear in the parable of the banquet (14:16–24). Without doubt, they constitute a relatively long story compared with others. In this respect, the fourth redactor was a well-trained scribe in writing an instructive document. The fourth redactor described the entrustment of money and its accounting in that the master entrusted three servants with money and made them manage what they were given. What is important is whether they made a profit or not. While two of them doubled the money, the other did not. As a result, the master was pleased with the first two servants, but not with the third. The master told the former that they were the good servants since they were faithful in the least things and they were rewarded. On the other hand, the master rebuked the latter for laziness and stupidity and deprived him of what he had. It is, however, noteworthy that the master heard his long lame excuse, which led only to the master's rebuke. This implies that there will be an eschatological judgment at the end of the world. The good servants of God will be rewarded, whereas the bad ones will be punished.

The fourth redactor developed several themes of the third redaction in the parable of the accounting. First of all, in this parable, the title "Lord" is applied to the master who seems to stand for Jesus as the third redactor described (Q^3 6:46–47; 7:6; 10:2; Q^4 19:16, 18, 20). Then, the return of the master makes readers think of the coming of the Son of Man (Q^3 12:39–40, 42–46; 17:23–24; Q^4 19:15). In addition, the accounting is reminiscent of the reward and punishment at the end of the world (Q^3 3:16–17; 12:42–46; 17:34–35; Q^4 19:17, 19, 22). In consequence, the fourth redactor supplemented the instruction originated in the third redaction with the parable of the accounting.

The fourth redactor revealed the economic situation of the disciples of Jesus with the parable of the accounting. The more profit a servant makes,

---

because the Lucan and Matthean versions are described in different ways. While Luke describes that ten servants received the same amount of money, Matthew depicts that three servants received different amounts of money. There are some who think that the Lucan one represents the original wording of Q (Robinson et al., *Critical Edition*, 524–55). However, in my judgment, the Matthean version is to be preferred.

the more it pleases the master. This kind of instruction is absolutely different from the idea that the disciples of Jesus should give more than what they were asked in the first redaction (Q^1 6:27, 29–30). On the contrary, the fourth redactor delivered the instruction that the master took what the lazy servant had and gave it to the one who already made the most profit. Then, the master finally said, "Everyone who has more, will be given, but as for the one who has nothing, even what he has will be taken away." Although the Lucan and Matthean versions use different units of currency, it cannot be denied that they are extraordinary amounts of money.[20] This indicates that the disciples of Jesus were exposed to a large amount of economic activity at the stage of the fourth redaction. This reminds readers of the devil who offered all the kingdoms of the world and their glory as the object of bargain (Q^4 4:5–8). In this respect, as Q went through a process of redaction, the economic status of the Q community was getting bigger.

N. ESCHATOLOGICAL AUTHORITY (Q 22:30)

Eschatological authority is described in Q^4 22:30 (Luke 22:30; Matt 19:28). This text follows Q^4 19:12–26 by the theme of eschatological reward. It is natural that Q ends with the eschatological reward to the disciples of Jesus. This text was added to the texts of the third redaction in order to emphasize the eschatological judgment at the end (Q^3 17:23–24, 26–27, 30, 34–35).

The fourth redactor does not designate the time when the twelve apostles would sit on the twelve thrones. It is simply described that it will happen at the time of the renewal of the world.[21] This seems to go along well with the third redaction in that it also does not designate a timetable for the eschatological judgment in detail. The disciples wished for eschatological victory over the world; however, they did not have the concrete scenario about it. It is, however, noteworthy that the eschatological promise was given to the disciples in Jerusalem which had been considered the center of Israel from a religious perspective. In this respect, the fourth redactor announced the hope for the eschatological victory over the twelve tribes of Israel.

The promise of twelve thrones completes the Israelites typology in Q. It started with the mentioning of the creation of the descendants of Abraham in the fourth redaction (Q^4 3:8bc). Then, the temptation story was added to the baptism story referring to the crossing of the Red Sea (Q^3 3:21–22) and the temptation in the wilderness (Q^4 4:1–13). In addition, the fourth redactor listed the twelve apostles who replaced the twelve patriarchs of the

---

20. Cf. Jacobson, *First Gospel*, 242.
21. Jacobson, *First Gospel*, 246.

Israelites (6:12–16). Moreover, they are promised to be seated on the twelve thrones to rule the twelve tribes. In this way, the number "twelve" dominated the story in the fourth redaction. As a result, the fourth redactor substituted the twelve tribes of the Israelites with the twelve apostles (22:20). In this way, the Israelites typology was completed. It seems that the fourth redactor received the traditions that the first redactor revealed the allusions to the holiness code embedded in Lev 19 (Q^1 6:27, 29–38),[22] the second redactor described the five petitions of the Lord's Prayer against the backdrop of the garden of Eden (Gen 2:4—3:24; Q^2 11:2-4), and the third redactor quoted the verses from Exod 23:20 (Q^3 7:27) or made an allusion to primordial time (Gen 1:1; 2:4a; Q^3 10:21). All of them are related with the Pentateuch which deals with the history of the forefathers of the Israelites. Having inherited these traditions of the previous redactors, the fourth redactor was able to connect the sayings and activities of Jesus with the Israelites in order to identify the disciples of Jesus as the twelve tribes of the Israelites—that is, the people of God.

Q ends with the most authoritative saying regarding the promise that the twelve thrones will reign over the twelve tribes. It seems to reflect that the occasion for writing was the crisis caused by Gaius Caligula around 40–41 CE. In association with the Sanhedrin, he tried to erect his statue in the Jerusalem temple. Facing the serious crisis, the Jews resisted his attempt even if they were sentenced to death. In the middle of the crisis, the fourth redactor also urged the disciples of Jesus in Jerusalem to protest against idolatry. At this point, the twelve thrones were promised to them representing the new Israelites, so that the disciples of Jesus could get victory over the Roman emperor's blasphemous attempt.

---

22. Allison, *Intertextual Jesus*, 33.

4

Conclusion

Q was extended further by the fourth redaction. The fourth redactor added texts to the previous redactions more than any other redactor. He did it in order to deliver his own theology. Responding to the contemporary circumstances, the fourth redactor tried to give his instruction to the disciples of Jesus.

It is necessary to list the texts that the fourth redactor interpolated into the main texts of the three previous redactions. They can be listed as follows: (1) the texts added to the first redaction are Q 3:8bc; 4:1–13; 6:12–16, 20a, 23c; 14:5; 7:28; 16:16–18; 7:35; (2) the texts added to the second redaction are 9:59–60a; 10:3; 11:24–26, 47–51; 12:4–5, 10–12; 16:13; 14:26–27; 17:33; (3) the texts added to the third redaction are 12:49, 51–56, 58–59; 13:28–30, 34–35; 14:11, 16–24, 34–35; 15:4–7; 17:1–2, 6, 37b; 19:12–26; 22:30. The texts listed above show that an abundant amount of sources were added to the previous redactions by the fourth redactor. The Moses/Exodus/Israelites typologies were applied to Jesus and his disciples, and the fourth redactor emphasized the eschatological judgment of reward and punishment.

The fourth redactor completed the biography of Jesus in Q. When the fourth redaction was complete, Q was finally formed as follows:

I. John the Baptist and Jesus

  A. The Ministry of John

    Q^1 3:2–4 (Luke 3:2–4 / Matt 3:1–3, 5–6)

    Q^1 3:7–8a (Luke 3:7–8a / Matt 3:7–9a)

    Q^4 3:8bc (Luke 3:8bc / Matt 3:9bc)

Q^1 3:9 (Luke 3:9 / Matt 3:10)

Q^3 3:16–17 (Luke 3:16–17 / Matt 3:11–12)

Q^3 3:21–22 (Luke 3:21–22 / Matt 3:16–17)

B. The Ministry of Jesus

  1. The Temptation

    Q^4 4:1–13 (Luke 4:1–13 / Matt 4:1–11)

  2. The Twelve Apostles

    Q^4 6:12–16 (Luke 6:12–16 / Matt 5:1a; 10:2–4)

  3. The Sermon

    Q^4 6:20a (Luke 6:20a / Matt 5:1b)

    Q^1 6:20b (Luke 6:20b / Matt 5:2b–3)

    Q^2 6:21 (Luke 6:21 / Matt 5:4, 6)

    Q^3 6:22–23b (Luke 6:22–23b / Matt 5:11–12b)

    Q^4 6:23c (Luke 6:23c / Matt 5:12c)

    Q^1 6:27 (Luke 6:27 / Matt 5:44a)

    Q^3 6:28 (Luke 6:28 / Matt 5:44b)

    Q^1 6:29–38 (Luke 6:29–38 / Matt 5:39–40, 42, 45–48; 7:1–2, 12)

    Q^3 6:39 (Luke 6:39 / Matt 15:14)

    Q^4 14:5 (Luke 14:5 / Matt 12:11–12)

    Q^3 6:40 (Luke 6:40 / Matt 10:24–25)

    Q^3 6:41–42 (Luke 6:41–42 / Matt 7:3–5)

    Q^3 6:43–45 (Luke 6:43–45 / Matt 7:16, 18; 12:33–35)

    Q^3 6:46–49 (Luke 6:46–49 / Matt 7:21, 24–27)

  4. The Activity

    Q^3 7:1–10 (Luke 7:1–10 / Matt 8:5–10, 13)

C. Jesus and John

  Q^3 7:18–27 (Luke 7:18–27 / Matt 11:2–10)

  Q^4 7:28 (Luke 7:28 / Matt 11:11)

  Q^4 16:16 (Luke 16:16 / Matt 11:12–13)

  Q^4 16:17–18 (Luke 16:17–18 / Matt 5:18, 32)

  Q^1 7:29–30 (Luke 7:29–30 / Matt 21:31–32)

Q^3 7:31–34 (Luke 7:31–34 / Matt 11:16–19a)

Q^4 7:35 (Luke 7:35 / Matt 11:19b)

II. Jesus' Disciples and Their Missions

  A. The Followers of Jesus

    Q^2 9:57–58 (Luke 9:57–58 / Matt 8:19–20)

    Q^4 9:59–60a (Luke 9:59–60a / Matt 8:21–22)

  B. The Manual for Ministry

    Q^3 10:2 (Luke 10:2 / Matt 9:37–38)

    Q^4 10:3 (Luke 10:3 / Matt 10:16a)

    Q^2 10:4–12 (Luke 10:4–12 / Matt 10:7–15 (11:24))

    Q^3 10:13–16 (Luke 10:13–16 / Matt 11:21–23; 10:40)

    Q^3 10:21–24 (Luke 10:21–24 / Matt 11:25–27; 13:16–17)

  C. The Lord's Prayer and Its Applications

    1. The Lord's Prayer

      Q^2 11:2–4 (Luke 11:2–4 / Matt 6:9–13)

    2. Confidence in Prayer

      Q^2 11:9–10 (Luke 11:9–10 / Matt 7:7–8)

    3. Confidence in the Father: The Vocative of God

      Q^2 11:11–13 (Luke 11:11–13 / Matt 7:9–11)

    4. The Kingdom of God: The Second Petition

      Q^2 11:14–15, 17–20 (Luke 11:14–15, 17–20 / Matt 12:22–28)

      Q^3 11:21–23 (Luke 11:21–23 / Matt 12:29–30)

      Q^4 11:24–26 (Luke 11:24–26 / Matt 12:43–45)

    5. Temptation: The Fifth Petition

      Q^2 11:16, 29–30 (Luke 11:16, 29–30 / Matt 12:38–40)

      Q^3 11:31–32 (Luke 11:31–32 / Matt 12:41–42)

      Q^3 11:33–35 (Luke 11:33–35 / Matt 5:15; 6:22–23)

      Q^3 11:39–46 (Luke 11:39–46 / Matt 23:4, 6–7, 23, 25–28)

      Q^4 11:47–51 (Luke 11:47–51 / Matt 23:29–31, 34–36)

      Q^3 11:52 (Luke 11:52 / Matt 23:13)

Q^3 12:2-3 (Luke 12:2-3 / Matt 10:26-27)

Q^4 12:4-5 (Luke 12:4-5 / Matt 10:28)

  6. Fear of God: The First Petition

    Q^2 12:6-7 (Luke 12:6-7 / Matt 10:29-31)

    Q^3 12:8-9 (Luke 12:8-9 / Matt 10:32-33)

    Q^4 12:10-12 (Luke 12:10-12 / Matt 10:18-19; 12:32)

  7. Daily Bread: The Third Petition

    Q^2 12:22-31 (Luke 12:22-31 / Matt 6:25-33)

    Q^3 12:33-34 (Luke 12:33-34 / Matt 6:19-21)

    Q^4 16:13 (Luke 16:13 / Matt 6:24)

  8. Forgiveness: The Forth Petition

    Q^2 17:3-4 (Luke 17:3-4 / Matt 18:15, 21-22)

D. Discipleship

  Q^4 14:26-27 (Luke 14:26-27 / Matt 10:37-38)

  Q^4 17:33 (Luke 17:33 / Matt 10:39)

III. The Son of Man and the Kingdom of God

  A. Preparation for the Son of Man

    Q^3 12:39-40 (Luke 12:39-40 / Matt 24:43-44)

    Q^3 12:42-46 (Luke 12:42-46 / Matt 24:45-51)

    Q^4 12:49, 51-56 (Luke 12:49, 51-56 / Matt 10:34-36; 16:2-3)

    Q^4 12:58-59 (Luke 12:58-59 / Matt 5:25-26)

  B. The Kingdom of God

    Q^3 13:18-21 (Luke 13:18-21 / Matt 13:31-33)

    Q^3 13:24-27 (Luke 13:24-27 / Matt 7:13-14, 22-23; 25:10-12)

    Q^4 13:28-30 (Luke 13:28-30 / Matt 8:11-12; 20:16)

    Q^4 13:34-35 (Luke 13:34-35 / Matt 23:37-39)

    Q^4 14:11 (Luke 14:11 / Matt 23:12)

    Q^4 14:16-24 (Luke 14:16-24 / Matt 22:1-10)

    Q^4 14:34-35 (Luke 14:34-35 / Matt 5:13)

    Q^4 15:4-7 (Luke 15:4-7 / Matt 18:12-14)

Q^4 17:1-2 (Luke 17:1-2 / Matt 18:6-7)

Q^4 17:6 (Luke 17:6 / Matt 17:20)

C. The Coming of the Son of Man

Q^3 17:23-24 (Luke 17:23-24 / Matt 24:26-27)

Q^3 17:26-27, 30 (Luke 17:26-27, 30 / Matt 24:37-39)

Q^3 17:34-35 (Luke 17:34-35 / Matt 24:40-41)

Q^4 17:37b (Luke 17:37b / Matt 24:28)

Q^4 19:12-26 (Luke 19:12-26 / Matt 25:14-29)

Q^4 22:30 (Luke 22:30 / Matt 19:28)

The final form of Q shows a well-structured document according to theme from a literary perspective. The fourth redactor did not change the literary structure of previous redactions; rather, he or she just interpolated many texts in order to describe Jesus as their religious leader. It seems that the fourth redactor delivered the instruction in the name of Jesus responding to the crisis that the Roman emperor Gaius Caligula attempted to raise his statue in the Jerusalem temple in 40-41 CE. Then, the fourth redaction seems to be written in Jerusalem by a well-trained scribe reflecting that the disciples of Jesus advanced from the region of Galilee to the center of Israel.

The fourth redaction provided the disciples of Jesus with several new instructions. First of all, the fourth redactor urged them to keep faith in God through observation of the law in spite of martyrdom due to the crisis caused by Gaius Caligula. Second, the disciples of Jesus are identified as the Israelites—that is, the new people of God. Third, the fourth redactor taught that the Spirit would guide and protect them from death. For this, the Spirit was personified in the fourth redaction. In this respect, the fourth redactor delivered his or her own instructions to the disciples of Jesus who faced the rapidly changing environment in Jerusalem around 40-41 CE.

Epilogue

Q seems to be redacted four times. Its quadruple redaction is detected based on the fact that Q undoubtedly shows logical gaps among the texts which make readers see the inconsistency of its literary flow. When the layers of redaction are separated from each other using the form critical, redaction critical, composition critical, socio-historical approaches, each will show its own literary and theological characteristic.

Q is well organized according to theological theme and was written for a specific purpose through editing.[1] Although Q seems to be composed through a highly complex process of redaction, its composition was accomplished quite simply through a series of supplements. It seems that the theologically trained scribes were involved in the redaction of Q. The first redactor listed the sources he collected in the first section of Q, which became the main texts of the first redaction regarding the ministry of John and Jesus. However, we are surprised by the fact that its amount is not much. It seems that John was more focused on than Jesus in the first redaction. Then the second redactor expanded Q by adding two beatitudes to the first one found in the first redaction and attaching his or her own sources—that is, the main texts of the second redaction regarding the summoning of the followers and their mission found in the second section of Q. This includes the manual for missionary journey, the Lord's Prayer, and its applications. Thereafter, another expansion was made by the third redactor, who interpolated his own sources into some parts of the first and second redactions and attached the main texts of the third redaction regarding the eschatological Son of Man and the kingdom of God found in the third section of Q. Finally, the fourth redactor added parts he wanted to convey in between the texts of the previous three redactions. No main texts of the fourth redaction are found in it. This is how Q was expanded by the supplementary redaction

---

1. The following texts were already used in my previous book (*Origin*, 18–20). I use them again with a slight modification here.

one by one. The following is a diagram that makes readers see the process of redaction.

1. The First Redaction ①①①
2. The Second Redaction ①②①① ②②②
3. The Third Redaction ①②③①③① ②③②③② ③③③
4. The Fourth Redaction ①②③④①③④① ②③④②③②④ ③③④③④

The diagram above shows the process of supplementary redaction and enlargement of Q done by four redactors. The final form of Q can be compared with the carpet carefully made of various kinds of thread by a craftsman. In other words, Q was expanded by well-trained scribes from a literary and theological perspective step by step. In consequence, they left the first writing about Jesus and made it possible to see the information about the historical Jesus and the theological interpretation imposed upon his teaching.

It seems that the redactors of Q followed the Jewish tradition. As is known to modern readers, a supplementary technique was used in the composition of the Pentateuch and the book of Isaiah. Critical scholars conclude that the Pentateuch is composed of the so-called J, E, D, and P documents. According to them, E was joined by J first, then D was added to them, and finally P was interpolated among them. A similar view is applied to the book of Isaiah which also underwent triple redaction among chapters 1–39, 40–55 and 56–66. In addition, it has been well-known that Psalms is composed of five books reflecting their redaction. Following the Jewish tradition, Q was expanded step by step. It is, however, to be noted that each new redactor did not modify the previous tradition, showing respect to his or her predecessors. In this respect, Q is to be considered a Jewish document regarding John and Jesus.

Q is the first stepping stone to understanding John and Jesus. Especially, Q helps readers take a closer approach than any other documents on the historical Jesus. However, this does not mean that every single teaching and action of Jesus written in this document actually happened. The texts of the first redaction convey no theological hand except the allusion to Lev 19. The radical aspect of instruction does not find its parallel in other Jewish documents. However, it seems that the second, third, and fourth redactors imposed theological meanings to Jesus. The texts of the second redaction show a theological hand in that the Lord's Prayer consists of five petitions alluding to the events that occurred in the garden of Eden. Jesus was identified as the Son of God and the Son of Man in the third redaction and defined as the one who represented the Israelites in the fourth redaction.

They imposed the theological aspect to Jesus, so that the texts of the third and fourth redactions might reflect their contemporary social situation and deliver instruction to meet the rapidly changing environment. To my judgment, only the first redaction seems to definitelycontain the words and actions of the historical Jesus and John. Only a small number of texts seem to originate in the historical Jesus. If my interpretation is plausible, then it provides New Testament scholars with a new approach to the historical Jesus.

From a perspective of redaction, each layer of Q seems to reflect the social environment in which Jesus or his disciples were involved. For example, the first redactor described John announcing the eschatological judgment to unspecified persons and Jesus addressing his instruction to poor people in the wilderness of the region of the Jordan. Everyone was allowed to come to them without any restriction at the stage of the first redaction. Then, the second redaction reflects the situation that Jesus summoned followers and sent them to the neighboring towns to proclaim the kingdom of God and heal the sick. Without doubt, they faced some challenges from the ordinary people. This shows that Jesus and his followers expanded their boundary from the isolated wilderness to the public places such as towns. Later, the third redactor mentioned the names of cities such as Capernaum, Chorazin, and Bethsaida. This means that the disciples of Jesus advanced the urban area but that they faced opposition from the religious leaders. It seems that the third redaction was completed in Capernaum—that is, the central city of the region of Galilee—before the death of Herod Antipas the Tetrarch in 39 CE. Finally, the fourth redaction reflects the historical event caused by the Roman emperor Gaius Caligula who attempted to erect his statue in the Jerusalem temple. Responding to the crisis, the fourth redactor urged the disciples to cope with the idolatry attempt by keeping the law and running the risk of persecution and even martyrdom. They had to completely rely upon God who worked through the Spirit. This was the only way to receive the promised reward that will be given to them. It can be concluded that the fourth redaction was completed by a well-trained scribe in Jerusalem around 41 CE. In consequence, Q itself shows how the early Jesus movement moved from unknown and isolated places to Jerusalem via the Galilean cities.

Bibliography

Allison, Dale C., Jr. "The Eye Is the Lamp of the Body." *NTS* 33 (1987) 61–83.
———. *The Intertextual Jesus: Scripture in Q*. Harrisburgh, PA: Trinity, 2000.
———. *The Jesus Tradition in Q*. Harrisburg, PA: Trinity, 1997.
———. "Matt. 23:39 = Luke 13:35b as a Conditional Prophecy." *JSNT*, n.s., 18 (1983) 75–84.
Arnal, William E. *Jesus and the Village Scribes: Galilean Conflicts and the Setting of Q*. Minneapolis: Fortress, 2001.
Attridge, Harold W. "Reflections on Research into Q." *Semeia*, n.s., 55 (1992) 223–33.
Batten, Alicia. "More Queries for Q: Women and Christian Origins." *BTB* 24 (1994) 44–51.
Bammel, Ernst. "Das Ende von Q." In *Verborum Veritas: Festschrift für Gustav Stählin zum 70. Geburtstag*, edited by O. Bocher und K. Haacker, 39–50. Wuppertal, Germany: Brockhaus, 1970.
Bonnard, Pierre. *L'Evangile selon Saint Matthieu*. CNT 1. 2nd ed. Neuchatel: Delachaux & Niestlé, 1970.
Boring, M. Eugene. *Sayings of the Risen Jesus: Christian Prophecy in the Synoptic Tradition*. SNTSMS 46. Cambridge: Cambridge University Press, 1982.
Brown, Raymond E. *An Introduction to the New Testament*. New Haven: Yale University Press, 2010.
Carlson, Charles E. "Wisdom and Eschatology in Q." In *Logia: Les paroles de Jésus*, edited by J. Dobobel, 101–19. Leuven: Leuven University Press, 1982.
Casey, Maurice. "The Jackals and the Son of Man (Matt 8.20//Luke 9.58)." *JSNT* 23 (1985) 3–22.
Catchpole, David R. "The Beginning of Q: A Proposal." *NTS* 38 (1992) 205–21.
———. "The Centurion's Faith and It's Function in Q." In *The Four Gospels 1992*, edited by F. van Segbroeck, 517–40. Leuven: Leuven University Press, 1992.
———. "The Mission Charge in Q." *Semeia*, n.s., 55 (1992) 147–74.
———. *The Quest for Q*. Edinburgh: T. & T. Clark, 1993.
Collins, John J. "The Kingdom of God in Apocrypha and Pseudepigrapha." In *The Kingdom of God in Twentieth-Century Interpretation*, edited by Wendell Willis, 81–95. Peabody: Hendrickson, 1987.
Cotter, Wendy J. "The Parable of the Children in the Marketplace, Q (Lk) 7:31–35." *NovT* 24 (1987) 289–304.
Crossan, John Dominic. *In Fragments: The Aphorisms of Jesus*. San Francisco: Harper & Row, 1983.

———. *The Historical Jesus: The Life of a Mediterranean Jewish Peasant*. San Francisco: Harper, 1991.

Dahl, Nils A. "Parables of Growth." *Studia Theologica* 5 (1951) 132–66.

Davies, W. D., and D. C. Allison Jr. *The Gospel according to St. Matthew*. Vol. 1, *Introduction and Commentary on Matthew I–VII*. ICC. Edinburgh: T. & T. Clark, 1988.

Del Agua, Agustin. "The Narrative of the Transfiguration as a Derashic Scenification of a Faith Confession (Mark 9.2–8 Par)." *NTS* 39 (1993) 340–54.

Di Lella, Alexander A. "The Structure and Composition of the Matthean Beatitude." In *To Touch the Text*, edited by M. Horgan and P. Kobelski, 237–42. New York: Crossroad, 1989.

Downing, F. Gerald. "Quite like Q." *Biblica* 69 (1988) 196–225.

Dunn, James D. G. *Baptism in the Holy Spirit*. Naperville, IL: Allenson, 1970.

———. *Christology in the Making: A New Testament Inquiry into the Origins of the Doctrine of the Incarnation*. 2nd ed. London: SCM, 1989.

Eddy, Paul Rhodes. "Jesus as Diogenes? Reflects on the Cynic Jesus Thesis." *JBL* 115 (1996) 449–69.

Eiberg-Schwartz, Howard. *The Savage in Judaism: An Anthropology of Israelite Religion and Ancient Judaism*. Bloomington: Indiana University Press, 1990.

Fleddermann, Harry T. "The Beginning of Q." In *SBLSP 1982*, edited by K. H. Richards, 153–59. Atlanta: Scholars, 1982.

———. "The Demands of Discipleship: Matt 8,19–22 par. Luke 9,57–62." In *The Four Gospels 1992*, edited by F. van Segbroeck, 541–61. BETL 100. Leuven: Leuven University Press, 1992.

———. "The Householder and the Servant Left in Charge." In *SBLSP 1986*, edited by K. H. Richards, 17–26. Atlanta: Scholars, 1986.

———. *Mark and Q: A Study of the Overlap Texts*. BETL 122. Leuven: Leuven University Press, 1995.

Han, Kyu Sam. *Jerusalem and the Early Jesus Movement: The Q Community's Attitude toward the Temple*. JSNTSS 207. London: Sheffield Academic, 2002.

Horsley, Richard. A. *Jesus and Spiral of Violence: Popular Jewish Resistance in Roman Palestine*. San Francisco: Harper & Row, 1987.

———. "Questions about Redactional Strata and the Social Relations Reflected in Q." In *SBLSP 1989*, edited by H. R. Kent, 186–203. Chico, CA: Scholars, 1989.

———. *Sociology and the Jesus Movement*. New York: Crossroad, 1989.

———. "Logoï Prophētōn? Reflections on the Genre of Q." In *The Future of Early Christianity*, edited by B. A. Pearson, 175–209. Minneapolis: Fortress, 1991.

———. "Q and Jesus: Assumptions, and Analysis." *Semeia*, n.s., 55 (1992) 175–209.

Humphrey, Hugh M. "Temptation and Authority: Sapiential Narratives in Q." *BTB* 21 (1991) 43–50.

Jacobson, Arland D. "Apocalyptic and the Synoptic Sayings Source Q." In *The Four Gospels 1992*, edited by F. van Segbroeck, 1:403–19. BETL 100. Leuven: Leuven University Press, 1992.

———. *The First Gospel*. Sonoma, CA: Polebridge, 1992.

———. "The Literary Unity of Q." *JBL* 101 (1982) 365–89.

Jülicher, A., and E. Fascher. *Einleitung in das Neue Testament*. Tübingen: Mohr, 1931.

Keck, Leander E. "The Spirit and the Dove." *NTS* 17 (1970) 41–67.

Kee, Howard Clark. *Jesus in History: An Approach to the Study of the* Gospels. 2nd ed. New York: Harcourt Brace Jovanovich, 1970.

Kelly, Balmer H. "An Exposition of Matthew 4:1–11." *Int* 29 (1975) 57–61.

Kloppenborg, John S. "Blessing and Marginality: The Persecution Beatitude in Q, Thomas and Early Christianity." *Forum* 2 (1986) 37–56.

———. *The Formation of Q: Trajectories in Ancient Wisdom Collections.* Philadelphia: Fortress, 1987.

———. "The Formation of Q and Antique Instructional Genres." *JBL* 105 (1986) 443–62.

———. *Q Parallels: Synopsis Critical Notes and Concordance.* Sonoma, CA: Polebridge, 1988.

———. *Q, the Earliest Gospel.* Louisville: Westminster John Knox, 2008.

———, ed. *The Shape of Q: Signal Essays on the Sayings Gospel.* Minneapolis: Fortress, 1994.

———. "Symbolic Eschatology and the Apocalypticism of Q." *HTR* 80 (1987) 287–306.

———. "The Tradition and Redaction in the Sayings Source." *CBQ* 46 (1984) 34–62.

Koester, Helmut. "GNOMAI DIAPHOROI: The Origin and Nature of Diversification in the History of Early Christianity." In *Trajectories through Early Christianity*, edited by James M. Robinson and Helmut Koester, 114–57. Philadelphia: Fortress, 1971.

Koester, Helmut, and James M. Robinson. *Entwicklungslinien durch die Welt des frühen Christentums.* Tübingen: Mohr-Siebeck, 1971.

Labahn, Michael, and Andreas Schmidt, eds. *Jesus, Mark and Q: The Teaching of Jesus and Its Earliest Records.* JSNTSS 214. Sheffield: Sheffield Academic, 2001.

Lambrecht, J. "John the Baptist and Jesus in Mark 1.1–1.15: Markan Redaction of Q?" *NTS* 38 (1992) 357–84.

Lewis, Jack Pearl. *A Study of the Interpretation of Noah and Flood in Jewish and Christian Literature.* Leiden: Brill, 1968.

Lührmann, Dieter. "The Gospel of Mark and the Sayings Collection Q." *JBL* 108 (1989) 51–71.

———. *Redaktion der Logienquelle.* Neukirchen-Vluyn: Neukirchener Verlag, 1969.

Mack, Burton L. "The Kingdom That Didn't Come: A Social History of the Q Tradents." In *SBLSP 1988*, edited by Kent H. Richards, 608–35. Chico, CA: Scholars, 1988.

———. *The Lost Gospel: The Book of Q and Christian Origin.* New York: HarperCollins, 1993.

Manson. T. W. *The Sayings of Jesus.* London: SCM, 1949.

Marcus, Joel. *The Way of the Lord: Christological Exegesis of the Old Testament in the Gospel of Mark.* Louisville: Westminster, 1992.

Meier, John P. "The Circle of the Twelve: Did It Exist during Jesus' Public Ministry?" *JBL* 116 (1997) 635–72.

Miller, Robert J. "The Rejection of the Prophets in Q." *JBL* 107 (1988) 225–40.

Neirynck, F. "The First Synoptic Pericope: The Appearance of John the Baptist in Q?" *ETL* 72 (1996) 41–74.

———. "Luke 14,1–6: Lukan Composition and Q Saying." *Evangelica II* (1991) 183–204.

———. "The Minor Agreeement and Q." In *The Gospel behind the Gospels*, edited by R. A. Piper, 49–72. NovTSup 75. Leiden: Brill, 1995.

Pagels, Elaine. "The Social History of Satan, the 'Intimate Enemy': A Preliminary Sketch." *HTR* 84 (1991) 105–28.

Piper, Ronald. *Wisdom in the Q-Tradition: The Aphoristic Teaching of Jesus.* SNTSMS 61. Cambridge: Cambridge University Press, 1989.
Polag, A. *Die Christologie der Logienquelle.* WMANT 45. Neukirchen-Vluyn: Neukirchener Verlag, 1977.
Pokorný, Petr. "The Temptation Stories and Their Intentions." *NTS* 20 (1973–74) 115–27.
Ra, Yoseop. *The Origin and Formation of the Gospel.* Eugene, OR: Wipf & Stock, 2015.
Robbins, Vermon. *Jesus the Teacher: A Socio-Rhetorical Interpretation of Mark.* Philadelphia: Fortress, 1984.
Robinson, James M. "Die Logienquelle: Weisheit oder Prophetie: Anfragen an Migaku Sato, Q und Prophetie." *EvT* 53 (1993) 367–89.
———. "LOGOI SOPHON: On the Gattungs of Q." In *The Future of Our Religious Past*, edited by J. M. Robinson, 84–130. New York: Harper & Row, 1971.
———. "The Sayings Gospels Q." In *The Four Gospels 1992*, edited by F. van Segbroeck, 361–88. BETL 100. Leuven: Leuven University Press, 1992.
Robinson, James M., et al. *The Critical Edition of Q.* Hermeneia. Minneapolis: Fortress, 2000.
Saldarini, Anthony J. "Political and Social Roles of the Pharisees and Scribes in Galilee." In *SBLSP 1988*, edited by David J. Lull, 200–209. Atlanta: Scholars, 1988.
Sanders, E. P. *Jesus and Judaism.* Philadelphia: Fortress, 1985.
Sato, Migaku. *Q und Prophetie: Studien zur Gattungs und Traditionsgeschichte der Quelle Q.* WUNT 2/29. Tübingen: Mohr, 1987.
———. "The Shape of the Q-Source." In *The Shape of Q: Signal Essays on the Sayings Gospel*, edited by John S. Kloppenborg, 156–79. Minneapolis: Fortress, 1994.
———. "Wisdom Statement in the Sphere of Prophecy." In *The Gospel behind the Gospels*, edited by Ronald A. Piper, 139–58. Leiden: Brill, 1995.
Schulz, Siegfried. *Q: Die Spruchquelle der Evangelisten.* Zürich: Theologischer, 1972.
Schürmann, Heinz. *Gottes Reich-Jesu Geschick: Jesu ureigener Tod im Licht seiner Basileia-Verkündigung.* Freiburg: Herder, 1983.
———. "QLk 11,14–36: Kompositionsgeschichtlich Befrage." In *The Four Gospels 1992*, edited by F. van Segbroeck, 563–86. Leuven: Leuven University Press, 1992.
———. "Observations on the Son of Man Title in the Speech Source: Its Occurrence in Closing and Introductory Expressions." In *The Shape of Q: Signal Essays on the Sayings Gospel*, edited by John S. Kloppenborg, 74–97. Minneapolis: Fortress, 1994.
———. "Zum Komposition der Redenquelle. Beobachtungen an der lukanischen Q-Vorlage." In *Der Treue Gottes Trauen: Festschrift für G. Schneider*, edited by C. Bussmann and W. Radl, 325–42. Freiburg: Herder, 1991.
Scott, Bernard Brandon. "Jesus as Sage: An Innovation Voice in Common Wisdom." In *The Sage in Israel and the Ancient Near East*, edited by John G. Gamomie, 339–415. Winona Lake, IN: Eisenbrauns, 1990.
Seeley, D. "Blessings and Boundaries: Interpretations of Jesus' Death in Q." *Semeia*, n.s., 55 (1992) 131–45.
———. "Jesus' Death in Q." *NTS* 38 (1992) 222–34.
Shireck, Robert. "Whose Exorcists Are They? The Referents of 'Your Sons' at Matthew 12.27/Luke 11.19." *JSNT*, n.s., 46 (1992) 41–51.
Steck, Odil Hannes. *Israel und das gewaltsame Geschick der Propheten: Untersuchung zur Überlieferung des deuteronomistischen Geschichtsbildes im Alten Testament,*

Spätjudentum und Urchristentum. WMANT 23. Neukirchen-Vluyn, Germany: Neukirchen Verlag, 1967.

Theissen, Gerd. *Studien zur Soziologie des Urchristentums*. WUNT 19. Tübingen, 1983.

———. *Gospels in Context: Social and Political History in the Synoptic Tradition*. Translated by L. M. Maloney. Minneapolis: Fortress, 1991.

Thrall, William Flint, and Addison Hibbard. *A Handbook to Literature*. Revised and enlarged by C. Hugh Holman. New York: Odyssey, 1962.

Tuckett, Christopher M. "The Beatitudes: A Source-Critical Study." *NovT* 25 (1983) 193–216.

———. "On the Stratification of Q: A Response." *Semeia*, n.s., 55 (1992) 213–21.

———. *Q and the History of Early Christianity: Studies on Q*. Edinburgh: Hendrickson, 1996.

Uro, Risto. "John the Baptist and the Jesus Movement: What Does Q Tell Us." In *The Gospel behind the Gospels*, edited by R. Piper, 231–57. Leiden: Brill, 1995.

Vaage, Lief. E. "The Son of Man Saying in Q: Stratigraphical Location and Significance." *Semeia*, n.s., 55 (1992) 103–29.

———. "Q1 and the Historical Jesus." *Forum* 5 (1989) 159–76.

Valantasis, Richard. *The New Q: A Fresh Translation with Commentary*. New York: T. & T. Clark, 2005.

Vassiliadis, Petros. "The Function of John the Baptist in Q and Mark." Θεολογία 46 (1975) 405–13.

Vermes, Geza. *The Dead Sea Scrolls in English*. 3rd ed. London: Penguin, 1987.

Verseput, Donald J. *The Rejection of the Humble Messianic Kingdom*. Frankfurt: Lang, 1986.

Vielhauer, Philipp. *Geschichte der Urchristlichen Literatur*. Berlin: de Gruyter, 1975.

Webb, Robert L. "The Activity of John the Baptist's Expected Figure at the Threshing Floor (Matthew 3.12 = Luke 3.17)." *JSNT*, n.s., 43 (1991) 103–111.

Wild, Robert A. "The Encounter between Pharisaic and Christian Judaism: Some Early Gospel Evidence." *NovT* 27 (1985) 106–24.

Williams, James G. "Parables and Chreia: From Q to Narrative Gospel." *Semeia*, n.s., 43 (1988) 85–114.

Wink, Walter. *John the Baptist in the Gospel Tradition*. SNTSMS 7. Cambridge: Cambridge University Press, 1968.

———. "Neither Passivity Nor Violence: Jesus' Third Way (Matt 5:38–42 / Luke 6:29–30)." *Forum* 7 (1991) 5–27.

Zeller, Dieter. "Redaktionsprozesse und weckselner 'Sitz im Leben' bein Q-Material." In *Logia*, edited by J. Delobel, 396–99. BETL 59. Leuven: Leuven University Press, 1982.

Ancient Document Index

Genesis

1:1	130, 138, 202, 237
1:11–12	53, 71
1:27	138, 161
2:2–3	160
2:4	130, 138, 202
2:4a	237
2:4—3:24	237
2:9	53
2:16	53
2:18—4:1	161
2:24–25	203
3:1–5	71
3:11–19	71
3:15	200
3:22	71
3:22–24	71
3:24	161
4:24	88n34
5:24	172
6:19–20	13n36
7:2–3	13n36
7:9	13n36
7:15	13n36
11:4	126
11:7	126
16:1–16	208
19:24	64
19:24–25	98
49:27	297n3

Exodus

4:22	28, 36, 68
8:19	75n7
9:15–16	75n7
16:1–12	188
16:35	186
17:1–7	190
19:1–3	195
20:7	68
22:25	34
22:26–27	34
23:20	117, 117n26, 237
32:1–14	191
33:11–23	133

Leviticus

2:5	160
6:16	160
10:12	160
19:2	36n16
19:15	36n18
19:18	33n10

Numbers

1:1—3:4	195
12:6–8	133
14:33–34	186
18:21–28	143
32:13	186

Deuteronomy

2:7	186
5:11	68
6:13	28, 68, 191, 193
6:15	191
6:16	28, 190

Deuteronomy *(continued)*

8:2	186
8:3	28, 187, 188, 193
8:4	186
9:10	75n7
12:6–17	143
14:22–29	143
19:15	35
24:12–13	34
26:12	143
29:5	186
34:1	190
34:1–4	191
34:10	133

Joshua

5:6	186

Judges

9:15	160n10

2 Samuel

7:11–14	102n9

1 Kings

17:7–16	63
19:7–8	63
19:19–21	56n1

2 Kings

2:8–11	97

Nehemiah

9:26	32n7

Job

16:21	58, 169

Psalms

2:7	101, 102, 102n9, 113
8:4	58, 169
58:1	58, 169
80:17	58, 169
91:11–12	194
117:26a	228

Proverbs

1:20ff	212
3:18	71
8:4	58, 169
8:22–31	203
8:31	58, 169
28:15	207n3

Ecclesiastes

14:26	160n10

Isaiah

1:11	64, 182
1:18	64, 182
3:16	64, 182
18:3–6	98
24:13	98, 124n1
29:18f	115
35:5f	115
40:3	22, 22n4, 22n5, 184
42:1	101, 113
45:1–3	23
61:1	100, 115
63:16	36, 68
65:1	28
65:25	207

Lamentations

4:20	160n10

Jeremiah

1:11	64, 182
2:5	64, 182
22:27	207n3
44:11	64, 182
49:33	58, 169
50:40	58, 169
51:33	98
51:43	58, 169

Ezekiel

1:1	100
2:1	58, 169
2:2	100
3:1	58, 169
3:16	64, 182
4:1	58, 169
7:1	64, 182
17:22–24	160, 160n10
22:27	207n3
30:8	97, 98
31:3–9	160
31:6	160n10

Daniel

4:11	160n10
4:18	160n10
7:13	172
7:13–14	169, 172

Hosea

6:11	124n1
11:1	28, 36, 68

Joel

2:3	97, 98
2:28–29	100
2:30	98
3:13	98
4:1–21	124n1

Jonah

1:17	79n20
3:5–6	126

Micah

4:11–13	98, 124n1
7:6	223

Zephaniah

3:3	203n3

Zechariah

3:1–5	194n20

Malachi

3:1	22n4, 117, 117n26, 118
4:1	97, 98
4:5	97, 118

Baruch

1:12	160n10

Sirach

1:15	227
14:26	160n10
29:11–13	152n30

Wisdom

1:4–6	190
1:4–7	204
2:17–20	190, 203

Tobit

4:8–11	152n30
12:8–9	152n30

1 Enoch

25:5	71
42:1–2	203n40
46:1–6	169n33
48:2–6	169n33

Testament of Levi

13:5–9	152n30
18:10	71, 161

Testament of Gad

1:3	207n3

Testament of Ben

11:1–2	207n3

Apocalypse of Moses

27:2–3	54n3
28:4	54n3
29:7	54n3
19:1	161

4 Ezra

9:1–25	124n1
9:29–37	124n1

2 Apocalypse of Baruch

14:12	152n30
24:1	152n30

Jewish Antiquities

18:264	193
18:266	193
18:272	193
18:280–283	194

Jewish War

2:200	194n21

Q

3:1–6	7
3:2	98, 184
3:2–4	5n15, 21, 21n1, 23, 25, 28, 29, 30, 32, 44, 46, 90, 101, 109, 117, 118, 122, 175, 238
3:2–17	21, 46
3:2—7:35	9, 15, 19, 46
3:4	22n4, 24, 39, 44, 96, 118, 124, 184, 228
3:7	35, 36, 37, 43, 52, 64, 74, 96, 98, 127
3:7–8a	7, 12, 13, 15, 23, 25, 28, 29, 30, 32, 35, 36, 37, 38, 44, 46, 69, 88, 90, 96, 99, 101, 175, 181, 238
3:7–9	4, 7, 10, 12, 13, 23, 23n6, 25
3:7—7:28	6
3:7—7:35	9
3:8a	33, 35n14, 38, 79, 88, 125
3:8b	234
3:8bc	12, 13, 15, 15n40, 23, 25, 28, 29, 30, 32, 37, 42, 43, 45, 46, 164, 167, 173, 181, 183, 186, 197n31, 201, 204, 206, 208, 225, 236, 238
3:8c	8, 28, 213, 228
3:9	7, 12, 15, 23, 24, 25, 28, 29, 30, 32, 35, 36, 37, 38, 44, 46, 52, 57, 82, 86, 88, 90, 96, 98, 99, 101, 108, 110, 127, 149, 175, 181, 206, 229, 231, 239
3:16	39, 40, 96, 118n29, 136, 155, 199, 208, 210
3:16a	7
3:16c	8
3:16–17	4, 7, 10, 12, 13, 25, 27, 28, 29, 31, 32, 38, 39, 40, 41, 42, 45, 46, 60, 61, 65, 76, 77, 80, 87, 95, 98, 99, 102, 103, 106, 109, 110, 112, 114, 118, 121, 124, 128, 136, 137, 154, 156, 157n4, 168, 174, 175, 183, 235, 239
3:17	7, 39, 98, 99, 107, 110, 111, 120, 124, 127, 136, 141, 143, 144, 149, 151, 152, 209, 216
3:21	99, 208
3:21–22	5n15, 27, 27n1, 28, 29, 31, 32, 40, 46, 66, 99, 101, 102, 103, 104, 109, 115, 126, 128, 129, 130, 132, 133, 134, 152, 174, 175, 183, 185, 186, 193, 215, 228, 239
3:21—6:16	27, 29
3:21—7:10	19, 27, 40, 46
3:22	28, 100, 103, 113, 131, 207
4:1	183, 208, 216
4:1–2	203, 215
4:1–3	193
4:1–12	231

4:1-13	4, 6, 8, 15, 15n40, 16, 27, 28, 29, 30, 32, 40, 46, 58, 59, 61, 77, 81, 82, 84, 150n28, 164, 164n19, 165, 172, 173, 183, 185, 192, 195, 217, 218, 219, 230, 234, 235, 236, 238, 239	6:20b-22	222
		6:20-23	16, 32, 33
		6:20-23b	16
		6:20-49	29
		6:20b-21	6, 11, 31, 32, 66n8, 103
		6:20b-22b	8
		6:20b-23	6, 7, 11, 30
		6:20b-23b	4, 7, 32
4:2	77, 184, 185, 193	6:20b-49	7
4:2b-13	6	6:21	7, 11, 30n4, 31, 32, 40, 49, 51, 52, 55, 57, 61, 63, 64, 69, 70, 72, 73, 85, 90, 102, 103, 116, 133, 156, 161, 175, 182n1, 188, 203, 239
4:3	28, 187, 193		
4:3-4	186, 187, 189		
4:3-12	216		
4:4	28, 187, 192, 199, 202, 223		
		6:21a	51, 52, 53, 69, 71, 73, 160, 186, 200
4:5	166, 190, 234n17		
4:5-8	195, 217, 218, 225, 236	6:21b	53, 54
4:6-7	191	6:22	39, 102, 103, 104, 105, 108, 121, 151,152, 168, 189
4:8	28, 191, 192, 199, 223		
4:9	28, 214		
4:9-11	189	6:22-23	6, 11, 31
4:9-12	61, 164, 167, 172, 188, 189, 203, 206, 207, 211, 212, 213, 227, 233	6:22-23b	5, 7, 31, 32, 33, 34, 37, 38, 39, 40, 42, 45, 46, 66, 77, 80, 83, 83n30, 84, 87, 102, 103, 105, 106, 107, 108, 109, 116, 121, 122, 126, 128, 130, 132, 133, 136, 141, 150, 155, 156, 162, 174, 175, 196, 197, 214, 215, 219, 239
4:9-13	228		
4:10-11	194, 223		
4:12	28, 190, 199, 202, 223		
4:13	77, 192, 208		
6:12	195		
6:12a	234n17		
6:12-16	15, 15n40, 27, 28, 28n3, 29, 30, 32, 40, 42, 43, 45, 46, 57, 61, 173, 195, 200, 204, 205, 206, 237, 238, 239		
		6:22b-23	183
		6:23ab	104
		6:23b	103, 152
		6:23c	4, 7, 8, 15, 16, 32, 40, 46, 81, 197, 198, 211, 227, 238, 239
6:13a	195		
6:13-16	59	6:27	33, 34, 35, 36, 37, 38, 39, 40, 44, 46, 47, 51, 52, 53, 62, 64, 70, 72, 74, 90, 105, 107, 109, 111, 112, 117, 133, 150, 158, 175, 182, 213, 228, 229, 236, 237, 239
6:13b-16	196		
6:20a	29, 30, 32, 40, 46, 69, 238, 239		
6:20b	7, 11, 30, 31, 32, 33, 35, 36, 37, 40, 44, 46, 47, 51, 52, 53, 61, 63, 69, 71, 75, 86, 87, 90, 102, 103, 104, 109, 111, 115, 116, 133, 156, 159, 161, 175, 201, 225, 229, 239		
		6:27-29	4
		6:27-30	33
		6:27-38	7, 33, 37, 37n19
6:20b-21a	69		

Q (continued)

6:28	33, 33n11, 34, 37, 40, 46, 104, 105, 108, 109, 122, 124, 129, 175, 239
6:29a	34
6:29b	34
6:29–30	34, 35, 51, 52, 53, 105, 117n25
6:29–36	36
6:29–38	36, 37, 38, 39, 40, 44, 46, 47, 62, 70, 74, 90, 105, 107, 109, 111, 112, 133, 150, 158, 175, 229, 236, 237, 239
6:30	34, 35, 35n15
6:31	35, 144
6:31–32	70
6:31–35	36
6:31–36	33, 35
6:31–38	224
6:32	35, 43, 44, 120
6:32–34	35
6:34	35, 70
6:35	35, 68, 75, 102, 130, 131
6:35–36	129
6:36	36, 68, 106
6:37	36, 70
6:37–38	33, 36
6:38	36
6:39	8, 37, 38n21, 41, 105, 119, 132, 134, 140, 141, 147, 164, 198, 239
6:39–40	6, 37, 38, 39, 80
6:39–42	105, 107, 175
6:39–45	45, 109
6:39–49	37, 39, 40, 45, 46, 174
6:40	37, 42, 106, 109, 114, 196, 239
6:40–41	8
6:41–42	37, 38, 38n21, 39, 80, 106, 119, 134, 141, 146, 239
6:41–45	39
6:42	8, 39, 81, 107, 108
6:43	39, 108, 231
6:43–44	38, 38n22, 107, 120, 130, 141, 146, 149, 171
6:43–45	6, 38, 107, 109, 110, 143, 175, 239
6:43–49	8
6:44–45	37
6:45	38, 39, 108, 142, 147
6:45b	108
6:46	40, 80, 109, 112, 124, 155, 162, 228
6:46–47	42, 128, 132, 134, 150, 163, 188, 235
6:46–48	209
6:46–49	37, 39, 40, 60, 61, 109, 111, 113, 113n15, 137, 157, 175, 217, 239
6:47	109
6:47–49	80, 140
6:48	119, 158
6:48–49	44, 80, 110, 120, 130, 143, 151, 154, 155, 156, 158, 171, 223
7:1	111, 113, 122, 189
7:1–10	4, 7, 8, 39, 40, 42, 46, 60, 61, 65, 80, 111, 113n15, 114, 114n17, 115, 119, 120, 122, 125, 126, 132, 135, 136, 137, 163, 164, 174, 175, 183, 187, 192, 226, 230, 234
7:3	111, 130
7:3–6	112
7:6	40, 80, 124, 128, 150, 155, 162, 188, 228, 235
7:7–9	112
7:9	117, 122, 138, 182, 213, 228
7:18–20	114
7:18–23	4, 8, 41, 42, 66, 114, 115n18, 116, 118, 168
7:18–27	45, 46, 65, 121, 154, 174, 176, 200, 239
7:18–28	41, 43, 114
7:18–35	7, 19, 41, 42n1, 46
7:21–23	115
7:22	42, 65, 117n25, 134, 139, 142, 143, 182, 187, 193, 233, 234
7:22–23	115n22
7:23	42, 66n8, 83, 116, 128, 133, 136, 151, 155, 156, 222, 232

ANCIENT DOCUMENT INDEX 259

7:24	184, 223	9:57–60a	8, 49, 56, 59, 60, 85n32
7:24–25	127	9:57a–60	84n32
7:24–26	116, 139	9:57–62	4
7:24–27	8, 42, 43, 61, 66, 116, 118, 119, 134, 166, 228	9:57—10:24	6
		9:57—12:34	9
7:24–28	4	9:57—11:13	9, 10n29
7:25–26	135	9:57—12:34	15, 49
7:26	136, 182, 199, 201, 210, 213, 228	9:58	79, 85, 104, 110, 121, 150, 151, 155, 168, 169, 207
7:26–27	128	9:59	205
7:27	6, 22n4, 43n5, 60, 66, 117, 118n29, 131, 133, 149, 150, 150n28, 187, 190, 237	9:59–60a	8, 56, 58, 59, 61, 81, 82, 157, 164, 172, 205, 206, 207, 211, 214, 218, 219, 222, 230, 238, 240
7:28	8, 42, 43, 46, 166, 199, 200, 201, 201n38, 202, 204, 210, 213, 215, 226, 228, 238, 239	10:2	8, 60, 61, 65, 66, 89, 123, 124, 125, 128, 130, 132, 144, 151, 155, 163, 174, 207, 212, 228, 235, 240
7:28b	43n5	10:2–3	60, 61
7:29	120	10: 2–11	4
7:29–30	41, 43, 44, 46, 47, 87, 90, 119, 163, 175, 199, 239	10:2–12	8
		10:2–16	66
7:30	44	10:2–24	49, 60
7:31	119, 137, 158, 213	10:3	61, 66, 81, 89, 164, 167, 172, 199n34, 207, 208, 211, 212, 214, 219, 227, 238, 240
7:31–32	44, 80, 119		
7:31–34	45, 46, 56, 66, 80, 119, 121, 123, 141, 143, 151, 157, 162, 171, 174, 176, 204, 240	10:3–11	8
		10:4	61, 85, 151
		10:4–5	141
7:31–35	4, 6, 8, 41, 44, 56	10:4–11	64, 65n5
7:32	119, 122, 130, 145, 146, 189	10:4–12	60, 61, 65, 66, 90, 103, 106, 109, 125, 127, 128, 132, 159, 177, 240
7:32–34	144, 149, 161	10:5	61, 62, 70, 140, 209
7:33	120, 185, 208	10:5–6	70, 222
7:33–34	44, 145, 170, 183, 189	10:5–8	85
7:34	120, 121, 121n36, 122, 150, 151, 155, 156, 168, 215	10:5–9	75
		10:6	62, 70
7:35	45, 46, 81, 203, 212, 212n9, 215	10:7	140
		10:7–8	62, 63, 70
9:57	82, 83	10:7–9	70
9:57–58	56, 57, 58, 59, 61, 62, 73, 79, 83, 85, 89, 90, 104, 109, 113, 121, 123, 130, 132, 163, 176, 192, 196, 205, 229, 240	10:8	100, 122
		10:8–9	63, 192
		10:8–10	98
		10:8–11	111
9:57b–58	8		

Q *(continued)*

10:9	63, 69, 70, 71, 74, 76, 83, 86, 103, 112, 115, 124, 148, 159, 163, 201, 225
10:10	70, 100
10:10–11	63, 64, 76, 103
10:11	122, 127
10:12	6, 64, 65, 65n5, 69, 72, 79, 83, 85, 96, 98, 99, 110, 111, 111n12, 117, 136, 137, 182, 199, 210, 213, 228
10:12–15	4, 6, 8
10:13	125, 141
10:13–14	87, 126, 127, 137
10:13–15	6, 8, 60, 65, 65n5, 80, 81, 125, 126n3, 127, 131, 137, 138, 167, 189, 232
10:13–16	66, 89, 130, 131, 174, 176
10:14	65, 136, 199, 210, 224
10:15	126, 127, 130, 144, 146, 148, 215, 229
10:16	8, 65, 65n6, 66, 77, 80, 83, 127, 128, 131, 132, 136, 150, 151, 162, 196
10:16–24	60
10:21	66, 69, 129, 131, 140, 141, 148, 149, 152, 160, 190, 202, 237
10:21b	130
10:21c	131
10:21–22	8, 66, 68, 129, 132, 133, 138, 150, 162, 186, 191
10:21–24	4, 66, 67, 81, 89, 128, 135, 174, 176
10:22	6, 131, 132, 133, 136, 171
10:23	66n8, 133, 222
10:23–24	8, 66, 68n2, 133, 135, 139, 198, 211, 227
10:24	134, 135, 143, 196, 211
10:29–32	8
11:2	68, 73, 76, 83, 86, 87, 102, 129, 148, 159, 192, 201, 215, 225
11:2a	68
11:2b	68
11:2c	69
11:2–3	69, 86, 187
11:2–4	4, 8, 67, 67n1, 68n2, 71, 73, 79, 89, 105, 109, 124, 129, 133, 138, 160, 161, 176, 200, 203, 225, 237, 240
11:2—12:34	49
11:3	69, 70, 73n5, 85, 86, 144, 189, 217
11:4	72, 78, 87, 88, 125, 145, 150, 158, 184, 185, 216
11:4a	70
11:4b	70
11:4c	70
11:9	72, 86, 162, 182, 212, 213, 228
11:9–10	67, 71, 73, 78, 79, 89, 91, 100, 117n25, 176, 209, 240
11:9–11	9
11:9–13	4, 8, 68n2, 189n7
11:9–20	124, 129
11:9–26	67
11:10	72
11:11	82, 110, 187
11:11–12	85, 102
11:11–13	10n29, 67, 73, 74, 78, 79, 83, 89, 90, 131, 176
11:12	182
11:13	74, 85, 96, 100, 104, 108, 129, 199
11:13–14	126
11:14	192, 208, 209
11:14–15	67, 74, 76, 78, 81, 90, 96, 98, 112, 113, 115, 115n22, 120, 135, 163, 177, 185, 187, 189, 192, 230, 240
11:14–20	8, 89
11:14–26	4, 10n29
11:14–32	6
11:14–52	9, 10n29
11:16	10n29, 67, 77, 78, 78n16, 79, 81, 91, 101, 104, 112, 112n12, 113, 126, 137, 139, 140, 142, 148, 158, 176, 184, 185, 192, 214, 240
11:17	111, 119
11:17–18	74, 75, 127

11:17–20	67, 74, 76, 78, 81, 90, 96, 113, 115, 115n22, 120, 135, 163, 176, 185, 189, 192, 230, 240	11:34	80
		11:34–35	80, 140, 141, 142, 215
		11:35	141
		11:39	142, 142n17, 147, 193
11:17–26	74	11:39–40	8
11:18	105, 191	11:39–41	80, 142, 143, 149
11:19	74, 211	11:39–42	9, 163n14, 193, 199, 202
11:19–20	75, 78, 183, 201	11:39–45	142
11:20	87, 147, 159, 191, 225	11:39–46	81, 87, 89, 148, 167, 174, 176, 210, 233, 240
11:21	135, 209		
11:21–22	158, 159	11:39–52	4, 6, 80
11:21–23	76, 77, 80, 84, 89, 135, 144, 151, 152, 154, 174, 176, 208, 240	11:42	8, 81, 143, 144, 152
		11:43	81, 144, 145, 229
		11:44	8, 81, 145, 206, 211, 211n6
11:21–24	137		
11:21–26	78	11:45–46	81
11:22	136, 199	11:46	8, 146
11:23	8, 77, 83, 136, 143, 151	11:47	211
11:24	208, 209	11:47–48	211
11:24–26	8, 77, 89, 208, 210, 210n4, 223, 238, 240	11:47–51	8, 16, 81, 82, 84, 89, 164, 167, 172, 210, 211n6, 212n9, 214, 219, 227, 233, 238, 240
11:25	209		
11:26	210		
11:29	213	11:49	211, 212, 216
11:29–30	67, 78, 78n16, 79, 81, 89, 90, 101, 111, 112, 112n12, 113, 119, 124, 126, 135, 137, 139, 140, 142, 148, 158, 176, 185, 192, 214, 240	11:49–51	81n26, 223, 228
		11:50	212
		11:50–51	212, 213, 214
		11:51	164, 164n18, 213, 214, 228
		11:52	81, 81n26, 87, 89, 141, 142, 161, 167, 174, 176, 210, 226, 233, 240
11:29–32	4		
11:29–46	129		
11:29—12:3	10n29, 77	12:2	81, 148
11:30	79, 80, 83, 104, 121, 150, 151, 155, 168, 170	12:2–3	8, 81, 82, 148, 149, 171, 174, 176, 214, 224, 241
11:31	139, 190, 203	12:2–7	4
11:31–32	79, 80, 80n2, 112n12, 137, 138, 139, 140, 141, 142, 143, 148, 159, 161, 164, 165, 170, 171, 174, 176, 193, 199, 213, 226n6, 240	12:2–32	9, 10n29
		12:2–34	6
		12:3	149
		12:4	214, 215
		12:4–5	82, 84, 89, 164, 172, 214, 215, 217, 219, 220, 225, 238, 241
11:31–35	89, 140		
11:32	139, 182	12:4–7	9, 129, 171
11:33	80, 140	12:4–12	10n29, 67
11:33–34	8	12:5	215
11:33–35	80, 80n23, 81, 139, 142, 148, 174, 176, 240	12:6	82, 83, 110, 130, 189, 206
11:33–36	4, 8		

Q *(continued)*

12:6–7	67, 82, 83, 84, 85, 86, 89, 90, 124, 149, 176, 192, 207, 214, 215, 224, 241
12:6–12	82
12:7	83, 85, 96, 199, 210
12:8	150
12:8–9	83, 84, 84n30, 89, 149, 150, 150n28, 151, 151n29, 154, 155, 156, 162, 168, 174, 176, 190, 215, 241
12:8–10	4
12:10	84, 215, 216
12:10–12	84, 89, 215, 217, 217, 238, 241
12:11–12	84, 167, 171, 216, 224
12:12	217
12:22	86, 117, 182, 213, 228
12:22–23	85, 215
12:22–28	86
12:22–31	9, 67, 84, 87, 89, 90, 124, 129, 131, 144, 151, 156, 176, 186, 189, 207, 217 219, 224, 241
12:22–34	10n29, 67, 84, 120
12:22b–31	85n32
12:22b–34	4
12:23	85, 215
12:23–24	96, 136, 199, 210
12:24	85, 149, 207, 223
12:24–28	85, 86, 110, 117n25, 130
12:25–26	85
12:27	85, 135, 139, 149, 170, 190, 223
12:28	86, 96, 206
12:29	86, 120, 162
12:29–31	86
12:30	86, 112
12:31	86, 148, 159, 201, 225
12:31–34	8
12:33	151, 152
12:33–34	87, 89, 151, 152, 154, 166, 174, 176, 217, 241
12:33—22:30	9
12:34	152
12:35–39	8
12:35—22:30	15
12:39–40	4, 154, 155, 157, 167, 168, 169, 174, 177, 228, 235, 241
12:39–46	158, 221
12:39–59	93, 153
12:39—22:30	9, 93, 153
12:40	8, 168
12:42	162
12:42–46	4, 8, 155, 157, 162, 167, 171, 174, 177, 218, 231, 235, 241
12:43	156
12:49	4, 157, 157n4, 157n5, 158, 174, 221, 222, 223, 233, 238, 241
12:49–53	8
12:51	8, 157n4
12:51–53	4, 157, 157n5, 158, 221, 223, 233
12:51–56	157, 158, 174, 238, 241
12:52–53	222
12:53	8, 223
12:54–55	157n5
12:54–56	4, 8, 157, 158, 223, 224
12:56	224
12:57–59	4
12:58	224
12:58–59	8, 158, 167, 174, 224, 225, 238
12:59	225
13:18	158
13:18–19	8, 203, 226, 234
13:18–21	5n15, 158, 160, 161, 171, 174, 177, 201, 224, 225, 226, 229, 231, 232, 241
13:18—17:2	93, 153, 158
13:19	207
13:20–21	8
13:23–35	6
13:24	4, 161, 212
13:24–27	8, 161, 164, 174, 177, 192, 202, 225, 226, 229, 230, 231, 232, 241
13:24–30	4
13:24–35	8
13:25	162
13:25–30	4
13:26–27	162

ANCIENT DOCUMENT INDEX

13:28–29	225, 226	17:6	167, 233, 233n17, 238, 242
13:28–30	164, 165, 166, 174, 225, 226, 229, 231, 238, 241	17:23–24	4, 167, 168, 169, 174, 177, 223, 228, 233, 234, 235, 236, 242
13:28—17:2	163		
13:29	231	17:23–27	6
13:30	226	17:23—22:30	93, 153, 167
13:34	227	17:24	169, 169n34, 215
13:34–35	4, 16, 164, 164n16, 164n18, 164n19, 165, 167, 174, 204n43, 226, 226n8, 227, 228, 229, 230, 233, 234, 238, 241	17:26	169n34, 170
		17:26–27	169, 170, 171, 174, 177, 189, 233, 234, 235, 236, 242
13:35	228	17:27	170
14:5	164, 164n21, 165, 166, 198, 199, 202, 207, 238, 239	17:26–30	4
		17:30	169, 170, 171, 174, 177, 233, 235, 236, 241
14:11	164, 174, 229, 238, 241	17:33	4, 5n15, 8, 165, 171, 218, 219, 220, 221, 229, 241
14:16–24	4, 8, 165, 166, 173, 174, 229, 230, 231, 232, 238, 241	17:34–35	4, 171, 174, 177, 233, 234, 235, 236, 242
14:26–27	4, 8, 165, 171, 218, 219n18, 221, 222, 238, 241	17:37	4, 172
		17:37b	172, 174, 234, 238, 242
14:26	218	19:12–26	172, 174, 234, 235, 236, 238, 242
14:27	219	19:15	235
14:34	231	19:16	235
14:34–35	4, 5n13, 8, 165, 166, 174, 231, 238, 241	19:17	172, 235
		19:18	235
15:4–5	232	19:19	172, 235
15:4–7	166, 167, 174, 198n34, 231, 232, 238, 241	19:20	235
		19:22	235
16:13	9, 166, 171, 217, 218, 238	22:30	15, 15n40, 29n3, 172, 173, 174, 236, 237, 238, 242
16:16	4, 7, 8, 166, 199, 201, 202, 204, 215, 226, 239		
16:16–17	167		
16:16–18	238		

Matthew

3:1–3	21, 46, 90, 175, 238
3:2	201n38
3:5–6	21, 46, 90, 175, 238
3:7–9a	46, 90, 175, 238
3:7–10	23
3:9bc	238
3:10	46, 90, 175, 239
3:11–12	25, 95, 175, 239
3:16–17	27, 99, 175, 239
4:1	184n3
4:1–11	28, 183, 239
4:3	186n4
4:6	186n4

16:17	166, 202
16:17–18	202, 239
16:18	166, 167, 202
17:1	232
17:1–2	167, 174, 232, 233, 238, 242
17:2	233
17:3	87, 88, 106
17:3–4	9, 49, 67, 87, 88, 89, 91, 124, 125, 129, 171, 176, 210, 216, 241
17:4	88

Matthew (continued)

5:1a	28, 195, 239
5:1b	29, 239
5:2b	47
5:2b–3	90, 175, 239
5:3	30n4, 47
5:3–4	30
5:4	90, 175, 239
5:6	30, 51, 53, 90, 175, 239
5:11–12b	83n30, 102, 175, 239
5:12b	197, 197n31
5:12c	239
5:13	165, 231, 241
5:15	80, 140, 176, 240
5:18	166, 167, 202, 239
5:25–26	157, 167, 241
5:32	166, 202, 239
5:39–40	33, 47, 90, 175, 239
5:39b	34
5:42	33, 47, 90, 175, 239
5:44a	47, 90, 175, 239
5:44b	33n11, 104, 175, 239
5:44–48	33
5:45–48	47, 90, 175, 239
5:46	120
6:9–13	67, 90, 176, 240
6:11	69n3
6:19–21	87, 151, 166, 176, 241
6:22–23	80, 140, 176, 240
6:24	166, 217, 241
6:25–33	84, 90, 176, 241
7:1–2	33, 47, 90, 175, 239
7:3–5	37, 105, 175, 239
7:7–8	90, 176, 240
7:7–9	71
7:9	182, 187
7:9–11	73, 90, 176, 240
7:12	33, 47, 90, 239
7:13–14	161, 177, 241
7:16	37, 175, 239
7:16–18	107
7:18	37, 175, 239
7:21	37, 68n1, 109, 175, 239
7:22–23	161, 162n13, 177, 241
7:24–27	37, 109, 239
7:28a	113n15
8:5–10	39, 111, 175, 239
8:11–12	164, 225, 241
8:13	39, 111, 175, 239
8:19–20	56, 90, 175, 240
8:21–22	58, 205, 240
9:27–30	78n16
9:32–34	78n16
9:37–38	60, 123, 176, 240
10:2–4	28, 195, 196n27, 239
10:7–15	61, 90, 176
10:16a	60, 207, 240
10:18–19	84, 171, 215, 241
10:24–25	37, 105, 175, 239
10:25	37
10:26–27	81, 148, 171, 176, 241
10:28	82, 214, 241
10:28–33	171
10:29–31	82, 90, 176, 241
10:32–33	83, 149, 176, 241
10:34	157n4
10:34–36	157, 221, 241
10:37–38	165, 241
10:37–39	171, 218
10:39	171, 219, 241
10:40	65, 127, 176, 240
11:2–6	114
11:2–10	175, 239
11:2–11	41
11:7–10	116
11:11	199, 239
11:12–13	166, 201, 239
11:16–19	44, 119
11:16–19a	175, 240
11:19b	203, 240
11:21–23	65, 176, 240
11:21–24	125
11:24	90, 176, 240
11:25–27	66, 129, 176, 240
12:11	164n21, 166, 198n34
12:11–12	164, 198, 207, 239
12:22–28	74, 78n16, 90, 176, 240
12:29–30	76, 135, 135n9, 176, 240
12:32	84, 215, 241
12:33–35	37, 107, 239
12:38	78n18
12:38–40	78, 90, 176, 240
12:40	79n20, 79n21
12:41–42	79, 137, 176, 240
12:43–45	77, 208, 240
12:50	68n1

Reference	Pages
13:16–17	66, 133, 176, 240
13:31–33	158, 177, 241
15:14	37, 105, 175, 239
16:1	78, 78n18
16:1–2a	78, 78n16
16:2–3	157, 158n5, 223, 241
16:4	78, 78n16
17:20	167, 167n27, 233, 242
17:20b	234n17
18:6–7	167, 232, 242
18:12–13	231
18:12–14	166, 241
18:14	68n1
18:15	87, 91, 125n2, 176, 241
18:21–22	87, 91, 176, 241
19:28	173, 236, 242
20:14–15	68n1
20:16	164, 225, 241
20:29–34	78n16
21:21	234n17
21:31	68n1
21:31–32	43, 47, 90, 175, 239
21:32	43n6, 120
22:1–10	165, 229, 241
22:7	97
23:4	80, 146, 176, 240
23:6–7	80, 144, 176, 240
23:12	165, 229, 241
23:13	147, 148, 176, 240
23:23	143, 176, 240
23:25–26	142
23:25–28	80, 176, 240
23:27–28	145, 145n23
23:27–36	211n6
23:29–31	210, 240
23:34–36	210, 240
23:37–39	164, 241
24:26–27	167, 177, 242
24:28	172, 234, 242
24:37–39	169, 177, 242
24:40–41	171, 242
24:43–44	154, 177, 241
24:45–51	155, 177, 241
25:10–12	161, 177, 241
25:14–29	172, 234, 242
27:3–10	197n30
27:37–39	226
28:16	197n30

Mark

Reference	Pages
1:2–3	22n4
1:2–5	2n3
1:9	2n3
1:10–11	2n3, 27n1
1:12–13	2n3
1:16–20	58n4, 196n26
2:13–14	196n26
3:16–19	2n3, 196n27
3:22–29	2n3
3:35	68n1
4:21–22	2n3
4:30–32	2n3
6:7–11	2n3
8:11–12	2n3
9:2	196n29
14:33	196n29

Luke

Reference	Pages
1:1–3	1
3:2–4	21, 46, 90, 175, 238
3:7–8a	46, 90, 175, 238
3:7–9	23
3:8bc	238
3:9	46, 90, 175, 239
3:16–17	25, 95, 175, 239
3:21–22	27, 99, 175, 239
4:1–13	28, 183, 239
4:2	184n3
6:12–16	28, 195, 239
6:16	197n30
6:20a	29, 239
6:20b	30n4, 47, 90, 175, 239
6:20b–23	30
6:21	90, 175, 239
6:21a	51
6:21b	53
6:22–23b	83n30, 102, 175, 239
6:23c	197, 197n31, 239
6:27	47, 90, 175, 239
6:27–28	33
6:28	33n11, 104, 174, 175, 239
6:29–38	47, 90, 175, 239
6:29a	34
6:39	239
6:39–42	105, 175
6:39–49	37

Luke (continued)

6:40	239
6:41–42	239
6:43–45	107, 175, 239
6:46–49	109, 175, 239
7:1	113n15
7:1–10	39, 111, 175, 239
7:18–23	114
7:18–27	175, 239
7:18–28	41
7:24–27	116
7:28	199, 239
7:29	43n6
7:29–30	43, 47, 90, 175, 239
7:31–34	44, 119, 175, 240
7:31–35	44
7:35	203, 240
9:57–58	56, 90, 175, 240
9:59–60a	58, 205, 240
9:61–62	56n1
10:2	123, 176, 240
10:2–3	60
10:3	207, 240
10:4–12	61, 90, 176, 240
10:13–15	65, 125
10:13–16	176, 240
10:16	65, 127
10:21–22	66, 129
10:21–24	176, 240
10:23–24	66, 133
11:2–4	67, 90, 176, 240
11:3	69n3
11:9–10	71, 90, 176, 240
11:11–13	73, 90, 176, 240
11:14–15	74, 90, 176, 240
11:16	78, 90, 176, 240
11:17–20	74, 90, 176, 240
11:21–23	76, 135, 135n9, 176, 240
11:24–26	77, 208, 240
11:29–30	78, 90, 176, 240
11:31–32	79, 137, 176, 240
11:33	140
11:33–35	80, 176, 240
11:34–35	140
11:39	142n17
11:39–41	142
11:39–46	176, 240
11:39–52	80
11:42	143
11:43	144
11:44	145, 145n23
11:46	146
11:47–51	210, 240
11:52	147, 148, 240
12:2–3	81, 148, 241
12:4–5	82, 214, 241
12:6–7	82, 90, 176, 241
12:8–9	83, 149, 176, 241
12:10–12	84, 215, 241
12:22–31	84, 90, 241
12:33–34	87, 151, 176, 241
12:39–40	154, 177, 241
12:42–46	155, 177, 241
12:49	157, 157n4, 221, 241
12:51	157n4
12:51–53	221
12:51–59	157
12:54–56	223
12:58–59	224, 241
13:18–21	158, 177, 241
13:24–27	161, 177, 241
13:26–27	162n13
13:28–30	164, 225, 241
13:34–35	164, 226, 241
14:5	164, 164n21, 198, 198n34, 239
14:11	165, 229, 241
14:16–24	165, 229, 241
14:26–27	165, 218, 241
14:34–35	165, 231, 241
15:4–7	166, 231, 241
16:13	166, 217, 241
16:16	166, 201, 239
16:16–17	167, 202
16:17	166
16:17–18	202, 239
16:18	166
17:1–2	167, 232, 242
17:3	125n2
17:3–4	87, 91, 176, 241
17:6	167, 167n27, 234n17, 242
17:23–24	167, 177, 242
17:26–27	169, 177, 242
17:30	169, 177, 242
17:33	171, 218, 219, 242
17:34–35	171, 177, 242

17:37b	172, 234, 242
19:12–26	172, 234, 242
22:30	173, 236, 242

John

10:12	207n3
14:22	197n30

Acts

1:18–19	197n30
20:29	207n3

1 Corinthians

15:5	28n3, 197

Galatians

1:13—2:10	189n6
1:16–19	214n13

1 Thessalonians

2:14	189n6
2:15	197n30

Revelation

14:15	124n1
22:2	71

www.ingramcontent.com/pod-product-compliance
Lightning Source LLC
Chambersburg PA
CBHW071246230426
43668CB00011B/1602